Schoenberg
and
His Circle

In memoriam Rudolf Kolisch

Schoenberg and His Circle

A Viennese Portrait

Joan Allen Smith

SCHIRMER BOOKS
A Division of Macmillan, Inc.
NEW YORK

Collier Macmillan Publishers
LONDON

Schirmer Books
A Division of Macmillan, Inc.
866 Third Avenue, New York, N. Y. 10022

Collier Macmillan Canada, Inc.

Library of Congress Catalog Card Number: 85-27821

Printed in the United States of America

printing number
1 2 3 4 5 6 7 8 9 10

Library of Congress Cataloging-in-Publication Data

Smith, Joan Allen.
    Schoenberg and his circle.

    Bibliography: p.
    Includes index.
    1. Schoenberg, Arnold, 1874–1951—Criticism and
interpretation. 2. Music—Austria—Vienna—20th century
—History and criticism. 3. Twelve-tone system.
I. Title.
ML410.S283S57 1986   780'.92'4   85-27821
ISBN 0-02-872620-0

Contents

List of Illustrations

~Preface~

The oral history project that forms the basis for this work was undertaken in an attempt to preserve from extinction recollections by people personally involved with the Vienna circle of Arnold Schoenberg in the period between 1900 and World War II, during which the twelve-tone method of composition was evolving. In its role as a device for ordering pitch-class and interval content, the twelve-tone method is one of the most influential musical developments of the twentieth century. The genesis of this method coincided with a number of important cultural events in other fields, creating a situation enticing to historians. Also striking is the conjunction of this active cultural climate with political upheaval and world conflict. Vienna during this time was a city of innovators in many fields. One need only to think of the names Wittgenstein, Carnap, Freud, Loos, Kokoschka, Schoenberg, and Karl Kraus to get some idea of the atmosphere of change and experimentation that prevailed there. This study is an attempt to place an event of major cultural importance, the development of the twelve-tone method, within a cultural-historical framework. The deep involvement, in some cases, of Schoenberg's friends and associates in other cultural events of similar significance makes this cultural climate of special interest.

An oral history of the evolution of the twelve-tone idea cannot delve equally satisfactorily into all of the issues necessary for a total historical explanation. Fundamentally non-analytical in nature, oral history is better at setting a scene than at providing technical detail. Recollections of events and encounters long past may show little identification with the long-since-metamorphosed personality who initially experienced them, and these events are now being retrieved from the transforming bias of voluntary memory. "The aspirations of yesterday were valid for yesterday's ego, not for today's."[1] Furthermore, importance to future generations is not always intuited by the selective memory process: major factors may be forgotten while relative trivialities (perhaps with which the narrator was personally connected) stand out strongly in the mind. A tendency to exaggerate the personal involvement of the individual in events later awarded historical significance seems also to be a human trait.

The strengths of oral history lie in the uniqueness of the material gathered and in the immediate and genuine quality of the recollections. One of the goals of the historian is to re-create the cultural or political flavor of a time so that the readers can imagine what it might have been like to have lived in a place and time different from their own. For this purpose, oral history adds a human dimension to the often sterile accounts drawn solely from formal documents.

Because Schoenberg's development as a musical innovator benefited from his noncompositional activities, the scope of the oral history project extended to subjects who were involved with Schoenberg in a number of musical and nonmusical capacities, including friends, students, and performers of his music. Material has been included from interviews not only with students of Schoenberg, Berg, and Webern, and other musicians involved with Schoenberg's work during his Vienna years, but also with people from other disciplines who knew Schoenberg personally and whose work Schoenberg found compatible with his own. This book is organized into four main sections, each dealing with a different facet of Schoenberg's life: his cultural surroundings, his involvement with performance, his teaching activities, and the evolution of the twelve-tone method. A final section concerns Schoenberg's life after his disclosure of the method and before his immigration to the United States.

The interviews were conducted between March 1972 and July 1974. Because the interview excerpts are almost verbatim transcripts of tape-recorded informal conversations, the subjects, who were often not speaking their native tongues, cannot be held responsible for grammatical inelegancies. The spoken language is never as tightly constructed as the written. Clearly, I can make no claims for the accuracy of people's recollections of events that occurred fifty years ago; it is equally clear that, in some places, their recollections conflict. Some subjects are obviously authoritative on technical musical matters (Erwin Ratz, Max Deutsch, Felix Greissle, Josef Trauneck), as are others on questions of performance practice (Rudolf Kolisch, Marcel Dick, Benar Heifetz, Eugen Lehner). Yet, because of the nonfactual nature of recollections in general, there is a sense in which all memorial reconstructions of the past have equal validity—they are not direct presentations but re-creations made dramatic by the subconscious *ossature* of each individual's persona. Although recollections totally at odds with firmly established historical fact have not been included or have been noted as inaccurate, the subjects, as much as possible, speak for themselves. I have chosen to suggest my preference, in the case of more obscure conflicting accounts, through organization and placement of material rather than through direct statement.

Editing of the interview material has been done with great care and restraint in order to preserve the flavor of the original. I have corrected tenses but left word order untouched, except in such places where the meaning was obscured. Translations of this and other material not otherwise credited are my own.

Interviews

ASKENASE, STEFAN. Munich, 5 November 1973.
CURJEL, HANS. Zollikon, Switzerland, 31 October 1973.
DEUTSCH, MAX. Paris, 21 November 1973.
DICK, MARCEL. Cleveland, Fall 1972.
GÁL, ERNA. London, 11 October 1973.

GALIMIR, FELIX. New York, 28 March 1972.

GREISSLE, FELIX. Manhasset, Long Island, 22 June 1973.

HEIFETZ, BENAR. Great Neck, Long Island, 6 December 1973.

KELLER, ALFRED. Rorschach, Switzerland, 2 November 1973.

KOKOSCHKA, OSKAR. Villeneuve, Switzerland, 30 October 1973.

KOLISCH, RUDOLF. Watertown, Massachusetts, 4 June 1973, 15 December 1973.

LEHNER, EUGEN. Newton Center, Massachusetts, 2 June 1973.

MORGENSTERN, SOMA. New York, 5 December 1973.

PISK, PAUL AMADEUS. Dallas, 3 November 1972.

PLODERER, WOLFGANG. Vienna, 19 November 1973.

RANKL, KRISTINA. London, 12 October 1973.

RATZ, ERWIN. Vienna, 8 November 1973.

SCHMID, ERICH. Geroldswille, Switzerland, 1 November 1973.

SEARLE, HUMPHREY. London, 16 October 1973.

SEIDLHOFER, BRUNO. Vienna, 10 November 1973.

STEUERMANN, CLARA. Cleveland, Fall 1972.

STIEDRY-WAGNER, ERIKA. Zurich, 27 October 1973.

TRAUNECK, JOSEF. Vienna, Summer 1974.

TRUDING, LONA. London, 18 October 1973.

VIERTEL, SALKA. Klosters, Switzerland, 28 October 1973.

Note

1. Samuel Beckett, *Proust* (New York: Grove Press, 1931), p. 3.

Notational Devices and Acknowledgments

Certain notational devices have been used to clarify a situation in which different types of source material are used. The interview material, quoted exactly (within the framework discussed in the Preface), is introduced by the speaker's name in capital letters, flush left, followed by a colon:

FELIX GREISSLE:

or

GREISSLE:

Subsequent lines of the same speech are indented from the left. Succeeding blocks of interview material are separated from one another by an extra line of space.

Extract material quoted entirely from other sources is set in smaller size type and indented from the left and right. When the speaker of such material is indicated, the form used is (Felix Greissle).

A biographical list has been included to identify many of the large number of people referred to in the text. This list comprises all of the people interviewed as well as all those appearing in the text whose names are followed by a superscript capital B (e.g., Erwin Stein[B]). The superscript B is used only with the first appearance of a name in each chapter. In the biographies themselves, the names of those interviewed are set in **boldface type.**

Because of the nature of my project, I have many people to thank for assistance. Foremost are the people whose words appear in these pages. Their contribution is truly a unique one, and the generosity they have exhibited in devoting themselves to the task at hand has been remarkable. In addition, I am grateful to the following people who allowed themselves to be interviewed but whose recollections do not appear: Herta Apostel, the late Helene Berg, Alexander Goehr, Victoria von Hagen, Hans Keller, Louis Krasner, the late Leopold Spinner, Peter Stadlen, and the late Hans Swarovsky. I want to thank Professors Milton Babbitt and Claudio Spies of Princeton University who have in many conversations allowed me the benefit of their knowledge and wisdom while lending frequent help and encouragement. The late Rudolf Kolisch was an important influence. His profound knowledge has added greatly to my understanding. For special assistance with interviewing or for reading portions of the manuscript, I am grateful to Paul Bickart, Robert Black, Regina Busch, Brenda Dalen, Mark DeVoto, Ronald Sabaroff, and David Satz. Cynthia Ovens and Lois Swanson assisted with the translations. I also wish to offer thanks to Nuria Nono, and to Ronald and Lawrence Schoenberg for permission to photograph and include items from the Arnold Schoenberg Institute. I am grateful to Herr Walter Szmolyan for assistance at the Schoenberg Archive in Mödling, to Hans Keller of the BBC, London, for making available an interview broadcast from the BBC Archives, to Lorna Kolisch for permission to include material from the Kolisch Collection at Harvard University, and to Jerry McBride of the Arnold Schoenberg Institute for assistance with the illustrations and helpful advice. Jody Rockmaker generously assisted in the reading of the galleys. Finally, for their patient and wise editorial advice to a first-time author, I am grateful to Maribeth Payne, Michael Sander, and Joan Pitsch of Schirmer Books.

Schoenberg
and
His Circle

Introduction

In the years preceding the appearance of the twelve-tone method of composition, Arnold Schoenberg (1874–1951) was faced with a specific set of musical problems, as he and his pupils Anton Webern (1883–1945) and, to a lesser extent, Alban Berg (1885–1935) began to compose works in which no tonal center was readily discernible. With the absence of tonal focus, the nature of a music that depended upon tension and release—and upon delay, expectation, and arrival—was thrown into question. Concepts of progression were endangered; the resulting paucity of time-span-oriented compositional concepts inhibited the production of large-scale works. While Webern attempted to provide continuity through the use of vocal texts and audible intervallic identities, Berg extended the organization of rhythmic unities within a context retentive of certain tonal ideas. The method eventually created by Schoenberg attempted directly to substitute an alternative organizational procedure for the pitch-class properties of tonal music.

Schoenberg described the twelve-tone method as "composition with twelve tones related only to one another." This method, a highly structured approach to the composition of nontonal music, involves the compositional use of an ordering of the twelve pitch-classes which, taken together with its four systematic transformations (transposition, inversion, retrogression, and retrograde-inversion), becomes the normative reference for, at least, all pitch-associated aspects of a given composition. Its adoption facilitated a resurgence in the use of large-scale forms—initially those familiar from tonal music. This followed experimentation with shorter works, made necessary by the lack of pitch organization for maintaining large-scale structures without a tonal framework. The gradual process of substituting this pitch structure for the organizational properties of tonal harmony

1

occupied Schoenberg's fertile mind during the first two decades of the twentieth century, and the resulting method constitutes perhaps the most important and original single innovation in compositional technique of this time.

Schoenberg developed his method in an atmosphere of intense and grandly fruitful intellectual activity. Significant developments were taking place in nearly every aspect of intellectual life, including philosophy, psychology, architecture, art, and literature, as well as music. Speculation regarding the aesthetic consistency of the twelve-tone method with these coincidental preoccupations leads to an examination of the pattern of events that preceded its inception. Included are the circumstances of the times (political, cultural, and economic) as well as the specific musical situation that created its immediate necessity. In the case of the twelve-tone method—an ingenious and original, if somewhat eclectic, solution to a specific and profound musical problem—the explanation is complicated by the complexity of the individual who was Schoenberg, as well as the multilayered implications of his time.

Although Schoenberg was aware of many contemporary trends, his personal involvement was primarily with the work of three men, Karl Kraus in literature, Oskar Kokoschka in painting, and Adolf Loos in architecture—men whose work in some respects paralleled his own. Loos probably did more than anyone else to insure communication among these four rather solitary figures. Perhaps because Loos was seldom awarded a commission to build, he devoted many hours to lending his support to creative work in various fields. He talked with Kraus in the Café Central and brought young artists, writers, and musicians to meet him. He attended Schoenberg's concerts and obtained commissions for Kokoschka. Alone of the nonmusical figures discussed in this study, he maintained an intimate, personal relationship with Schoenberg and the members of his circle. It is therefore of extreme importance to understand the significance of this father of modern architecture whose work has been too long neglected. The relationship of Kraus to the Schoenberg circle was primarily formal. By virtue of his magazine *Die Fackel*, Kraus had greater public visibility than most of his contemporaries. Although personally acquainted with the Schoenberg circle and sympathetic with its work, Kraus was a private figure who did not socialize extensively outside of his own immediate group. His major influence upon Schoenberg and his pupils lay in the contents of his magazine, which they all read avidly, and in his attitude toward language, which they adopted in their own writing. Although Kokoschka was less theoretical in his thinking than either Kraus or Schoenberg, his views on painting were certainly of interest to Schoenberg. Schoenberg was clearly sympathetic to Kokoschka's intentions to portray the inner rather than the outer persona, and his own paintings reveal an individual style quite removed from and in some respects more revolutionary than Kokoschka's. Kokoschka was more sociable than Kraus, and his recollections disclose a warm and personal knowledge of Schoenberg.

Schoenberg's awareness of other significant figures of early twentieth-century Vienna was more limited. Interaction with philosophers and their works was especially rare. Although the logical positivists of the Vienna Circle (including Moritz Schlick, Rudolf Carnap, and Viktor Kraft) were active in Vienna during Schoenberg's time there, it is not clear that he was even aware of their existence. One philosopher not a member of this circle, Karl Popper[B], attended concerts of the Verein für musikalische Privataufführungen organized by Schoenberg and his disciples, but there is no evidence that he ever met with Schoenberg socially.* Any meeting between Schoenberg, Berg, or Webern and Ludwig Wittgenstein, whose *Tractatus* was highly admired by both

---

*Lona Truding, a Schoenberg pupil interested in philosophy, recalled Popper's attendance at these concerts:

LONA TRUDING: Popper! He's a wonderful man! Extraordinary. . . . He's as great as a man as he is as a thinker; or he is great because he is a great thinker. . . . I would say . . . he didn't fit in. He was an outsider in the best sense of the word. He was a marvelous man. He came to these concerts, but he was not in close relationship. I think he wasn't related with any of that particular circle. But I think he was more in connection with—have you ever heard of that painter Itten[B]?—with that school and the Bauhaus.

the Vienna circle and Karl Kraus, is similarly undocumented. Wittgenstein was interested in music (his brother Paul was a pianist), the family had known Brahms, and Wittgenstein also knew both Kraus and Loos, either of whom might have introduced him to the Schoenberg circle.[1]

Schoenberg and his disciples were seemingly much interested in modern psychology. Freud's works were read and discussed, and Webern even consulted the analyst Alfred Adler in 1913.[2] With the exception of Berg, however, there appears to have been no personal connection between Freud and members of the Schoenberg school.

Berg's attitude toward Freud was ambivalent. Although he once consulted Freud for a medical problem,[3] he seems not to have pursued the relationship.* Berg's great admiration for Karl Kraus, who feuded with a follower of Freud, Fritz Wittels, and consequently attacked Freud's views vociferously in *Die Fackel*, possibly prevented him from viewing Freud's work objectively. He had a glimpse of the idea that Kraus might not be reliable on this issue when Webern consulted Adler and described his experience to Berg. Berg reported in a letter to Schoenberg of 10 October 1913 that much of what Webern had told him seemed "very plausible and sympathetic—it seems totally different from what Kraus attacks."[4]

Schoenberg would have been interested in Freudian theories, if only because he himself loved to theorize, and Freud's ideas would have given him an interesting starting point. In an interview, Salka Viertel's characterization of Schoenberg is revealing:

SALKA VIERTEL: They talked about Freud, they talked a lot about Kraus, they talked a lot about Jung. They dis-

---

*But see Berg's letter to Helene Berg of 29 November 1923 where, in response to news of her receiving psychiatric treatment, he wrote, "Tell the doctor I've forbidden it, and say that if there had been any question of psychoanalytic treatment, we should have gone to Dr. Freud or Dr. Adler, both of whom we have known very well for many years." Alban Berg, *Letters to His Wife*, ed. and trans. Bernard Grun (London: Faber and Faber, 1971), p. 335.

cussed it, but I never thought it was done in some kind of unliterary and uninformed way. I mean, somebody read something. Certainly, my brother [Edward Steuermann[B]] was very much interested in psychology. He never was psychoanalyzed and never wanted to be. He was very skeptical about it but somewhere very interested. But Schoenberg would invent immediately another method, another science. He was incredibly inventive. Such a conversation with him would be fascinating because he would focus on something about which nobody had thought before. That was his magic really, this constant effectiveness. . . . He played tennis, for example, and he had some special strokes. He was very—sometimes it [what Schoenberg said] sounded childish, but it had always some spark in it which only a genius could have.

Without further documentation, it is impossible to assess the influence of Freudian concepts upon Schoenberg. It is clear that Schoenberg met often and interacted intellectually with Adolf Loos, and to a lesser extent, Karl Kraus and Oskar Kokoschka. It would be inaccurate to say that these four men constituted a circle. There is a loose but vital connection among them, and the connection was reciprocal. Because of the excitement of their interaction, their relationships are investigated in the opening chapters of this study.

Although Schoenberg's involvement with Kraus, Loos, and Kokoschka yielded significant exchanges of ideas and undoubtedly contributed to the direction of his thoughts, he worked mainly alone and with his own students. His pedagogical activities, and especially his complicated intimacy with Berg and Webern, were also important to his creative development. He was a skilled teacher, whose methods were as innovative as his subject matter was traditional. He considered his music to be based firmly upon that of earlier periods, and his students consequently received from him a solid musical background, as well as a comprehensive philosophical outlook, which still appears very important to them.

That he owed much in his musical thinking to interaction with his students is a fact which he readily admitted.

Schoenberg was involved in problems of performance as director of his Verein für musikalische Privataufführungen, an organization whose stated goal was to provide intelligible performances of new and unfamiliar works in a receptive atmosphere. Many long hours of work by him and his students were required to achieve this goal. This fervent activity immediately preceded the disclosure of the twelve-tone method, and the Society was thus an important factor in its development.

Some mystery surrounds the actual inception of the twelve-tone method and Schoenberg's relationship to it. Although his students do not recall any discussion of it prior to the famous meeting of 1923 where the method was first publicly revealed, they remember in some detail the meeting and Schoenberg's subsequent attitude toward teaching the method. Schoenberg considered the method a private affair and for some time resisted describing it both publicly, to his own students, and regarding certain of its more intricate aspects, to anybody.

One of the questions that immediately confronts the student of early twentieth-century Vienna is that of an explanation for the many new cultural and intellectual developments occurring simultaneously not only in Vienna but in Berlin and Paris as well. Why should this period be so amazingly rich in new ideas and achievements? How does this intense activity relate to World War I? Are the achievements of major figures in different disciplines related through their respective reflections of the same cultural and political influences? In her essay, "Tradition and the Modern Age," Hannah Arendt develops the thesis that our tradition of social thought, which had its genesis in Plato and Aristotle, came to an end with the theories of Karl Marx.[5] She explains this view as follows:

> The beginning was made when, in *The Republic*'s allegory of the cave, Plato described the sphere of human affairs—

all that belongs to the living together of men in a common world—in terms of darkness, confusion, and deception which those aspiring to true being must turn away from and abandon if they want to discover the clear sky of eternal ideas. The end came with Marx's declaration that philosophy and its truth are located not outside the affairs of men and their common world but precisely in them, and can be "realized" only in the sphere of living together, which he called "society," through the emergence of "socialized men."[6]

This interpretation, which Arendt develops in detail, suggests that during the latter part of the nineteenth century a crisis in social thought resulted in the decline of a tradition that had been a part of Western civilization nearly from its inception, leaving in all areas of intellectual endeavor a vacuum inviting feverish activity.

That turn-of-the-century Vienna nonetheless placed much stress upon classical values may be interpreted as an attempt to bolster a thing already past its flowering rather than the celebration of a living mode of thought. Thus Arendt writes:

The end of a tradition does not necessarily mean that traditional concepts have lost their power over the minds of men. On the contrary, it sometimes seems that this power of well-worn notions and categories becomes more tyrannical as the tradition loses its living force and as the memory of its beginning recedes; it may even reveal its full coercive force only after its end has come and men no longer even rebel against it.[7]

Hence we find in the nineteenth century a glorification of the past in a society which, no longer able to adopt the ideals of a tradition as its own, yet celebrated them at a time when its basic tenets were about to be irretrievably lost.

Despite the suggestion that by the beginning of the twentieth century the traditions of the past were irrelevant to modern life, these traditions continued to hold a predominant, if not lively, spot in the curriculum of schools and universities in Vienna. This situation has been graphically described by the author Stefan Zweig in his autobiography *The World of Yesterday:* "It was a dull, pointless learning that the old pedagogy forced upon us, not for the sake of life, but for the sake of learning. And the only truly joyful moment of happiness for which I have to thank my school was the day that I was able to shut the door on it forever."[8] It was this education that tormented most talented Viennese youths of the early 1900s, and it is perhaps not surprising, therefore, that there existed a general urgency to achieve something new. The idealistic drive for change, common to the young of any time, must have received a special impetus from a decrepit monarchy, itself the embodiment of a tradition no longer meaningful, and from the rapid changes brought about by the rise of science and technology.

World War I was in many respects an idealized war. In addition to economic motivations, there existed at the time a strong feeling that a cleansing of the collective soul was essential and that the war, when it came, was necessary in order to clear the way for a new society. The war was thus to be a final death and celebration of death for an entire way of life. The falseness of this celebration was recognized only by a few, especially the journalist Karl Kraus, who maintained one of the few continual cries of outrage throughout the war.

If the transformations in philosophy and psychology and similarly those in literature, music, and architecture were at least in part compensations, conscious or not, for an alienation from tradition, it seems appropriate that many of these new developments comprised in one way or another simplifications of past styles (although they sometimes resulted in new complications). Adolf Loos, for example, was much influenced by the classical forms of architecture, especially those of the Romans. Schoenberg, Berg, and Kokoschka all insisted that their activities maintained links with past tradition. Arendt says of this in relation to Karl Kraus:

> It seems tempting to believe, and would indeed be a comforting thought, that those few who ventured out onto the

most exposed positions of the time and paid the full price of isolation at least thought of themselves as the precursors of a new age. That certainly was not the case. In his essay on Karl Kraus, [Walter] Benjamin[B] brought up this question: Does Kraus stand "at the threshold of a new age?" "Alas, by no means. He stands at the threshold of the Last Judgment." And at this threshold there really stood all those who later became the masters of the "new age"; they looked upon the dawn of a new age basically as a decline and viewed history along with the traditions which led up to this decline as a field of ruins.[9]

Both Kraus and the author Walter Benjamin adopted the technique of juxtaposition in an attempt to express more than the literal meaning of a given text—to suggest rather than to state explicitly, "so as not to ruin everything with explanations that seek to provide a causal or systematic connection."[10] Benjamin left behind him a large collection of quotable excerpts which he intended to use in a work made up entirely of such items, juxtaposed so as to highlight the special meaning that he saw in them. Hannah Arendt attributes this procedure to Benjamin's understanding of the end of tradition:

> Walter Benjamin knew that the break in tradition and the loss of authority which occurred in his lifetime, were irreparable, and he concluded that he had to discover new ways of dealing with the past. In this he became a master when he discovered that the transmissibility of the past had been replaced by its citability and that in place of its authority there had arisen a strange power to settle down, piecemeal, in the present and to deprive it of "peace of mind," the mindless peace of complacency.[11]

This method of eroding the present, by presenting the language of the present in a context that enhances its meaning, was used extensively by Kraus in his journal *Die Fackel.*

Kraus appears to have understood both the breach in tradition and the hopelessness of a loss which was already at that time, before the war years, beyond recall. In his journal, he reprinted newspaper stories and advertisements with little or no comment, their very appearance in that context being itself a statement. At times, Kraus compared in print disparate items from the newspapers in such a way that the juxtaposition itself lent meaning to the quoted material which it lacked in its original context. In these quotations, it was not only the subject matter but the language in which it was expressed that Kraus considered significant. Arendt tells us that this method, which relied upon the sensibilities of the reader for the necessary interpretation, was considered by Benjamin to be in the nature of a purge:

> This discovery of the modern function of quotations, according to Benjamin, who exemplified it by Karl Kraus, was born out of despair—not the despair of a past that refuses "to throw its light on the future" and lets the human mind "wander in darkness" as in Tocqueville, but out of the despair of the present and the desire to destroy it; hence their power is "not the strength to preserve but to cleanse, to tear out of context, to destroy."*[12]

The juxtapositional techniques of Kraus and Benjamin served as models for the current study, which contains interview narrative interspersed with explanatory and historical commentary. Oral history has been since the time of Herodotus a juxtapositional method, contrasting accounts by various witnesses of recent events. Presenting the interview material in a juxtapositional form, therefore, serves the

*The juxtaposition method has been used more recently in a film concerning the occupation of France during World War II, *The Sorrow and the Pity*. In this film, made in 1969, the director Marcel Ophuls interviews people whose lives were variously affected by the Occupation. Included are members of the occupying forces and the Resistance; townspeople in the small town of Clermont-Ferrand, which was the headquarters for the Vichy government; and surviving Jews, including the later Prime Minister Pierre Mendes-France. Selections of interviews with these participants in the war drama are juxtaposed to actual newsreel footage along with very few staged scenes. The nonverbal composite of this juxtaposed material creates an exegetical impression impossible to attain by more conventional verbal means.

dual purpose of relating form to method and harmonizing with the views of those under discussion. The impetus for the study was a desire to investigate the genesis of the twelve-tone idea. Its purpose, however, is not to provide a new body of facts concerning the development of the twelve-tone method, although this does indeed occur. Rather it is to recreate as far as possible, through the recollections of the participants, the nonspecific flavor of that time of brilliant creation in a nonetheless decaying culture and the humanity of those struggling to achieve a rebirth.

Notes

1. For a discussion of Wittgenstein's relationship to Kraus and Loos, see Paul Englemann, "Kraus, Loos, and Wittgenstein," in *Letters from Ludwig Wittgenstein with a Memoir* (New York: Horizon Press, 1968), pp. 122–132; or William M. Johnston, *The Austrian Mind: An Intellectual and Social History, 1848–1938* (Berkeley: University of California Press, 1972), pp. 209–213.

2. Hans Moldenhauer and Rosaleen Moldenhauer, *Anton von Webern: A Chronicle of his Life and Work* (New York: Alfred A. Knopf, 1979), pp. 178–181.

3. Theodor W. Adorno, *Alban Berg: Der Meister des kleinsten Übergangs* (Vienna: Verlag Elisabeth Lafite; Oesterreichischer Bundesverlag, 1968), p. 25.

4. Quoted in Mosco Carner, *Alban Berg: The Man and the Work* (London: Gerald Duckworth, 1975), p. 21.

5. Hannah Arendt, "Tradition and the Modern Age," in *Between Past and Future: Eight Exercises in Political Thought* (New York: Penguin Books, 1978), pp. 17–40.

6. Ibid., p. 17.

7. Ibid., p. 26.

8. Stefan Zweig, *The World of Yesterday* (London: Cassell, 1953), p. 30. For similar views held by Alban Berg, see Joan Allen Smith, "The Berg-Hohenberg Correspondence," in *Alban Berg Studien* (Vienna: Universal Edition, 1981), vol. 2: *Alban Berg Symposion Wien 1980: Tagungsbericht*, ed. Rudolf Klein, pp. 189–197.

9. Hannah Arendt, "Walter Benjamin: 1892–1940," trans. Harry Zohn, in *Men in Dark Times* (New York: Harcourt Brace Jovanovich, 1968), p. 191.

10. Ibid., p. 202.

11. Ibid., p. 193.

12. Ibid., p. 193.

~ PART I ~

The Cultural Ambience

It was like for us youngsters then a transition from—Schoenberg had such a marvelous word for it: "*Ach, so blumenreiche Romantik*," the "Oh-so-flowery Romanticism"— . . . to a new "Age of Reason" or to a new age of consciousness.

Lona Truding

≈ 1 ≈

Schoenberg's Vienna

There is such a thing as a spirit of time, one calls it *Zeitgeist*, and this *Zeitgeist* expresses itself in a definite style and Schoenberg, or Kokoschka[B], or Gropius, or that French one, Corbusier, these great personalities were instruments for that particular *Zeitgeist* to bring into culture what the *Zeitgeist* thought necessary. . . . That *Zeitgeist* is beyond a single individuality, so one cannot say they had a kind of common agreement to compose in a new vein or something; . . . but it was in the spirit of the time . . . which really brought certain individualities together to express what has to come into that time.

Lona Truding

While the nature of an intelligible *Zeitgeist* may be difficult to unveil in certain historical periods, the Vienna of the early 1900s possessed a more clearly defined intellectual character than have most cities at most times.[1] The Emperor Franz Joseph, whose reign stretched from December 1848 to November 1916, had long lent an air of security and per-

15

manence to the Viennese way of life. Franz Joseph was a dignified if unimaginative leader devoted to duty. He worked eight to ten hours daily signing documents and holding audiences and slept on a narrow camp bed. At the same time, he maintained all of the elegance of traditional Habsburg entertainment. Throughout the military failures of his reign, his very predictability helped to hold the Empire together. He stood for security and perpetuity, and he was deeply respected, especially in his later years. His family life was minimal. Ill-suited by her intelligence and independence to the stifling traditionalism of court life, the Empress Elisabeth preferred to spend her time riding in the country and looking after her health in various European spas. Abdicating control even of her own children to the Emperor's domineering mother the Archduchess Sophia, she spent much of her time abroad. Although in his later years the Emperor took to breakfasting with the actress Katharina Schratt (1855–1940), he grieved deeply when Elisabeth was senselessly assassinated by an Italian anarchist in 1898.

Relations between Franz Joseph and his only son the Crown Prince Rudolf (1858–1889) were strained, and the Crown Prince was excluded from political affairs. A sensitive and intellectual liberal, Rudolf was popular with the Viennese public. The circumstances concerning his death with that of the Baroness Mary Vetsera at Mayerling on 5 November 1888 have never been explicated by scholars. Unhappily married to the Princess Stephanie, Rudolf was publicly snubbed by Franz Joseph shortly before his death when he appealed to Pope Leo XIII for an annulment. Denied a voice in politics, unhappy in marriage, and ignored by his father, Rudolf had little of value to occupy his life.

The bureaucratic structure supporting the monarchy was formidable and, as the Emperor aged, increasingly out of control. Although he acceded to demands for constitutional rule in 1860 and 1867, and allowed universal male suffrage in 1907, Franz Joseph kept a tight rein on wealth and privilege. Relations between the Emperor and the heir presumptive Archduke Franz Ferdinand (1863–1914) were difficult owing to the latter's meddling in politics and his morganatic marriage to Sophie Chotek. Franz Ferdinand was disliked by the Viennese for his arrogance, his authoritarianism, and for a clericalism encouraged by Sophie. Stefan Zweig described the character of the archduke:

> Franz Ferdinand lacked everything that counts for real popularity in Austria; amiability, personal charm and easy-goingness. I had often seen him in the theatre. There he sat in his box, broad and mighty, with cold, fixed gaze, never casting a single friendly glance towards the audience or encouraging the actors with hearty applause. He was never seen to smile, and no photographs showed him relaxed. . . . His wife was equally unfriendly. They were surrounded by an icy air; one knew that they had no friends, and also that the old Emperor hated him with all his heart because he did not have sufficient tact to hide his impatience to succeed to the throne.[2]

In order to avoid political repercussions, the Viennese had stressed the romantic aspects of the death of Rudolf. Mourning for the dead Crown Prince far exceeded that accorded Archduke Franz Ferdinand, whose murder with Sophie at Sarajevo in 1914 sparked off World War I.

The aristocracy, a strictly hierarchized group whose access to the royal family was rigorously controlled by rank, lent to the Viennese social calendar a glitter and frivolity totally at odds with what was to come later. Following the lives of the rich and privileged was a favorite pastime of the Viennese middle classes. Since the artistic and educational institutions of Vienna were controlled by the same bureaucracy as the governmental machine, the aristocracy could corrupt the judicial and university systems through a protection system that insured the most favorable decisions for those of its own rank. This system led to censorship in the theatre and injustice in the courts where libel suits were commonplace.

During the last days of the Empire, previously strict censorship was somewhat relaxed through the growing ineptitude of the bureaucratic establishment. Although criticism of the government was forbidden, articles banned in one paper often slipped by in another simply because the censorship authorities were slipshod. Once printed, an article could be quoted by the other papers. Papers often printed articles favorable to the aristocracy in order to curry support at court. The papers, not widely sold, were commonly read in the cafés which subscribed to a wide variety and also handled mail. The leading paper in Vienna, the *Neue Freie Presse*, which could compete intellectually with any paper in Europe, expressed the artistic and intellectual aspirations of the Viennese. Articles by Ibsen, Shaw, Hauptmann, Zola, and Strindberg found their way into its pages. Politically it was liberal but necessarily cautious. It was this caution, and a tendency to extol the literary at the expense of social justice, which outraged Karl Kraus.

The character of the monarchy acted as a pervasive influence upon all aspects of Viennese life. There was a general attitude of security and moderation, and most people did not worry about the future. As Robert Musil described it, change was gradual:

> Of course cars also drove along these roads—but not too many cars! The conquest of the air had begun here too; but not too intensively. Now and then a ship was sent off to South America or the Far East; but not too often. There was no ambition to have world markets and world power. Here one was in the centre of Europe, at the focal point of the world's old axes.[3]

Perhaps because the monarchy seemed secure and unambitious and the military uninspiring, the Viennese preferred to devote themselves to the goal of artistic supremacy. Thus, the means for cultural experimentation were at hand at a time when a sense of coming chaos provided a unifying stimulus. In pre-war Vienna, the cultural atmosphere encouraged an exchange of information in a closely knit intellectual community and supported major developments in diverse endeavors ranging from architecture to cafeterias.

Arnold Schoenberg, who was to be responsible for the development of the twelve-tone method, was born and raised in this imperial city. His early musical training arose primarily from playing chamber music; as a composer, he was almost entirely self-taught. The man who most influenced Schoenberg during his youth was his friend and teacher Oskar Adler[B]. Adler, who enriched Schoenberg's school years with instruction in violin, viola, and the rudiments of harmony, had many interests, including philosophy and astrology, and may have introduced Schoenberg to the works of Schopenhauer and Kant. Schoenberg, in his essay "My Evolution," described his debt to Adler:

> Through him I learned of the existence of a theory of music, and he directed my first steps therein. He also stimulated my interest in poetry and philosophy and all my acquaintance with classical music derived from playing quartets with him, for even then he was already an excellent first violinist.[4]

Besides Adler, Schoenberg's only other music teacher was his friend and later brother-in-law, Alexander von Zemlinsky[B]. Zemlinsky had studied at the Vienna Conservatory and first encountered Schoenberg when they were both involved in the amateur orchestra Polyhymnia, Zemlinsky as conductor and Schoenberg as the only cellist. Zemlinsky recalled the meeting:

> The orchestra had chosen me as its conductor. It was not large: a few violins, one viola, one cello, one double-bass— or only half a one, really. . . . At the single cello desk sat a young man, fervently ill-treating his instrument—not that the instrument deserved any better; it had been bought with three painfully saved-up Gulden at Vienna's so-called Tandelmarkt. This cellist was none other than Arnold Schoenberg. At that time Schoenberg was still a junior bank clerk, but he was not overzealous in his profession, preferring music paper to the paper-money at the bank.[5]

Schoenberg studied harmony and counterpoint with Zemlinsky until about 1900. Alma Mahler[B], widow of the composer, who also studied composition with Zemlinsky, considered him an excellent teacher:

Alexander von Zemlinsky was one of the finest musicians and a magnificent teacher. When I went to him for lessons—usually he came to our house—I often met his favorite student, Arnold Schönberg. "He'll be the talk of the world someday," said Zemlinsky. And that is exactly what Schönberg, the composer, has become, aside from teaching and influencing others, such as Alban Berg, Anton von Webern, Ernst Krenek[B]. To this entire musical generation Zemlinsky was the teacher par excellence. His technical brilliance was unique.[6]

Zemlinsky introduced Schoenberg to a number of important musical influences, including Wagner, and by the time Schoenberg returned to Vienna in 1903 following a stay of a year and a half in Berlin, he had already composed a number of important works. These include *Verklärte Nacht* (1899), the *Gurrelieder* (1901), and *Pelleas und Melisande* (1903). Upon his return to Vienna, Schoenberg became actively involved in promoting performance activities. In 1904 he began to teach, first at the school for girls run by Dr. Eugenie Schwarzwald[B], and then privately. Two of his earliest pupils were Anton Webern and Alban Berg. Together with the performers Edward Steuermann[B] (1892–1964) and Rudolf Kolisch (1896–1978), Webern and Berg were to form the basis of a group of disciples who remained loyal to Schoenberg throughout his career.

The writing of all of these composers was at first tonal, deriving from the music of Wagner and Mahler. Gradually, however, the use of distantly related chords and a progressive freeing of modulatory techniques resulted in works in which the cadential structure of tonal music was seriously disrupted. The most influential work by Schoenberg during this period was the Chamber Symphony, Op. 9, completed in 1906. As the structural unification provided by harmonic progression disappeared, works became extremely short, and efforts to develop new unifying features became paramount. This process resulted quite early (by 1911) in pieces where all twelve tones appeared in a self-contained manner. The use of twelve-note chords and themes after this time was frequent and it is this development that precipitated the genesis of the twelve-tone idea. It was to be another decade, however, before the concepts of ordering and permutation (essential to the twelve-tone method) made their appearance.

When examining the activities of the Schoenberg circle of composers in the years preceding the emergence of the twelve-tone method, one must consider the unique cultural climate that surrounded these musical endeavors. The nature of this method was in subjective, though intangible, ways determined and enhanced by the exposure of composers to the ideas of nonmusicians. Obvious superficial similarities exist among the works of the intellectuals and artists of the time, primarily because of a similarity of social and political stimuli. More subtle and meaningful comparisons, related to the void created by the separation from previous traditions, become evident through a more flavorful, if less detailed, sampling of that curious and *sui generis* cultural soup which then constituted Viennese cultural life.

For Schoenberg, perhaps the most important nonmusical association, although not the closest personal one, was with the poet and social critic Karl Kraus (1874–1936).[7] Kraus, who turned to journalism and literature after an unsuccessful beginning as an actor, was in his early years a contributor to the Viennese newspaper the *Neue Freie Presse.* In 1899 Kraus, by then at odds with the establishment, refused a lucrative permanent position at the *Neue Freie Presse* to found his own journal, *Die Fackel* (The Torch). The first issue appeared in April of 1899. In the beginning there were numerous contributors, including Peter Altenberg[B], Richard Dehmel[B], Egon Friedell[B], Oskar Kokoschka, Adolf Loos, August Strindberg, Frank Wedekind, Franz Werfel, and Arnold Schoenberg. However, Kraus wrote most of the material himself, and from 1911 until the last issue in 1936, the magazine was entirely his own work.

Die Fackel was an immediate and tremendous success. Although always highly controversial, it was read and widely discussed far beyond Kraus's own immediate circle by many who could not have been said to agree with his political and moral views. This popularity continued until shortly before World War II, and Schoenberg, Berg, and Webern were all avid readers. In a letter of 4 August 1909 to his future wife, Helene Nahowski, Berg described his admiration for *Die Fackel:*

> Reading this whole issue gave me a joy of spirit such as I have rarely known, free from all dross and disappointment. I think of the mediocre productions of Wagner and Strauss at the Vienna Opera, the concerts this year, where Mahler's symphonies are being so wretchedly performed. Against all this mass of disappointments in every field, here is a masterpiece—the latest issue of the *Fackel!* Oh, if only you like it half as much as I do![8]

In the pages of *Die Fackel,* Kraus waged war against decadence and corruption in the political and social life of Vienna. His chief targets were the newspapers, which published an endless stream of trivial and sensational news at the expense of serious coverage of major issues. Although Kraus was involved in numerous lawsuits filed by individuals lampooned in his pages, the press responded to his criticisms by maintaining a conspiracy of silence regarding his name and activities.

When World War I came, Kraus filled the pages of *Die Fackel* with sharp political criticism and realistic reporting. By now an established and mature writer, Kraus focused his satirical powers upon global issues. He was at this time forty years old, a highly controversial but respected figure recognized throughout Austria but essentially unknown beyond its frontiers. It was Kraus's uncompromising and courageous pacifism during this war period that gave him his international reputation and significance as a writer. His ability to feel and express the overwhelming suffering of all humanity in that most agonizing of wars and his persistence in setting forth the idiocies and inhumanities of his own people gave Kraus moral stature. It is his uncompromising purity in a time of global insanity that lends the sometimes dated work of Karl Kraus its force and relevance today.

Kraus's personal influence was less than that of his writings. A solitary figure, he worked all night and slept during the day, emerging in the evening to sit in the cafés for dinner followed by coffee. It was considered a great honor to be invited to sit at his table while he refined punctuation for the next issue of *Die Fackel.* Berg and Schoenberg both met Kraus before 1910, but personal interaction was limited due to Kraus's working habits.

Although Kraus's schedule made extended conversation difficult, he had a few friends with whom he felt especially close both personally and artistically. One of these friends was the architect Adolf Loos (1870–1933). Born in Brno, Loos arrived in Vienna at the age of twenty-six, after study in Bohemia, military service, and three years in the United States, where he lived with relatives and earned money through washing dishes and other odd jobs. In Vienna he found the established architect Otto Wagner (1841–1918). After many years of designing buildings in the then-fashionable neo-Baroque style, Wagner proposed, in a lecture published as *Modern Architecture* in 1895,[9] that "it may be regarded as proved that art and artists always represent their own epoch." Thus, "all modern forms must correspond to new materials and the new requirements of our time, if they are to fit modern mankind."[10] This defense of modernism was a radical departure from conservative Viennese habit, which concentrated upon copying the more ornate styles of the past, and much closer to the ideas of the American architect Louis Sullivan, whose work Loos would have encountered during his stay in the United States. Although Wagner's own work never equalled in modernity the promise of his words, he nonetheless inspired his students and those around him with a new ideal.

Wagner's two most famous disciples were Joseph Maria Olbrich (1867–1908) and Josef Hoffmann (1870–1956). It was Olbrich who designed the striking new exhibition building for the Secession Movement in 1898, a flat, cube-like structure with a splendidly sculpted art nouveau dome. The Secession had been founded by the circle around the painter Gustav Klimt[B] in 1897 as a reaction against a conservative establishment and in support of the English Arts and Crafts Movement.[11] Hoffmann joined the Secession several months after its founding and, after Olbrich's departure in 1899 to assume a post in Darmstadt, became the leading figure in the younger generation of Viennese architects. He and Klimt withdrew from the Secession in 1905, leaving the group considerably impoverished. But there had been eight years of exhibitions—by such painters as Munch and Van Gogh—and an active Arts and Crafts Movement culminating in the foundation of the Wiener Werkstätte by Hoffmann in 1903, one year before Berg and Webern began study with Schoenberg.

The focus of the art nouveau–inspired Secession Movement was the belief that ornament of the past was unsuited to modern times and that a new contemporary ornament arising from the present and appropriate to its materials should be developed. From this belief evolved the nearly two-dimensional, often erotic decorations found on wall surfaces of buildings such as the Secession and in the more florid designs employed by the Arts and Crafts designers of the Wiener Werkstätte.

Loos, who admired Otto Wagner, was for a time friendly with the Secessionists but soon quarreled with them and often criticized them in print. Like the artists and craftsmen of the Secession, he admired the designs of the English, but his admiration had as its genesis a love for simplicity rather than an aversion to technology.

Although Loos had much in common with the Secession architects in their rejection of the ornamental styles of the past and their use of simple cube-like constructions without window borders, he differed sharply from them in his view of ornament. The Secession approach to decoration—although certainly differing outwardly from the neo-Baroque and other mimetic fashions and noteworthy for its attempt to utilize modern materials to reflect contemporary culture—nevertheless did not advocate a substantial dogmatic digression from the original masquerading function of ornament in those historicist styles. Loos felt that buildings and their contents should be allowed to reveal their structural elements through their function and materials (an ideal not far removed from Louis Sullivan's "form follows function") unobscured by irrelevant decoration. In this he was close to Otto Wagner, whose statement "What is impractical can never be beautiful" was echoed by Loos.[12] Rather than inventing new ornament, Loos wanted to eliminate all ornament that did not serve to enhance and clarify the formal structure of an object. This desire to reveal structure rather than to obfuscate it, a desire exemplified also in the sparse, undecorative style of Webern's music, followed closely Kraus's ideas of language. As Kraus himself put it:

> All that Adolf Loos and I did—he literally, I linguistically—was to show that there is a difference between an urn and a chamberpot, and that in this difference there is leeway for culture. But the others, the "positive ones," are divided into those who use the urn as a chamberpot and those who use the chamberpot as an urn.[13]

Perhaps Loos's most important extracurricular contribution to intellectual and artistic well-being in Vienna was his work on behalf of young artists and writers. Long a supporter of the Bohemian poet Peter Altenberg[B], Loos was often also helpful to Schoenberg and his disciples, with whom he became close. More than Kraus, he associated himself with musical events, and although hard of hearing, he attended many of Schoenberg's concerts.

Loos's assistance and encouragement were especially important to the painter Oskar Kokoschka (1886–1980). Kokoschka was earning his living decorating fans and designing post cards when Loos first met him in 1908 at an exhibition sponsored by Kokoschka's employer the Wiener Werkstätte, the Kunstgewerbeschule, and a group around Gustav Klimt. Kokoschka had been a pupil at the Kunstgewerbeschule, where he learned drawing, lithography, ceramics, and bookbinding, but not painting, which he taught himself. Interested exclusively in the human figure, he rebelled against what he considered the inhuman approach of the

Kunstgewerbeschule and the Wiener Werkstätte where, under the direction of Josef Hoffmann, a botanical style predominated. As Kokoschka himself said in an interview:

> In both these institutions [the Kunstgewerbeschule and the Wiener Werkstätte] I was the only one who drew *only* figures, I never fell for the vogue for ornamental decoration. Joseph Hoffmann was right in the middle of it, he had just designed the decorations for Klimt's studio in the Feldmühlgasse, all in the geometric style, nothing but squares and oblongs. Loos didn't have to tell me anything about his crusade against ornament, I never had any taste for it, no more than for abstract art today. It's all unhuman.[14]

In the first Kunstschau, Kokoschka displayed four large tapestry designs called *Die Traumtragenden* (The Bearers of Dreams), a skull-like self-portrait head with visible nerve endings and a gaping mouth, and the illustrations for a book *Die Träumenden Knaben* which had been published earlier in the year by the Wiener Werkstätte and which ranks as one of its finest achievements. The meeting between Loos and Kokoschka was recorded by both architect and painter:

> (Oskar Kokoschka) In my opinion Loos was outstanding both as a creative personality and as a critic. My meeting with him during the Kunstschau of 1909 [*sic*] was decisive not only for my career but also for my life. It may seem immodest, but I must say of Loos what Dante said of Vergil: he led me through the heaven and hell of life as a faithful companion and guide. He was the most important architect of the modern movement. . . . But he never received a public commission. . . .
> So Adolf Loos had time to help me. "You must paint!" He had a wide circle of supporters and acquaintances, whom he was able to interest in my work. To paint his portrait—to come into such close contact with so great a man and artist—was a major experience for me.[15]

> (Adolf Loos) I met him in the year 1908. He had designed the poster for the Vienna "Kunstschau." I was told that he

was employed by the *Wiener Werkstätte* to do fan painting, designs for post cards and the like, in the German
way—art in the service of commerce. It was immediately
clear to me that here one of the greatest sins against the
holy spirit was being perpetrated. I had him called. He
came. What was he doing now? He was making a bust. (It
was ready only in his brain.) It was purchased by me. How
much did it cost? A cigarette. Agreed. I never haggle. But
finally we agreed on fifty Kronen. . . .

When my "Haus auf dem Michaelerplatz" was being
constructed, my enthusiasm for Kokoschka was regarded
as proof of my worthlessness.[16]

Kokoschka's contributions to the Kunstschau were the
scandal of the exhibit and received much adverse publicity
in the press. Klimt supported Kokoschka strongly, however,
and Loos offered financial support which allowed him to
leave the Wiener Werkstätte in order to paint full-time.

In addition to giving Kokoschka his start in painting,
Loos introduced him to Viennese intellectual life. It was
through Loos that Kokoschka met Karl Kraus and the circle
around him. Kokoschka appreciated the literary activities of
this circle, and his work impressed Kraus who gave him his
support. Kokoschka would see Kraus at the Café Central,
where he sat with Altenberg, or perhaps more often he
would join Loos at the Café Museum or the Café Herrenhof
where Loos was a regular customer along with Else Lasker-
Schüler, Max Oppenheimer, and Alban Berg. Prior to World
War I, the coffee house served as the principal meeting
place for the exchange of ideas, the reading of newspapers,
and for conversational stimulation.

Although Kokoschka spent a great deal of time with the
Kraus circle, his concerns were less intellectually connected
to the objective of social change. As he himself wrote, "It is
not my trade to unmask society, but to seek in the portrait
of an individual his inner life, that measure of all things, and
never to rob humanity of its value."[17] Thus his reaction to
World War I, in contrast to the pacifistic social outcry of
Kraus, was more individual: after the war, he refused to

shake hands with any man whom he felt might have killed someone in battle.

Kokoschka was also well acquainted with the Schoenberg circle and painted both Schoenberg and Webern. According to Remigius Netzer, Schoenberg said of Kokoschka: "Kokoschka is one of those strong natures who can afford to express *themselves,* aware that they are thereby making their contribution to the expression of everyone and everything: the universe itself. This is without any doubt the task of the great artist."[18]

The relationships among the four characters who form the primary focus of this study—Schoenberg, Kraus, Loos, and Kokoschka—were neither continuous nor always intimate. They did not together constitute any sort of "circle" or "ism." Although they did not often meet to discuss their ideas, they did follow each other's work. (Their mutual respect is celebrated in the *Festschrift* articles which they wrote for each other's birthdays.) None of them had a large circle of followers in his own discipline. Schoenberg, who came closest to this, had disciples because he had students, but in essence he worked alone. Each of these four was, in an important sense, an outcast, made so by his own originality and by the strength and uncompromising nature of his vision. What they share is not to be found by examining their personal relationships to each other but rather by seeing how their time affected them in similar ways. All four men were isolated by their lack of acceptance and linked together by the evils of the time and the strength of their mutual understanding. Karl Kraus expressed this feeling of insularity: "I hear noises which others don't hear and which disturb for me the music of the spheres, which others don't hear either."[19]

Of the people interviewed on the subject of Schoenberg's relationship to Karl Kraus and Adolf Loos, only Oskar Kokoschka knew Schoenberg during the early days of his career when his involvement with these figures was closest. When I arrived to visit Kokoschka at his house in Switzerland, he was busy washing dishes. He came out from the kitchen, dish cloth in hand, and offered me tea. After we had settled, he talked freely and with great warmth about his friendship with Schoenberg, prompted occasionally by his gracious wife Olga. He had an openness of manner and a humanity that was immediately endearing. Despite being far more accustomed to interviews about his own life, he was eager to talk about Schoenberg and his feelings about Schoenberg's work. When I visited him later with Rudolf Kolisch, he again welcomed me generously.

Kolisch himself was a remarkable figure. A musical intellectual in the best sense, his remarks on Schoenberg are especially thoughtful. His interview style, hampered by his own reticence and, on my part, by two large Great Danes, does not convey the depth of his knowledge. He talked much more freely over lunch in his old-fashioned Brookline kitchen, or on the way to the dentist, when he felt able to speak without the concern of speaking for posterity. The brother-in-law of Schoenberg, Kolisch had personal knowledge of the complexities of Schoenberg's personality from 1918 until Schoenberg's death in 1951. This personal intimacy was shared by Schoenberg's son-in-law Felix Greissle, who was also a pupil. While Kolisch was a performer, Greissle's expertise was in the area of theory.

Erwin Ratz was a highly gifted and intelligent man. More accustomed to speaking than Kolisch, he is important in this study for his knowledge of Schoenberg immediately following the war years. Salka Viertel was the sister of Edward Steuermann. When I visited her in her mountain retreat in Switzerland, she was retired from an eventful life but still opinionated and full of energy. She had visited Schoenberg often with Steuermann when she was a fledgling actress in the company of Max Reinhardt. Intelligent, witty, and vivacious, she had a lively mind and an acute political sense.

The other three people who appear in this chapter had more distant relationships with Schoenberg. Lona Truding studied with Schoenberg at the Schwarzwald School in the early twenties. She knew Schoenberg in a classroom situation and saw little of him socially. Her value in this study is in her knowledge of the Schwarzwald School and in her involvement with the cultural environment that surrounded it. Kristina Rankl was married to Karl Rankl, a student of Schoenberg. Most of her recollections relate to Rankl's own memories. However, as a friend of the Kolisch family, she has contributed her own thoughts on post–World War I Viennese culture. Wolfgang Ploderer is the son of a member of the Schoenberg circle, Rudolf Ploderer. His recollections are those of a child but nonetheless perceptive. He has remained in Vienna, unlike the other people in this chapter, and his memories are thus untainted by the necessity to adopt a new culture.

LONA TRUDING: Now if I should say something of the times in which Schoenberg lived, our totally new approach to everything, then I could only say that it was like for us youngsters then a transition from—Schoenberg had such a marvelous word for it: "*Ach*, so blumenreiche Romantik," the "Oh-so-flowery Romanticism". . . —to an age of "utility" isn't quite the right word, "natural-ism" is also a bad word, but I would say a certain lack of ornaments. You know, for instance, the new building which came up through the Bauhaus. . . . Well, that was our age—Bauhaus. . . .From the emotionalism of Ro-manticism, it was a transition to a new "Age of Reason" or to a new age of consciousness. . . . And that is what we represented. For example, we wanted to do away with all of the ornaments on buildings. Any kind of ornamentation on architecture made me sick. I could only bear plain lines.

KRISTINA RANKL: The first airplane flew and the motor started to be driven around Vienna, the electromobile, and things like that which were all frightfully exciting. And, if your gift lay on the technical side, well, that's where everybody drifted to, and whether it was science or music, . . . every part of society was busy sort of going towards the one or the other, because that was the exciting time. . . . They were all fairly closely linked, you see. They all knew each other and they were all part of that big middle, not the aristocracy . . . but the broad population of the—for a better word I must call it the intelligentsia, of the bourgeois well-to-do if you like, although Schoenberg was never well-to-do by any means, but he had quite a large group of supporters who came from a medical-legal-press background. They were his followers and admirers.

JOAN ALLEN SMITH: So you didn't talk much about politics?

SALKA VIERTEL: Yes, of course we talked about politics. Europeans always talk about politics, but they were all very influenced by Karl Kraus, and Karl Kraus was not a reactionary, certainly not. He was another kind of revolutionary. . . . First the World War I was such an enormous event in all our lives, after fifty years of this sloppy monarchy and very mild opposition, and the socialist movement was not very great. It existed very strongly in Germany, but also Rosa Luxemburg and Karl Liebknecht—and then the whole world was collapsing, and everything was going to pieces, and people were dying by thousands, by millions, so every one of these people was against it—against the regime, against the useless . . . sacrifices. They were all ready to frater[nize] . . . one didn't hate the enemy. . . . They didn't like the Prussians, but they were for winning the war.

SMITH: But Karl Kraus was a pacifist, was he not?

VIERTEL: They were also pacifists.

SMITH: I know that Schoenberg had many friends in art and literature and other nonmusical fields. Which ones do you think were most influential as far as Schoenberg was concerned?

RUDOLF KOLISCH: I think Loos was. . . . And Kraus of course was. Ja, but the relationship with Kraus was very ambivalent.

SMITH: Was Kraus closer to Berg than to Schoenberg?

KOLISCH: No. I don't know whether there was a private connection between Berg and Kraus. Berg was an ardent admirer—unconditional—total! But I don't remember any private relationship. Well, private relationship with Kraus was, you know, a very special and difficult matter. He slept during the day and was awake only at night, and he really didn't see anybody.

SMITH: Did Schoenberg have a relationship with Altenberg, Kraus, or Kokoschka, or with other great men of this time?

ERWIN RATZ: Yes, sure, but actually relatively little. Most nearly to Karl Kraus, but it wasn't as if they saw each other every week; it was once every two months that such an occasion came about.

(Heinrich Fischer) The nature of this unceasing struggle by a solitary fighter will perhaps become clearer if I attempt a brief sketch of Kraus's private life as I saw it during the thirteen years of our friendship. His private life was actually almost non-existent. For thirty-five years he sat night after night at his desk and worked until well on in the morning. This mode of life, which meant continually immersing oneself in papers, might well have become unnatural, even hostile to life—there was certainly something demonic about it—had Kraus's work not always been so intimately bound up with reality. The inexhaustible substance of his humour also preserved him from growing rigid and abstract. This is how I see the personality of Karl Kraus when I think of him: the biting sharpness of a critical intellect which suddenly changes into the serene naïveté of a child; passionate anger at the misdeed of some rogue of the moment or of some newspaper scribe, which without warning dissolves into laughter at the stupidity of man. And what laughter it was! It was no sniggering little laugh that he could possibly control. His whole body would shake and he would be unable to calm down again, the newspaper would slip out of his hand and with his face covered he would go on laughing to himself. And then the first words would suddenly burst forth, a joke, a comment, and in a moment the squalid reality of the day was transmuted into the realm of the spirit. It was a unique experience to see his thoughts now in full flood; Kraus was scarcely able to control and fix them. With the stump of a pencil he would hastily scribble notes in the margin of the newspaper and then thrust it into his pocket; that fellow was dealt with and could not escape any more. At such times it was clear that polemic was for Kraus both a moral and artistic necessity. Whatever malice or stupidity the day brought within his purview left him no peace until it had been dealt with. Nothing weighed more heavily upon him than the thought of the thousands of newspapers in his room which still awaited their transmutation into satirical art.[20]

SMITH: How do you explain that you had so much in common? . . .

OSKAR KOKOSCHKA: It probably was because we all were on the edge of society. We didn't belong to society. We were well-known, well-known—too well-known maybe— but on the edge. We didn't belong. So we were like a disease, you know. Don't touch. So of course that makes a bond. We stuck together. Karl Kraus was a frightening figure in Vienna. No one would have dared to talk to him. . . . They were frightened by his edition the *Fackel*. . . . He was a cruel man, so he was frightening for the Viennese. . . . And that's why Loos never could build— the greatest architect! The others imitate him—Corbusier—imitate him, but he never got an offer really to build something important. Little flats he would find so exciting but usually left them without being paid. He didn't dare even to ask for money at that time. . . .

SMITH: Did you have much to do with Karl Kraus?

KOKOSCHKA: Yes. With Karl Kraus, it was rare. He was absolutely intolerant with everybody, and he gave permission to see him in the café at a certain time in the evening when he ate his dinner. He ate a sausage, a very sharp sausage. . . . And then there were three or four men—always Adolf Loos and always Altenberg. . . . Kraus was very intolerant so everybody had to stand his test when he had read the new edition of the *Fackel* that he could explain every phrase, even the comma, whether it's in the right place. And I, as a fledgling of Adolf Loos, had permission to come, but as a fool, I wasn't asked. I could sit there, and when I made a remark, it was like a remark of a, not a wisecracker, but like from the moon!—fallen from the moon! And Kraus wrote, when I published something at that time, maybe *Murder, Hope of Women*, he wrote about it in the *Fackel.* It was a terribly great decoration; it was better than all the golden medals that he wrote something about me. He was very rude also. He was stepping over cadavers. And I never was frightened by him. And I painted him twice. I painted him once during his meals in the evening in the coffee house and then, after the war, in the house which I owned in Vienna. Then he came in the afternoon with Loos. Loos accompanied him always.

SMITH: I heard that Kraus was very difficult to get along with also—that he made many enemies and that some of his enemies were former friends. Would you say that that's true?

KOLISCH: Well, it's hard to call it difficult to get along with—somebody who was, you know—whose idea it was not to get along and to attack. I found him extremely easy to get along with.

SMITH: Would you say that you knew him better than did either Schoenberg or Berg?

KOLISCH: No, I couldn't say that. . . . But again, you know, there was practically no private connection. I did have some private connection, but these others didn't have that. You know what one understands by that—meeting somebody, talking to him, going out with him. . . .

SMITH: You don't think that Schoenberg spent much time talking with Kraus in the cafés or anyplace else?

KOLISCH: No. . . .

(Richard Neutra) Loos had exactly the expression which Kokoschka has made immortal in his line drawing. He would sit, a very far-distant-reaching look in his eyes, in the old restaurant behind St. Stephan's cathedral, where we used to meet; or in the Schwarzwald Schule, where he taught when he was 40 and I a student. He would speak in a very low voice and sometimes accentuate a humorous turn—and there were many humorous turns—with a very slight smile.

One had to listen attentively over the noise in the restaurant to hear him, or over the noise on the marble top of the bar counter in the Kärntner Bar. Loos himself would not drink anything alcoholic; he would drink "ein Glas Obers"—a tumbler of raw cream, which had been prescribed for his ailing stomach. His face was wrinkled and at the same time young. His hair was slightly curly and blond, hardly tinged with gray when I first knew him, but not very plentiful. He was at that time married to a very pleasant young Scottish woman, who was, like he, a quiet person. . . . He never had any quarrel, it seems at least not in my presence. He was the most soft spoken person I have ever met.[21]

SMITH: Loos came to the concerts?

KOLISCH: Loos came to the concerts, ja, and was very—not passive audience, but had a very partisan attitude—was always fighting for the cause. . . .

SMITH: Why do you think he was so interested?

KOLISCH: I don't even believe that he had a particular, special organ for music. I think he experienced it only as a more abstract phenomenon and felt the importance, and felt what was akin to his work in his field. . . .

SMITH: And was Schoenberg deeply interested in what Loos was doing?

KOLISCH: Yes. Very much so.

SMITH: Do you think that they saw the work that each of them was doing as being similar in some way to the work that was being done by the other?

KOLISCH: Well, similar in the sense that it was new and different, but not similar in particular technical categories, if you mean that by similarity. . . . Ja. Well, of course you know some of the polemic ideas were similar, like the liberation from the ornament, ja? These you could of course consider as definite similarities.

KOKOSCHKA: Loos was maybe the first, the only one in Vienna, who understood Schoenberg. Why I don't know. It was in the air already.

(Alban Berg)

14 September 1919

... Then to Mödling, where we had very gay celebrations for Schoenberg's 45th birthday.... Loos particularly was in top form—honestly, his face becomes more and more superb. Of course he is aging visibly, but his features are taking on all the signs of special greatness and saintliness. He talked for hours—nearly a monologue—wonderful stuff: about politics and the history of civilization, all with the light, graceful raconteur's manner, almost anecdotal, yet somehow full of profundity. What a shame you weren't there to hear him.[22]

SMITH: I know that Schoenberg had a lot of friends in other fields than music, like Adolf Loos—

FELIX GREISSLE: Not friends! He had Loos, not too frequently; Kraus also, but not too frequently. As a matter of fact, I got to know Kraus, and Kraus sometimes let me do some of the things.... I saw him more often.... [Schoenberg] didn't see Kraus too frequently any more [after 1918]. He saw Loos a little bit, not too much. He saw Kokoschka only when he painted him; actually he had known Kokoschka from before. Schoenberg was wholly with his pupils. He didn't want to see too many other people. He didn't see too many. Webern saw many more. Webern had friends—Hildegard Jone and a few other people. So we were all rather isolated, forcibly. And they didn't want to know from us too much—ja? And Schoenberg was—it was very difficult—Schoenberg had dropped a lot of people. Schoenberg also was—it was very difficult to be together with him; he was very demanding, and most people were not ... fit.

WOLFGANG PLODERER: The coffee house played the great roles through the whole nineteenth century, I think, until in the twenties of this century, say till the beginning thirties, but then it was finished. I think in some way it was also the wireless which was in some way responsible for killing the café life, because one of the bases of the coffee house life was that one got there all the papers from Switzerland, from Germany, from France, from England, etc. They were all lying there and one of the first things was to get information in the coffee house, because one couldn't get all these papers. This was too expensive for the average man. And people went to the coffee house to read all the foreign papers and to form an idea, and this was the foundation. On the other hand, it was the literates and the composers and the artists meeting all together in the coffee houses. Many of them were Jews, and as you know, the Jews were practically annihilated in Austria by the Nazis. Then, of course, already in the last years, when Austria was still not under German domination, most of them emigrated and so all of this came to an end.

Notes

1. For a discussion of the Viennese cultural climate, see William M. Johnston, *The Austrian Mind: An Intellectual and Social History, 1848–1938* (Berkeley: University of California Press, 1972); or Ilsa Barea, *Vienna: Legend and Reality* (London: Secker and Warburg, 1966).

2. Stefan Zweig, *The World of Yesterday* (London: Cassell, 1953), p. 216.

3. Robert Musil, *The Man Without Qualities*, vol. 1, trans. Eithne Wilkins and Ernst Kaiser (London: Pan Books, 1979), p. 32.

4. Arnold Schoenberg, *Style and Idea*, ed. Leonard Stein, trans. Leo Black (London: Faber and Faber, 1975), p. 80.

5. Willi Reich, *Schoenberg: A Critical Biography*, trans. Leo Black (London: Longman Group, 1971), pp. 4–5.

6. Alma Mahler Werfel, *And the Bridge is Love* (New York: Harcourt Brace, 1958), p. 13.

7. For information about Kraus, see Wilma Abeles Iggers, *Karl Kraus: A Viennese Critic of the Twentieth Century* (The Hague:

Martinus Nijhoff, 1967); or Harry Zohn, *Karl Kraus* (New York: Twayne, 1971).

8. Alban Berg, *Letters to His Wife*, ed. and trans. Bernard Grun (London: Faber and Faber, 1971), p. 80.

9. Otto Wagner, *Moderne Architektur* (Vienna, 1895); quoted in Ludwig Münz and Gustav Künstler, *Adolf Loos: Pioneer of Modern Architecture*, trans. Harold Meek (New York: Frederick A. Praeger, 1966), p. 14.

10. Quoted in Münz and Künstler, *Adolf Loos*, p. 14.

11. For a more detailed description of the founding of the Secession Movement, see Peter Vergo, *Art in Vienna 1898–1918* (London: Phaidon Press, 1975); or Horst-Herbert Kossatz, "The Vienna Secession and Its Early Relations with Great Britain," *Studio International* 181 (January 1971):9–20.

12. Quoted in Münz and Künstler, *Adolf Loos*, p. 14.

13. Karl Kraus, *Werke*, ed. Heinrich Fischer, vol. 3: *Beim Wort Genommen* (Munich: Kösel Verlag, 1955), p. 341; Quoted in Karl Kraus, *Half-Truths and One-and-a-Half Truths: Selected Aphorisms*, ed. and trans. Harry Zohn (Montreal: Engendra Press, 1976), p. 69.

14. "A Colloquy between Oskar Kokoschka and Ludwig Goldscheider," in Ludwig Goldscheider, *Kokoschka*, 3d ed. (London: Phaidon Press, 1963), p. 13.

15. Oskar Kokoschka, *My Life*, trans. David Britt (London: Thames and Hudson, 1974), p. 35. Reprinted by permission of F. Bruckmann KG Publishers, Munich. Original edition © 1971 Verlag F. Bruckmann KG, München. English edition under license, © 1974 Thames and Hudson Ltd., London.

16. Adolf Loos, "Oskar Kokoschka," in *Die Potemkin'sche Stadt: Verschollene Schriften 1897–1933*, ed. Adolf Opel (Vienna: Georg Prachner Verlag, 1983), pp. 229–230.

17. Kokoschka, *My Life*, p. 23.

18. Remigius Netzer, "Postscript," in Kokoschka, *My Life*, p. 217.

19. Kraus, *Half-Truths and One-and-a-Half Truths*, p. 30.

20. Heinrich Fischer, "The Other Austria and Karl Kraus," in *In Tyrannos: Four Centuries of Struggle against Tyranny in Germany*, ed. Hans J. Rehfisch (London: Lindsay Drummond, 1944), p. 324.

21. Richard Neutra, review of *Adolf Loos: Pioneer of Modern Architecture*, by Ludwig Münz and Gustav Künstler, in *Architectural Forum* 125 (July–August 1966):88–89, 116.

22. Berg, *Letters to His Wife*, pp. 246–247.

~ 2 ~

Kraus, Loos, and Kokoschka

The creative work of Schoenberg, Loos, and Kokoschka is seminally related to that of Karl Kraus, the most public of these figures. Kraus's work reached an extensive audience, and he was widely read and discussed in his own time. Every issue of his magazine *Die Fackel* was a major event, and it was read with the same painstaking care that Kraus lavished upon its publication. Kraus instilled in his readers an appreciation for detail and a concern for exact meaning, values that translate easily to other disciplines. He also maintained throughout his professional career a deep understanding of the sociological relationship between art and the character of the times, a concern that was to become important to Schoenberg with the rise of National Socialism.

Kraus's real passion was the German language, and all of his other work derives from that consuming interest. As he saw it, corruption of society was reflected in, or even caused by, corruption of the language. "'He masters the German language'—that is true of a salesman. An artist is a servant of the word."[1] Kraus devoted his life to saving the German language from degradation by restoring its beauty and simplicity.[2] For models, he concentrated not upon the language of the people but upon the works of Goethe, Nietzsche, and a few other major literary figures. Kraus's famous war oration, written and published in 1914, shows clearly how his literary style was actively inseparable from meaning:

> In these great times which I knew long before they had become great and, if time permits, will be small once again; which, because in the realm of organic growth such transformations are impossible, we had better call fat times and surely hard times; in these times when things happen that could not be imagined, and in which the unimaginable must indeed happen because it would not, if one were able to imagine it; in these serious times which were dying with laughter at the thought that they might become serious; which, overtaken by their own tragedy, reach out for distractions and, catching themselves in the act of doing the unspeakable, grope for words; in these loud times which resound with the abominable symphony of deeds that bring forth reports, and reports that are responsible for deeds; in these times here and now you should not expect from me any word of my own. Nor should I be capable of saying anything new; for in the room where someone writes the noise is so great, and whether it comes from animals, from children, or merely from mortars shall not be decided now. He who addresses deeds violates both word and deed and is twice despicable. This profession is not extinct. Those who now have nothing to say because it is the turn of deeds to speak, talk on. Let him who has something to say step forward and be silent.*[3]

In his devotion to a view of language presupposing inseparable identity with the thought expressed (a view cer-

---

*Walter Benjamin said of Kraus's work that "Everything Kraus wrote is like that: a silence turned inside out, a silence that catches the storm of events in its black folds, billows, its livid lining turned outward." Walter Benjamin, "Karl Kraus," in *Reflections: Essays, Aphorisms, Autobiographical Writings*, ed. Peter Demetz, trans. Edmund Jephcott (New York:

tainly arguable), Kraus shows his integrity as both writer and thinker down to the smallest detail. For him, all literary and political matters from the morality of war to the placement of the comma were, as Walter Benjamin pointed out, "within the sphere of justice."[4] Kraus was extremely influential, and Schoenberg, Webern, and especially Berg adopted his stylistic stance. Schoenberg himself admitted his debt to Kraus in a copy of his *Harmonielehre* (1911):

> In the inscription with which I sent Karl Kraus my *Harmonielehre*, I stated: "I have learned perhaps more from you than one may learn from anyone if one still wishes to remain independent . . .", or words to that effect. Even if this assuredly does not describe the extent of my esteem for him, it nonetheless testifies to the level of that esteem.[5]

Schoenberg and Berg were both prolific writers. Schoenberg's *Harmonielehre*, first published in 1911, caused considerable stir and reflects, perhaps more than his later

---

Harcourt Brace Jovanovich, 1978), p. 243. One of the most interesting analyses of Kraus's first sentence is by Erich Heller, who is also responsible for most of the translation used here:

> The main clause is, of course, "In these great times you should not . . . ," but the predicate is postponed again and again, just as in a world where wartime deeds and mendacious reports feed on each other, endlessly multiplying through their obscene couplings, the "great times" could return to their proper scale only after an unconscionable delay. Indeed they would not return until the will to perform bloody deeds of war was as exhausted as the imagination must have been before the deeds could be done. The construction of the sentence is the product of Karl Kraus's superbly realized ambition not merely to express his thought but to do it so precisely that language itself would appear to be the thinker, would catch the rhythm of events in the rhythm of words, and make sentences the mirror of the world they describe—the mirror as well as the judgment passed on the world.

Erich Heller, "Dark Laughter," *New York Review of Books* 20 (3 May 1973):21.

works, the integrity and stylistic precision characteristic of the writings of Kraus. In addition to books on harmony and counterpoint, Schoenberg authored hundreds of articles, mostly still unpublished, but many of which appeared in newspapers and journals, including *Die Musikblätter des Anbruch* (the journal of Universal Edition), *Melos* (founded in 1920 by Hermann Scherchen), *Die Musik*, and *Pult und Taktstock.*[6] Schoenberg's writings include articles on numerous philosophical, biographical, and political topics outside of music, as well as libretti for his own vocal works.

Berg began his literary career by writing extensive analytical guides to Schoenberg's Chamber Symphony, Op. 9; the *Gurrelieder;* and *Pelleas und Melisande.* In June of 1920, in response to an article by the composer Hans Pfitzner, he published "Die Musikalische Impotenz der 'neuen Aesthetik' Hans Pfitzners" in *Anbruch.*[7] This article led to an offer of editorship of the journal. Because his financial situation was at that time precarious, he accepted, with misgivings about the time involved. Although he was only editor of *Anbruch* for one year, he continued throughout his life to write articles and commentary on his own compositions. His study of *Die Fackel* is evident in the clarity of his work on libretti for his operas *Wozzeck* and *Lulu.* Although he took no active role, Berg was also instrumental in the founding of the journal *23*, edited by his pupil Willi Reich. This journal, which appeared between 1932 and 1937, aimed to be a musical equivalent of *Die Fackel.*

Loos was a lifelong friend of Kraus and was often quoted in *Die Fackel.* Himself an active writer, who carried his desire for simplicity to the extreme of no longer capitalizing nouns, he admired the clear, essential style of Kraus, whom he described in an essay of 1913:

> He stands at the threshold of a new age and shows the way to mankind, which has removed itself so far from god and nature. With head in the stars, feet on the earth, he strides, his heart in agony over human misery. And cries

out! He fears world destruction. But, since he is not silent,*
I know that he has not given up hope. And he will continue
crying out and his voice will penetrate into the coming
centuries, until it is heard. And humanity will eventually
have to thank Karl Kraus for its survival.[8]

In addition to a journal, *Das Andere,* Loos wrote numerous
articles, especially before 1900, and gave lectures which
were well attended. The articles were later published as two
collections, *Ins Leere gesprochen* (essays, 1897–1900) and
Trotzdem (essays, 1900–1930).[9] For two years Loos was head
of the Vienna housing department, and in 1919 he published
a symposium, *Richtlinien für ein Kunstamt* (Guidelines for
an Arts Council), in which an essay by Schoenberg about the
formation of such a council appeared.[10]

Although Adolf Loos made much of his modernism, he
was, like Schoenberg, firm in his ties to the past. Devoted to
antiquity, Loos wanted not to create new forms but to strip
the old ones of nonfunctional decoration which concealed
the beauty of their structure: "New forms? How dull! It is
the new spirit that matters. Even out of old forms it will
fashion what we new men need."[11] Loos favored the buildings of the traditionalist Romans over those of the inventive
Greeks, praising Vitruvius and criticizing the Greeks for too
much originality and not enough social consciousness:

> It is not fortuitous that the Romans were unable to invent
> a new order of columns, a new system of ornament. They

*In 1936, faced with the menace of Hitler, Kraus, realizing that satire is
no longer possible when the impossible has in fact occurred, did become
silent. See "Warum Die Fackel nicht erscheint," *Die Fackel,* nos. 890–905
(July 1934), p. 1. Kraus's fears for the German language have been
realized today in the anglicization of German common speech encouraged by the media. His view that the decline of language accompanies the
loss of cultural integrity is one that seems particularly relevant as Western language in general loses its specificity and flexibility in an age where
technological advancement has outstripped moral judgment.

had already progressed too far. They borrowed all that
from the Greeks and adapted it for their own purposes.
The Greeks were individualists. Each building had to have
its own mouldings, its own decoration. The Romans, however, thought in a social manner. The Greeks could hardly
administer their towns, the Romans mastered the globe.
The Greeks wasted their inventive powers on the orders,
the Romans used theirs on the plan. And those who can
produce a good plan don't bother with new mouldings.[12]

In keeping with his views of classical architecture, Loos consistently employed marble in his buildings. He often added
interior friezes and exterior columns and main cornices,
such as those on the building on Michaelerplatz, constructed
in 1910.

Perhaps Loos's most important contribution to the modern architecture was his "plan of volumes." This approach
involved architects' plans, traditionally two-dimensional, in a
three-dimensional context which resulted in a realization
that all space in a house need not be the same height. Ludwig Münz described Loos's views:

> Adolf Loos introduced to the world a new and essentially
> higher conception of space: free thinking in space, the
> planning of rooms situated on different levels and not tied
> in to a continuous storey level, the juxtaposition of rooms
> with one another to form a harmonious, indivisible whole
> and a spatially economical structure. The rooms, accord-
> ing to their purpose and use, not only have different sizes
> but also different heights. Loos can therefore create more
> living space within the same confines, since the same cubic
> capacity on the same foundations and under the same
> roof can now contain more rooms within the same exter-
> nal walls.[13]

Evolving gradually over Loos's career, this conception eventually made inevitable the planning of a house from the
inside out. Thus not only was the tradition of continuous
floors abandoned but also the concept of symmetrical and

level windows and doors on the outside. The ideal Loos house came to be designed around a central pair of connected areas—a large high one for social gatherings and a small one for privacy.* It was an especially appealing characteristic of Loos's designs that they provided places where one person could gain the feeling of privacy even in the most crowded conditions. The reading nook, the single chair before a corner fireplace, a spot under the stairs all served to allow the individual a place for reflection or dreaming.

Loos felt strongly that architecture and interior design should serve both the physical and spiritual needs of the people living in it and using it rather than the abstract demands of art and taste. He described this belief in his short tale of the poor rich man and returned to the theme many times.[14] In an essay entitled "Architecture," written in 1910, he outlined his views more explicitly:

> A house has to please everybody, in contrast to a work of art which need not please anybody. The work of art is the artist's private affair. The house is not. The work of art is born without any existing need. A house fulfills a need. The work of art is responsible to nobody, the house to everybody. The work of art wants to tear you out of your comfortable existence. The house is to serve your comfort. The work of art is revolutionary, the house is conservative.†[15]

---

*Of incidental interest is the following remark of Loos, quoted in Henry Kulka, "Adolf Loos, 1870–1933," *Architects' Yearbook* 9 (New York: Chemical Publishing, 1960), p. 15:

> Formerly, an architect was forced to build a W.C. as high as a ballroom and only by halving the height could he achieve a lower room. Just as men will one day succeed in playing three-dimensional chess, so will future architects solve planning problems by compositions in space.

†Elsewhere Loos also said:

> Only a portion of architecture is a branch of the arts: the tomb and the monument. Utility architecture is divorced from art. Is this sad news for you? I myself only accepted this truth after a

Although other aspects of Loos's work may seem super-ficially more connected to the activities of Schoenberg, such as his commitment to the elimination of nonstructural ornament (window borders, decorative detail, and so forth), it is in his "plan of volumes" that Loos approached most closely the problems which ultimately faced Schoenberg, Berg, and Webern. It would be possible to compare the sim-plification process that accompanied the transition from tonal chromaticism to the early atonal music of these com-posers with the elimination of ornamentation in architecture and the decorative arts by Loos and the Wiener Werkstätte (to be discussed presently). There is, however, a major dif-ference. The problem of simplification for Loos involved, prior to the evolution of his "plan of volumes," principally nonstructural architectural units. It was his precise objection to these features that they obscured the structure of the build-ing. The chromatic simplification which could be considered analogous to this modification (although in actuality certain non-pitch-related aspects such as orchestration were a part of this change) resulted in a neutralization of the most basic structural features of tonal music. Thus Schoenberg was faced with a much more profound problem than Loos—how to substitute a new organization for the loss of the articulative means (provided by tonal harmony) which had been obscured but by no means eliminated by the chromaticism of the late nineteenth century. This fundamental structural reorganiza-tion was of the degree faced by Loos in his "plan of volumes"; the latter ultimately necessitated the elimination from within of much of what had been considered fundamental to exter-nal building appearance. It is not surprising that the evolution

---

heartbreaking struggle. But now I realise that the artist creates of his own free will, while the architect serves men's physical and mental needs. I became a perfectly happy man when I at last realised that I was merely a builder with a classical education. Now I understand art and have reverence for it. Art is the highest activity of man.

Quoted in Henry Kulka, "Adolf Loos, 1870–1933," *Architects' Yearbook* 9 (New York: Chemical Publishing, 1960), p. 8.

of the twelve-tone method, which represented at least a temporary solution to the problem of structure in nontonal music, took longer to emerge than the corresponding developments in architecture or that the intermediate process was more painful. It is interesting to note that the initial musical result, including such works as Schoenberg's Wind Quintet and Berg's *Lyric Suite*, which constituted a revival of traditional structural forms in a new guise, was in some respects less radical than the process that led to its inception.

Although extremely influential as an architectural theorist, Loos had few opportunities to put his ideas into practice. In fact, before 1910 only interior designs of shops, the Café Museum across from the Secession building, and private flats were carried out. In the period 1904 through 1906 he began the extensive remodeling of the Villa Karma, which was completed by another architect after Loos withdrew from the project.[16] It was not until 1910 that Loos built his first private house, the Haus Steiner, in Vienna.[17] His most famous building, the "Haus am Michaelerplatz," a store with flats above, caused a storm of opposition when it was constructed during 1910 and 1911.*[18] A few other private houses and more apartments followed, but Loos was never allowed to construct a public building. Schoenberg, in a letter seeking recognition for Loos on his sixtieth birthday, remarked that in his travels he had seen many Loos-like buildings by other architects but none by Loos.[19]

*Peter Vergo, in his book *Art in Vienna 1898–1918* (London: Phaidon Press, 1975), p. 172, quotes the following review from the *Neue Freie Presse* of 4 December 1910:

Seldom has a work of architecture called forth such universal opposition, not even the "cabbage dome" of the Secession. What is more, from the lowest point of the threshold to the bridge tiles on the roof, there isn't a trace of anything Viennese about the new house. The ground floor and mezzanine of proud marble, massive columns hewn from a single block, the lofty street façades, which fill the spaces between the huge panes of glass, all made of the noblest material, costly marble, and above it all, a bare plaster wall, without the shadow of an ornament, pierced by tasteless window-openings, a desolate poverty above all this marble splendour.

Loos's views of architecture extended to other aspects of daily life. Influenced by what he considered the advanced development of the American farmer, he took a stand against the still semifeudal condition of the Austrian peasant. In an effort to raise the Austrian farmer to the modern level of the city dweller, Loos published a journal entitled *Das Andere: ein Blatt zur Einfuehrung abendlaendischer Kultur in Oesterreich* (The Other: a Paper for the Introduction of Western Culture into Austria) in which he opposed national dress and wrote articles on such subjects as standing, lying down, walking, cooking, and eating. Although this journal lasted for only two issues (it was published in 1903), Loos never abandoned his efforts to effect social change. He yearned to give people time to be alone even in cramped surroundings and to save the poor from the drudgery of everyday life, giving them time for more elevating or contemplative activities. In a smaller way, Schoenberg was also interested in such matters. His fertile mind produced designs for skirt hangers, music stands, and chess sets; he built furniture and, possibly owing to his friendship with Loos, became interested in various aspects of mass transit.[20]

While still engaged in his earliest interior projects, Loos launched Kokoschka's portrait career with a trip to Switzerland in 1909. Loos was at this time married to an English woman who had tuberculosis. She was living in a sanatorium in Switzerland, and Loos took Kokoschka there. Kokoschka painted portraits of the Duchess and Count Montesquieu-Rohan and Besse Loos. In 1910 Loos sent Kokoschka again to Switzerland to paint the portrait of the well-known biologist August Forel. Kokoschka was allowed to work at the end of the day, after Forel had completed his labors.

> Every evening Forel carefully weighed out nuts and apple peel, which he solemnly ate. . . . And sometimes he did indeed nod off. Then I could really study the way he sat in his chair, and see how the wrinkles on his face increased and deepened. Suddenly he seemed ancient. . . . His face, and especially his hands, fascinated me. . . . The eye grew

clearer. I searched it profoundly, for it was the eye of a seeker wont to see beyond the appearance of things. It was the window of a brain whose intelligence I was trying to portray. My biggest problem was how to reproduce the scholar's knowledge when I myself was so ignorant.[21]

Although an early work, this painting is one of Kokoschka's finest and is characteristic of his attitude toward portraiture.

Back in Vienna, Loos continued his tireless efforts to secure commissions for Kokoschka or, when a work was not commissioned, to find buyers. Throughout the remainder of his life, Kokoschka remained grateful to Loos for his generosity and always considered him to have been one of his greatest influences. As he wrote many years after Loos's death: "Knowing Loos was an experience that determined one's fate. The generations that came later have had fewer chances to know wise men, because people everywhere, the older this century grows, conform more and more to the same pattern."[22] During these years, from 1908 to 1914, Kokoschka resumed his teaching at the Kunstgewerbeschule and painted a number of both obscure and well-known people including Adolf Loos, Anton Webern, Peter Altenberg[B], and Karl Kraus. Through this same period, Schoenberg completed several important works, including the Five Orchestral Pieces, Op. 16; a monodrama, *Erwartung;* the *Gurrelieder;* and *Pierrot lunaire,* while Berg completed his String Quartet, Op. 3, and suffered through the catastrophic premiere of his *Altenberg Lieder.*[23] An incessant seeker after the inner life, Kokoschka attempted in his portraits to reveal the *penetralia mentis* of the individual—he was said to paint not what a person was but what he or she would become—rather than to portray substantive physical reality, a goal that lent to his work a radiant and visionary quality undimmed by his subdued use of color.

This concern with inner vision—with the direct perception of the subject's essence—remained a constant in Kokoschka's artistic confrontation throughout his changes of style. In his autobiography, he described his way of seeing, which applied not only to portraits but to landscape painting as well:

> What used to shock people in my portraits was that I tried to intuit from the face, from its play of expressions, and from gestures, the truth about a particular person, and to recreate in my own pictorial language the distillation of a living being that would survive in memory. . . . I depend very much on being able to capture a mental impression, the impression that remains behind when the image itself has passed. In a face I look for the flash of the eye, the tiny shift of expression which betrays an inner movement. In a landscape I seek for the trickle of water that suddenly breaks the silence, or a grazing animal that makes me conscious of the distance or height of a range of mountains, or a lonely wayfarer whose shadow lengthens as evening falls. It would be too high-flown to call these things decisive experiences: they are simply what make me a *seeing* observer of nature.[24]

This view is strangely similar to that of August Strindberg, a playwright much in fashion in Kokoschka's circles, who wrote in his autobiography: "One should paint what one feels inside and not go out and draw logs and stones, which certainly in themselves are insignificant, and only in passing through the sensibilities of the subject can one get any form."[25]

In addition to painting, Kokoschka also wrote several plays, beginning in 1907. Heavily influenced by Strindberg (a favorite of Alban Berg), Kokoschka's plays were nonetheless both innovative and influential. *Sphinx und Strohmann* (later revised as *Job*) was written in 1907 on a wager, while *Mörder Hoffnung der Frauen* (*Murder, Hope of Women*) was initially performed in conjunction with the second Kunstschau exhibition in 1909. Both Loos, to whom it was dedicated, and Kraus attended.

Through the play's main characters—an anonymous man and woman—Kokoschka explores in dream-like symbolic language the relationship between the sexes. This theme, which was to concern Kokoschka throughout his life, especially during the period of a stormy romance with Alma Mahler[B] (the widow of the composer), was also a topic of great interest to other Viennese figures and to one of their literary heroes, August Strindberg. Karl Kraus, aware of the intense feminist activity of the time, felt that women had their own place in the scheme of life. Wilma Abeles Iggers, in her book on Kraus, has described his views:

> Kraus saw a basic difference between man and woman in their very nature, and in spiritual and mental organization. Woman was to him aesthetic and sensuous, but as a socially responsible and intelligent human being she was somewhere between uninteresting and non-existent. Of the two components of the totality of cultural life, women embodied nature, and man *Geist* (spirit or intellect). Thus woman experienced the world, and particularly man, in an essentially and sometimes exclusively erotic manner, so that her other senses were dulled and her inhibitions excluded. Man, on the other hand, lived mainly through his mind and through his imagination. The function of the physical was to man only that of inspiring and fertilizing the mind.[26]

Kraus opposed the political and social emancipation of women and considered the intellectual woman to be unfeminine:

> The interesting woman and the erotic farce mark the intellectual limits of Christian sexual freedom; nothing is less interesting than the former, and nothing is sadder than the latter. In them the transgression pays tribute to the prohibition.

Or:

> As long as a woman does not write, she preserves the appearance of sexual attraction, and the addition of repulsive intellectuality which enables her later to be a writer,

may even produce the suspicious mixture which deludes the fools.[27]

The theme of the essence of sexual difference, which so occupied Sigmund Freud at the same time, as well as such Scandinavian figures as Ibsen, Strindberg, and Munch, was taken up by Schoenberg in his opera *Die glückliche Hand.* It also pervaded the works of the playwright Frank Wedekind, whose dramas on this subject, *Erdgeist* (Earth Spirit) and *Die Büchse der Pandora* (Pandora's Box) were used by Alban Berg for the libretto of his opera *Lulu.* In the character of Lulu, Berg created through Wedekind's work a complex blending of the pure idealized feminine (as seen by men) with the truly individual character of Lulu—a victim of her own sexuality who is ultimately destroyed by the inevitability of her failure to conform in her femaleness to a male-dominated and -determined social structure.

Although Kokoschka's plays, all written between 1907 and 1918, were well-received by his intimate acquaintances—if hated and misunderstood by the more general theatre-going public—he stopped writing plays at the close of the war. He never returned to this activity, although he continued to write, creating small articles, some fables, and an autobiography.

Kraus was also involved with the theatre, giving public readings which became immensely popular. At first he read his own writings and works of his contemporaries, such as Gerhart Hauptmann, Frank Wedekind, Liliencron, and Else Lasker-Schüler. Later he expanded to the Schlegel and Tieck translations of Shakespeare, which he abridged slightly, and to Goethe and Nestroy. He also performed the operettas of Offenbach, which he knew from his childhood and which he updated considerably.* All of these works were performed—read or sung—with himself playing all the roles and, in the case of Offenbach, with a single pianist on

---

*Several people have remarked upon the similarity of Kraus's singing voice to Schoenberg's *Sprechstimme.*

the stage. Albert Bloch recalled hearing a remarkable performance of *Measure for Measure* in the early twenties:

> On a bare stage, a chair behind a little table, upon which there is nothing but the book or heap of papers from which the reading is to be given. The theater is darkened, only the table remains in light. The reading begins: short pauses between the first two and final two acts, a somewhat longer interval between the third and fourth. Five acts of Shakespeare, through which the audience sits breathless, spellbound, breaking its silence only with bursts of applause after each act. . . . The reader, book in hand, his short-sighted eyes close to the text, *acts out* the drama, seated there behind the little table. There is no need of dramatic gesture, nor can there be any, beyond an occasional movement of the right hand, which must turn the leaves of the book held in the left; but this reader may rely entirely upon the resources of his voice and its inflections. There are some twenty characters in *Measure for Measure*, five of them women, all of them greatly diversified; but never once is the hearer in doubt, under the voice of this extraordinary reader.[28]

A friend of Karl Kraus and a beneficiary of his financial support was the Berlin art critic and impresario Herwarth Walden. Introduced by Kraus, Kokoschka went to Berlin in 1910 to become Walden's assistant on his art magazine *Der Sturm.* While in Berlin, Kokoschka was introduced to the wider world of German painters, meeting those of the group *Die Brücke* (Nolde, Heckel, Kirchner, Pechstein, and Schmidt-Rottluff) and becoming involved in the intellectual life of the Café Grössenwahn. For the first time he met painters who shared his concerns, and although he shortly returned to Vienna and always maintained his independence, he benefited greatly from these two years of stimulating exchange with some of the foremost exponents of what was called German Expressionism.

Long before the artists of *Die Brücke* had developed their goals, Kokoschka had established his individuality through his use of traditional forms in untraditional ways. Character-istic of this approach is the *Still Life with Sheep and Hya-cinth* (1907) in which Kokoschka uses a standard form (the still life) to invoke complicated issues of life and death through the appearance of nontraditional subject matter and unpleasant objects (a sheep carcass, a mouse, for example). The odor associated with the hyacinth adds to the unsavory association. Again, in the landscape *Dent du Midi* (1909), the associations suggested by the unusual lighting and coloring overwhelm the more conventional subject matter and become the real thematic material of the paint-ing. Kokoschka said of this painting:

> What a light there is in that snowscape! The impres-sionists wouldn't have been able to do such a thing, they have an altogether different idea of light—how the *eye* is struck by sunbeams and reflections—while here it is *sen-sibility* on which light impinges, it's a spiritual light, a light as of the morning, the morning of life. Only there can one feel light like that.[29]

The practice of suiting traditional forms to nontraditional means was also adopted by Loos, in his use of classic fea-tures, and by Schoenberg and his disciples, as will be dis-cussed in Chapter 9.

In Berlin, Kokoschka also made the valuable acquaintance of the famous art dealer Paul Cassirer, who was to be his dealer for many years. Kokoschka held his first one-man show at the Cassirer Gallery in 1910. With the help of Walden and Cassirer, Kokoschka returned to Vienna in 1911 in order to mount an exhibition of twenty-five of his paintings and to produce one of his plays, *Der brennende Dornbusch* (The Burning Thornbush). In 1912, the year of Schoenberg's *Pierrot lunaire,* he delivered a lecture entitled "On the Na-ture of Visions," one of his earliest and most extensive the-oretical statements. In this lecture, Kokoschka made clear the stress that he placed upon the inner voice over the out-ward stimulus:

The consciousness of visions is not a mode of perceiving and understanding existing objects. It is a condition in which we experience the visions themselves.

In visions consciousness itself can never be grasped. It is a flux of impressions and images which once called forth give power to the mind.

But the consciousness of visions has a life of its own, accepting but also rejecting the images which appear to it.

. . . Thus we have to listen with complete attention to our inner voice in order to get past the shadows of words to their very source. "The Word became flesh and dwelt among us." And then the inner source frees itself, sometimes vigorously, sometimes feebly, from the words within which it lives like a charm.

. . . Consciousness is the source of all things and all ideas. It is a sea with visions as its only horizon.[30]

Although he continued to be attacked in the press, Kokoschka gradually gained public support during these years, and until the intervention of World War I, was active in his work. It was during this time that he became romantically involved with Alma Mahler.[31] This tumultuous affair, lasting from 1912 until 1915, was the inspiration for some of Kokoschka's finest paintings, including a remarkable double portrait and the visionary work entitled *The Tempest*, perhaps Kokoschka's most famous creation.

When the first world war began, Kokoschka enlisted at least partly to escape the dregs of this affair. His friend Loos arranged for him to join the cavalry, considered less dangerous than the infantry. The painting *The Tempest*, which had recently been sold, provided the funds for horse and uniform. Kokoschka received a serious head wound and was bayoneted through the lung at the Polish front. Years of recuperation followed, first in Sweden and then in Dresden.

After his recovery, Kokoschka returned briefly to Vienna and then embarked upon a series of travels. Perhaps wishing—because of his country's ruin and his own instability—to remove himself from that painful youthful "quest [of self] without mastery in naked unsatisfaction,"[32] he produced during these expeditions the series of landscape works comparing most strongly in visionary quality with the earlier portraits. Despite these works and the later large mythological paintings that followed World War II, some writers have felt that Kokoschka never fully recovered his genius following his war injuries. Although Kokoschka was isolated from both Kraus and Schoenberg by this trauma and his subsequent travels, he shared with them in his early years a friendship perhaps made closer by the commonness of their cause and the opposition to them in both the press and the public.

The creative ideals of Schoenberg, Kraus, Loos, and Kokoschka arose from the Vienna of the Habsburg monarchy. The complexities of the governmental bureaucracy and the intricacies of politics within cultural institutions engendered a desire for simplicity and honesty. From the longevity of the monarch himself came a need for change and an excitement about the future. Frivolity and corruption in the press gave Karl Kraus his voice, a voice that awakened many others. Adolf Loos, through his concern for other struggling creative minds, provided a vital connecting link.

Of the students of Schoenberg interviewed for this study, Max Deutsch and Rudolf Kolisch were the most heavily involved in Viennese cultural life. Max Deutsch knew the language of the *Harmonielehre* intimately through his many years of teaching it in Paris. Although he left Vienna after a falling-out with Schoenberg, Deutsch devoted the rest of his life to disseminating Schoenberg's teachings and conducting his music. He was a wise and generous man. Kolisch was perhaps the most closely associated with Kraus of all of Schoenberg's pupils. As his father, a well-known Vienna physician, was a personal friend of Kraus, Kolisch often met Kraus socially. Kolisch's own writing style and his philosophical outlook were strongly influenced by his knowledge of Kraus, as well as by his friendship with the philosopher Theodor Adorno.[B] Marcel Dick, the first permanent violist with the Wiener Streichquartett, was primarily active in Viennese musical life. He attended Kraus's readings and performances of Offenbach.

MAX DEUTSCH: For instance, the *Harmonielehre* written in German is a very special style of writing in German. This special style, you had four people—Schoenberg the musician, Karl Kraus the writer, Adolf Loos the architect, and Peter Altenberg the poet—four people, this German writing.

JOAN ALLEN SMITH: Would you say that the writing style of Schoenberg and Berg was influenced by Kraus?

RUDOLF KOLISCH: Yes, especially Berg's. . . .

SMITH: At one point, Schoenberg says that he owes to Kraus maybe more than any man should and still remain independent. What do you think he meant by that?

KOLISCH: I know about that. Well, that refers of course to his relationship to language.

SMITH: Do you think that he means only the German language or that Schoenberg somehow applied Kraus's use of the German language to a musical language?

KOLISCH: No, not that. . . . It should not be put this way, because it's not *use* of language, because it was just his idea that one cannot use language—language uses you! . . . But his thoughts about language influenced all of them very deeply. Ja, and also the ethical categories which are connected with it—no? . . . There is practically nobody who was not affected by it.

SMITH: Do you think that Schoenberg ever made any attempt to relate what he was doing in music—changing the musical language in any sense—to what was occurring in art or in literature, or even in science?

KOLISCH: Ja, well it's of course a relevant question. . . . I don't know, you know, how much these deliberations were consciously Schoenberg, but he undoubtedly felt that there was some parallelism. He must have felt that his exploits in painting were very, very, you know, close to his music. . . .

SMITH: You, and other people too, have talked about how

influenced Berg was by Kraus or by Schoenberg. Do
you think that Berg was then a rather dependent sort of
person?

KOLISCH: No, I wouldn't say that. But he was, you know,
he was possible to influence. He was ready and open
for influence. So was also everybody except Schoenberg. . . . Schoenberg did the influencing.

SMITH: Do you think that this limited Schoenberg—that he
was not open to other people's ideas?

KOLISCH: No. You can't say that he was not open. He was
open to ideas—Mozart, Schubert, Brahms—

SMITH: What about his contemporaries?

KOLISCH: No. No. . . . He never learned except from himself—students of course, students and by himself. . . .

SMITH: You say that these people all wrote in the same
way, in the same style?

DEUTSCH: In [the spirit of] the general Austrian, Viennese
culture.

SMITH: Do you think that this spirit extended to what Loos
was doing in architecture and Schoenberg in music?

DEUTSCH: Ja, it is the sense of two things. First, in a general
manner, necessity—what is necessary—and the second
term is intensity—necessity and intensity. That is the
criterion that you can find in the works of these four
men [Loos, Kraus, Kokoschka, and Schoenberg]. And
that is, too, Schoenberg's way to teach for the students—
what is absolutely necessary. Write down what is necessary! And don't write down what you are really not
very . . . [clear about]. And the second thing is intensity. Those are the two criteria.

SMITH: What do you mean by intensity in this case?

DEUTSCH: . . . Intensity can be *pianissimo;* it can be *fortis-
simo.* It is the inner way to bring out what you have to
tell.

WOLFGANG PLODERER: Karl Kraus plays a very big role in Alban Berg's life too. He liked Karl Kraus very much. I am a great admirer of Karl Kraus too. . . . I also went to his—when he was talking. I have a very good memory of Karl Kraus. He was a magnificent personality. He was wonderful. . . . He was a very great man; he was a very good speaker, and he was the keeper of the German language, I must say. And the German language has deteriorated today as well as English and French and all languages.

MARCEL DICK: We, the younger ones, were all Karl Kraus adherents—enthusiasts. Schoenberg and Karl Kraus met—kept personal contacts of sorts, but they preferred to admire each other from a distance, which they did.

SMITH: But Berg was closer to Kraus, wasn't he?

DICK: Berg was closer to Kraus, Webern probably not at all. Steuermann was very close to Kraus. He played the piano to accompany him, I think, during some of his lectures.* Offenbach operettas were one of his best things. I remember Offenbach operettas read by Karl Kraus and which I have seen afterwards on the stage, and I must say that my impression is still Karl Kraus. Also he read pieces by Nestroy, and he had a personality which made you feel that you see the whole thing on stage in a marvelous representation.

FELIX GREISSLE: Kraus, for instance, Kraus, who was very strict with other people about their literature—unbelievably strict—Kraus gave lectures and he loved Offenbach, and he gave the whole *Périchole* and sang everything himself. And Nestroy he did and sang all the music at that time of Mueller, and he sang it out of memory, and he had measures of 4/4 that had only seven eighths—things like that—or nine eighths, he stuck one in somewhere—things like that. And at one time, when I

*The most frequent pianist for Karl Kraus was Franz Mitler.

corrected that, he was so furious at me, he didn't talk to me for a long time. And there he was a terrible amateur, and he never tolerated amateurism in other things.

DICK: Offenbach, ja. He did Nestroy before that, then Offenbach. It was absolutely a unique experience— never before or since.

SMITH: What were these things like? Can you describe them?

DICK: A man sitting there reading and . . . surrounding the stage is full of people and characters, and one is alive and does things—just all that with his voice; his projection was unbelievable!

Notes

1. Karl Kraus, *Werke,* ed. Heinrich Fischer, vol. 3: *Beim Wort Genommen* (Munich: Kösel Verlag, 1955), p. 116. Quoted in Karl Kraus, *Half-Truths and One-and-a-Half Truths: Selected Aphorisms,* ed. and trans. Harry Zohn (Montreal: Engendra Press, 1976), p. 64.

2. For further discussion of Kraus and the German language, see Erich Heller, "Karl Kraus: Satirist in the Modern World," in *The Disinherited Mind: Essays in Modern German Literature and Thought,* exp. ed. (New York: Harcourt Brace Jovanovich, 1975), pp. 235–260.

3. Karl Kraus, "In dieser grossen Zeit," *Die Fackel,* no. 404 (December 1914), p. 1.

4. Walter Benjamin, "Karl Kraus," in *Reflections: Essays, Aphorisms, Autobiographical Writings,* ed. Peter Demetz, trans. Edmund Jephcott (New York: Harcourt Brace Jovanovich, 1978), p. 254.

5. Arnold Schoenberg, *Schöpferische Konfessionen,* ed. Willi Reich (Zurich: Verlag der Arche, 1964), p. 21. See also Anton Webern, *The Path to the New Music,* ed. Willi Reich, trans. Leo Black (Bryn Mawr, Pa.: Theodore Presser; London: Universal Edition, 1963), pp. 9–10.

6. Some of these articles have been reprinted in Arnold Schoenberg, *Style and Idea,* ed. Leonard Stein, trans. Leo Black (London: Faber and Faber, 1975); and *Gesammelte Schriften,* vol. 1: *Stil und Gedanke: Aufsätze zur Musik,* ed. Ivan Vojtech (Reutlingen: S. Fischer, 1976).

7. Alban Berg, "Die musikalische Impotenz der 'neuen Aesthetik' Hans Pfitzners," *Musikblätter des Anbruch* 2 (June 1920); reprinted in Willi Reich, *Alban Berg*, trans. Cornelius Cardew (New York: Harcourt, Brace and World, 1965), pp. 205–218.

8. Adolf Loos, "Karl Kraus," in *Trotzdem: 1900–1930*, ed. Adolf Opel (Vienna: Georg Prachner Verlag, 1982), p. 119.

9. Reprinted as Adolf Loos, *Ins Leere Gesprochen: 1897–1900*, ed. Adolf Opel (Vienna: Georg Prachner Verlag, 1981); *Trotzdem: 1900–1930*, ed. Adolf Opel (Vienna: Georg Prachner Verlag, 1982).

10. Schoenberg's essay appears in Arnold Schoenberg, *Style and Idea*, pp. 369–373.

11. Paul Engelmann, "Kraus, Loos, and Wittgenstein," in *Letters from Ludwig Wittgenstein, with a Memoir*, ed. B. F. McGuinness, trans. L. Furtmüller (New York: Horizon Press, 1968), p. 128.

12. Adolf Loos, "Architektur," in *Trotzdem: 1900–1930*, p. 103. Quoted in Ludwig Münz and Gustav Künstler, *Adolf Loos: Pioneer of Modern Architecture*, trans. Harold Meek (New York: Frederick A. Praeger, 1966), pp. 175–176.

13. Quoted in Münz and Künstler, *Adolf Loos*, p. 139.

14. Adolf Loos, "Vom armen, reichen Manne," *Neues Wiener Tagblatt*, 26 April 1900: reprinted as "Von einem armen, reichen Manne," in Adolf Loos, *Ins Leere Gesprochen: 1897–1900*, pp. 198–203. English translation in Münz and Künstler, *Adolf Loos*, pp. 223–225.

15. Adolf Loos, "Architektur," in *Trotzdem: 1900–1930*, p. 101.

16. For more about the Villa Karma, see Jacques Gubler and Gilles Barbey, "Loos's Villa Karma," *Architectural Review* 145 (March 1969): 215–216; or Münz and Künstler, *Adolf Loos*, pp. 79–88.

17. A description of this and other Loos building projects appears in Münz and Künstler, *Adolf Loos*.

18. The construction of the Haus am Michaelerplatz is described in detail in Hermann Czech and Wolfgang Mistelbauer, *Das Looshaus* (Vienna: Verlag Löcker und Wögenstein, 1976).

19. In a letter to Dr. Alexander Amersdorfer of 6 November 1930, in Arnold Schoenberg, *Letters*, ed. Erwin Stein, trans. Eithne Wilkins and Ernst Kaiser (New York: St. Martin's Press, 1965), p. 145.

20. For further description of Schoenberg's handicrafts, see Ernst Hilmar, ed., *Arnold Schönberg Gedenkausstellung 1974* (Vienna: Universal Edition, 1974), pp. 359–362; or Nuria Schoenberg Nono, "The Role of Extra-Musical Pursuits in Arnold Schoenberg's Creative Life," *Journal of the Arnold Schoenberg Institute* 5, no. 1 (June 1981):47–53.

21. Quoted in J. P. Hodin, *Oskar Kokoschka: The Artist and His Time* (London: Cory, Adams and Mackay, 1966), pp. 96–97.

22. Oskar Kokoschka, "In Memory of Adolf Loos," in Münz and Künstler, *Adolf Loos*, p. 11.

23. For a description and first-hand accounts of that premiere, see Egon Wellesz, *Arnold Schönberg*, trans. W. H. Kerridge (London: J. M. Dent and Sons, 1925; reprint ed., New York: Da Capo Press, 1969), pp. 34–35; Special Schoenberg Number, *Musikblätter des Anbruch* (Vienna: Universal Edition, 1934), pp. 321–323; Konrad Vogelsang, *Alban Berg: Leben und Werk* (Berlin: Max Hesses Verlag, 1959), pp. 17–18.

24. Oskar Kokoschka, *My Life*, trans. David Britt (London: Thames and Hudson, 1974), p. 33. Reprinted by permission of F. Bruckmann KG Publishers, Munich. Original edition © 1971 Verlag F. Bruckmann KG, München. English edition under license, © 1974 Thames and Hudson Ltd., London.

25. August Strindberg, *The Son of a Servant Woman*, quoted in Walter Sorell, *The Duality of Vision: Genius and Versatility in the Arts* (London: Thames and Hudson, 1970), p. 265.

26. Wilma Abeles Iggers, *Karl Kraus, A Viennese Critic of the Twentieth Century* (The Hague: Martinus Nijhoff, 1967), p. 158. Iggers has written an extensive investigation of Kraus's views on the role of women. See "The Social Role of Woman," in *Karl Kraus*, pp. 155–170. For aphorisms on the subject of women, see Kraus, *Half-Truths and One-and-a-Half Truths*, pp. 91–106.

27. Iggers, *Karl Kraus*, p. 160.

28. Albert Bloch, "Karl Kraus' Shakespeare," *Books Abroad* 11 (1937):21–22.

29. "A Colloquy between Oskar Kokoschka and Ludwig Goldscheider," in Ludwig Goldscheider, *Kokoschka*, 3d ed. (London: Phaidon Press, 1963), p. 14.

30. Oskar Kokoschka, "On the Nature of Visions," in *Voices of German Expressionism*, ed. Victor H. Miesel (Englewood Cliffs, N.J.: Prentice-Hall, 1970), pp. 98–100.

31. For more on the relationship between Alma Mahler and Oskar Kokoschka, see Alma Mahler Werfel, *And the Bridge is Love* (New York: Harcourt Brace, 1958), pp. 72–82, 86, 131–132; and Oskar Kokoschka, *My Life*, pp. 72–79, 116–117.

32. Rene Char, *Hypnos Waking; Poems and Prose*, quoted in Hannah Arendt, *Between Past and Future: Eight Exercises in Political Thought* (New York: Penguin Books, 1978), p. 4.

⁓ PART II ⁓

Performance

The only success which the composer is to have here is that which should be of the greatest importance for him: to be understood through his work.

Prospectus, Verein für musikalische Privataufführungen, 1918

❦ 3 ❦

Early Performances

The performance ended in a wild struggle in which blows were exchanged. It found its echo in the law courts, where a well-known operetta-composer, called as a witness, said, "Well, I laughed myself, and why shouldn't one laugh at what is obviously funny?" And another, a practicing doctor, declared that the effect of the music was "for a certain section of the public, so nerve-racking, and therefore so harmful for the nervous system, that many who were present already showed signs of severe attacks of neurosis."[1]

Egon Wellesz[B], the Austrian composer and musicologist, used these words to describe the first performance of two of Alban Berg's *Five Orchestral Songs on Picture-Postcard Texts by Peter Altenberg*. The violent disturbances, which along with vituperative reviews in the press accompanied many of the Schoenberg circle's early performances, kindled in Schoenberg much resentment against his native city. Performances were often accompanied by so much shouting from the audience that it was impossible to hear the works being performed. In at least one instance, that of the above-mentioned *Altenberg Lieder* concert, which took place on 31 March 1913, the situation became so acute that the concert could not be completed. Egon Wellesz, who as a student of Schoenberg was present at a number of these concerts, recalled:

> I . . . witnessed the tragedy of persistent attack on every new work that appeared. I saw also the disappointment of the composer and his circle of friends, which was quite small at first, but soon increased. They never could explain the fanatical antagonism of the critics and of a section of the audience towards Schönberg's music. They thought the seriousness and forceful expression of his music were sufficiently compelling at least to command respect, when on the contrary it met with ill-considered and malicious rejection. . . .
>
> In wider circles and among the younger generation now growing up, no idea can be formed of the attacks to which Schönberg was subjected, and of the suffering he had to endure.[2]

The pieces that engendered so much hostility at this time were early nontonal works widely varying in style. In Berg's *Altenberg Lieder,* fleeting tonal implications are largely masked by thick textures or unconventional progressions. The songs, all very brief, are principally organized around a series of short motives. Throughout the piece, rhythmic, dynamic, and textural aspects become strategic as articulative instruments, and while there are certain key pitches that play important roles in the piece, its primary goal cannot be said to be dramatic presentation of a coherent harmonic or otherwise pitch-focused structure. One of the earliest pieces to contain twelve-pitch simultaneities, this first orchestral work of Berg contains much that anticipates the compositional procedures to be employed in his opera *Wozzeck.*[3]

Although Gustav Mahler did not feel that he completely understood Schoenberg's music, he was an early supporter. He attended Schoenberg's concerts and, by his presence, lent them respectability. He also recommended Schoenberg's music to the Rosé Quartet, which ultimately participated in a number of Schoenberg performances.

On one of these occasions, the first performance of the String Quartet, Op. 10, which took place on 21 December 1908, there was a considerable uproar followed by scathing notices in the press. Schoenberg wrote a response,[4] which he attempted to have published in *Die Fackel,* but the piece was refused by Kraus in the following letter:

> I have no close connection with your art but, for the sake of the faith that you have professed in it, I would like to dissuade you from such brawls with critics. If I wanted to introduce observations of Vienna musical life into *Die Fackel,* I would use them only in a form which avoided the appearance of an internal polemic against a particular reporter. Nobody asks for evidence from you, however, that you are wielding a polemical pen and it is really not even good for you to introduce such evidence in various places in your article. I am returning it with full knowledge that I am depriving myself of an interesting contribution, but I believe that I am obliged to do so. Something other than the question of whether you want to use retaliation against a single critic is the question of whether you should defend yourself against material wrongdoing. And I am of the view that a complaint over the suppression of your open letter is your good right. If you want to state in so many words the fact that a 56th rate critic had disrupted your concert and what happened further, then *Die Fackel* is open to you. . . . I would not recommend naming the full names of the culprit [?]. One could write a book about a nonentity, but to address oneself directly to such a nonentity, no matter how briefly, dignifies him with greatness.[5]

In another essay on this performance, written about the same time, Schoenberg described what he felt to be the injustice of a situation in which people protest so loudly that they cannot hear what they protest against.

> However, on December 21st a new method of determining market-value burst upon the world. It is indeed the custom hereabouts to evaluate without being competent

to do so. But to prevent the object under evaluation from being even considered—to bar its entry into the world—to approach an unknown work with one's judgement already prepared: that, surely, is to simplify the juridical process too radically.

My only appeal against this wrong must be an appeal to the non-participants' sense of justice; the non-participants who perhaps have no suspicion of how exactly the disturbers on December 21st *knew in advance that they were going to dislike the work;* the non-participants who perhaps do not even suspect (any more, alas, than I can prove) that the crucial thing behind this *a priori* rejection was—dissonances, of a kind absent from my work: dissonances in the politics—not the work—of art. How else is one to explain why music critics—who should, after all, demand to hear a work repeatedly, so as to form a clear impression of it—tried to prevent even this single performance, by shouting "Stop!"?[6]

Pierrot lunaire, which received its first performance in Berlin on 16 October 1912, was somewhat more successful. It had been commissioned by the Viennese actress Albertine Zehme[B], who had already formed an attachment to the Pierrot role.[7] (Although Erika Stiedry-Wagner, who later performed *Pierrot* with Schoenberg, was also an actress, now the part is usually performed by a singer.) Originally she had asked Schoenberg merely for a piano setting of the Hartleben translation of the poems by Albert Giraud, but Schoenberg kept adding parts until the final setting for speaker and five players was determined. After the premiere, the ensemble went on tour, playing in eleven cities in Germany and Austria. Some of the performances were conducted by Schoenberg and some by Hermann Scherchen[B]. The reaction from the audience was generally favorable, but the bad press continued into the twenties.

Following the experience of so much hostility, the immediate success of the *Gurrelieder* was very encouraging to Schoenberg. The first performance, conducted by Franz Schreker[B], took place on 23 February 1913 in the large Musikvereinssaal in Vienna. The enthusiasm with which this work was received marked Schoenberg's first unqualified success.

Despite his occasional victories, Schoenberg never forgot these early years of prejudice, and the effects were deeply etched in his character. They made him secretive and defensive about the twelve-tone method, contributed to his decision to stay in Berlin in 1912, and certainly added to the severe feelings of persecution that he experienced throughout his life.

Of the performers who made it their specialty to perform Schoenberg's works, those closest to him were Edward Steuermann[B] and the members of the Kolisch Quartet. Players from the Kolisch Quartet and its predecessor, the Wiener Streichquartett, who were interviewed include Marcel Dick, Eugen Lehner, Benar Heifetz, and of course Kolisch himself. The Galimir Quartet, in which Felix Galimir played first violin, was formed later, after Schoenberg was spending little time in Vienna. This group had closer contact with Berg. As the sister of Edward Steuermann, Salka Viertel often visited Schoenberg in Berlin. She was familiar with *Pierrot lunaire* from its beginnings. Although she never took the part of Pierrot herself, she had very definite opinions about its performance.

LONA TRUDING: If any composer recognized Schoenberg as a great musician and composer, this composer, even if Schoenberg wouldn't think highly of him, would become a great friend of Schoenberg. . . . I often wondered if Schoenberg in his ultimate judgment of other composers was not influenced by their attitudes towards him or his music. That was something which I at times suspected. . . . I should not allow myself that vanity should conquer truth. But is it vanity or is it only a lifeline in a man's extremely stormy life of misunderstanding and misinterpretation as Schoenberg has had it? I mustn't forget that. And that, of course, cut very deeply in his life. And I know from my own experience that we had sometimes to get Schoenberg out of a concert hall by a back entrance and had to shield him with our very bodies against all the things which were thrown at him.

JOAN ALLEN SMITH: In the twenties, when you were playing these first performances, what reactions did you get from people? I know that there were many scandals. . . .

MARCEL DICK: Right. You took your life in your hands on each and every occasion. . . . At that time, only very large, vociferous, and rather violent disturbances were the stuff . . . shouting and so on, but knifing happened earlier—not any more.

SMITH: There had been knifings though, really?

DICK: Oh, don't you know that famous—well it's not a story—event . . . what happened when Alban Berg's *Sieben frühe Lieder*, the *Seven Early Songs*, were first performed, with piano of course at that time, not with orchestra? . . . There was a performance . . . and it so happened that Mahler was in the audience, and next to Mahler was sitting a very remarkable person, which gentleman by the name of [Josef] Polnauer[B]. . . . Now later he became a legend.

SMITH: I was told that everyone tried to sit next to him at concerts because he was large and could protect them.

DICK: Right. Right, and he was sitting next to Mahler, who was small of stature, and there was . . . Polnauer, who wasn't a musician, certainly not professionally; he was a government official. And Mahler was very disturbed by the shouting invectives of a person behind him in the audience . . . so Mahler turned around and said, "You are not supposed to hiss when I applaud." To which he answered back quite brazenly, "I hiss also at your unprintable symphonies!" Whereupon, Polnauer let it fly—he gave it to him—whereupon the attacked person brought out a knife and sliced Polnauer's face open, and he carried the scar with great pride to the end of his days. . . . Well, . . . *Pierrot lunaire* was still a most provocative piece, and you could not get through a *Pierrot lunaire* performance presentation whether Schoenberg conducted it or Erwin Stein[B], who took over eventually, without violent disturbances in Vienna. Not in Paris. In Paris, they were less personally involved in affairs musical than in Vienna. Music was everybody's business.

FELIX GALIMIR: There was one who was very—he was an employee of the railroads in Vienna, but he was such an enthusiastic musician that, after he retired, he became a very well-known teacher of theory in Vienna. . . . Polnauer. . . . He was an [official] for the *Bundesbahn;* he was an employee. But he was so enthusiastic; in his office there were only scores. And he loved music of all sorts. He was really quite an extraordinary guy. He was also very strong, and in the first performances, when it was questionable if there might be some scandals, everybody always was grouped around Polnauer because they were sure there is a strong man who could defend them when it came to—because there were often real fights. There were fist fights.

SMITH: Were you present at any of these occasions?

GALIMIR: Oh yes. There were quite a few. . . . But I think it was nice to have these fights, not in the form that you hit each other in the face or you punch in the nose, but you expressed a conviction of something, and not this nondescript no applause. You didn't like it, you started to boo and the other one, the enthusiastic guy, was mad that you booed. You know, it showed enthusiasm—there was such a real partisanship, you took sides, which is necessary to do sometimes. And not this—all right I didn't like it and you forget about it. It makes a much bigger impression that way.

SMITH: You never did *Pierrot* yourself. You were an actress who was interested in music. . . . I wondered if you ever thought of doing *Pierrot* yourself.

SALKA VIERTEL: No, I never would think about it. I didn't like the text of *Pierrot* very much. It didn't interest me, and I never would have had the patience to go through all that. I knew it by heart because I was always the first one to read it. Schoenberg would send every day some music pages—he lived in Zehlendorf and we were in Berlin—and so Edward [Steuermann] would immediately open it and go to the piano, and I would read the text and he would play the melody. . . .

SMITH: Do you know what Schoenberg thought of that first performance of *Pierrot* with Zehme?

VIERTEL: That I don't remember. Of course I was very much involved with the fighting with the public in the audience because, really, people were whistling, which in Europe is a sign of disapproval. And I think Schoenberg—nobody was terribly happy about Mrs. Zehme, the originator of the whole thing, but certainly the orchestra players were all first-class artists and he conducted. . . .

SMITH: Why did people come to the concerts if they were not interested?

VIERTEL: Well, to make scandal. They were interested, I suppose. I remember that the cellist, Grunfeld, it was— one Grunfeld was a pianist, famous pianist, and this was the cellist Grunfeld—stood next to me after *Pierrot lunaire* and screamed, "Erschiessen! . . . Erschiessen!" Shoot this man!

SMITH: And Schoenberg was on the stage while people were screaming?

VIERTEL: Yes. It was not everybody yelling.

SMITH: And did he ignore them or yell back?

VIERTEL: No, he didn't yell back at them. He was thanking those who pushed forward and applauded. And Madame Zehme was also very dignified. . . .

SMITH: What happened when you were in the audience at Schoenberg performances where there were disturbances?

VIERTEL: One was absolutely taking part in it. One booed the booers and one had—it was really not so bad only we were not used to it.

SMITH: And afterwards, what happened? Did everyone just go home?

VIERTEL: No, nobody went home. We went to a café and continued to argue. It was so distinct who was booing. . . . It was a distinct divide between the bourgeois and conservative and the young people who wanted something new. Actually, it's not different.

SMITH: Did it bother him that his music was not well received?

EUGEN LEHNER: Well, according to his words, not, because he was confident of posterity. Once he said, "I'm afraid that posterity will do just as much harm to me in overestimating me as the present does harm to me by underrating me." And then, to a certain extent, he was right. They overrated his analytical and his theoretical contributions but not his contribution as a creative artist, because that is really his contribution. It does not matter the volume of an artist's output but the quality of it.

In 1918, Schoenberg conducted ten open rehearsals of his Chamber Symphony, Op. 9. This unusual undertaking was suggested and organized by one of Schoenberg's most intelligent and gifted pupils, Erwin Ratz. Its purpose was to increase understanding of Schoenberg's music by providing a context in which an audience could gradually become intimately acquainted with one piece. It was hoped that the audience reaction, which was often hostile and sometimes violent at Schoenberg concerts, might thereby be improved. Ratz engaged musicians, made arrangements for a hall and tickets, and distributed, through the concert manager and bookseller Hugo Heller[B], a brochure describing the event as follows:

Arnold Schoenberg, at the request of Hugo Heller Concert Management, has agreed to perform his Chamber Symphony, introduced in Vienna several years ago by the Rosé Quartet and the Wind Ensemble of the Court Opera, in a manner new to current concert format. Rather than giving a single performance, Arnold Schoenberg plans to hold a series of ten open rehearsals. In the final rehearsal, the work will be played in its entirety at least once without interruption.

In this way the listener is offered the opportunity to hear the work often enough to grasp it in detail as well as in its entirety. It will also be of interest to the audience, and especially to musicians, to be able to follow the performance preparation of such a difficult work from the very beginning.

The rehearsals were well-attended by nonmusicians as well as by Schoenberg's private pupils and students from his Schwarzwald School seminar. Among those present were: Alma Mahler[B], Rudolf Ploderer, Franz Werfel, Johannes Itten[B], Paul Stefan[B], Hugo Kauder[B], Adolf Loos, and various current and former Schoenberg pupils including Ratz, Ernst Bachrich[B], Webern, Berg, and Josef Schmid. Also attending the last concert was Schoenberg's military superior. The rehearsal idea did not meet with universal approval, however, and the project was boycotted by Rosé[B], composer Erich Korngold[B], and pupils of the well-known composer Franz Schreker.[8] The press was in general excluded, although a few reviewers did attend the later rehearsals.[9]

ERWIN RATZ: So then I asked Schoenberg if it wouldn't be possible to change this situation by holding open rehearsals of a Schoenberg work; then we would find people with a totally different relation to Schoenberg's music, and that is how it happened. These discussions took place in April or May—[I] began to look for musicians—at that time we got the best people in Vienna—who were willing to do the Chamber Symphony under Schoenberg's direction. And it was through this, you see, that I found a group of people to finance it. You see, the bill was not small. . . . Ten rehearsals with the best musicians, hall rental fees—and I also succeeded in obtaining this money. This was the main point. And then I arranged to engage the musicians for certain days and informed Schoenberg to please on such and such a day. . . . Most of the rehearsals were held in the smaller Musikvereinssaal, the room known today as the Brahmssaal, but I noticed on the schedule that the Brahmssaal was already occupied on two occasions and we had to settle for the Konzerthaus. But it is uninteresting which room it was in. And I was fortunate enough to engage the services of the largest concert agency in existence at that time, the bookseller Hugo Heller. Today there really is no such concert agency; today everything is in the hands of the Konzerthaus and Musikfreunde, whereas at that time, there were still these private concert agencies. He was excited about the idea and allowed me the use of his rooms, and you can see, this plea for help which I sent to the people, to those who were interested, caused many people to come. And the effect was truly as I expected. Even the people who at first couldn't get anything out of it said after three or four rehearsals, "That sounds like Mozart." Now you must imagine you will never again hear the Chamber Symphony as it sounded under Schoenberg. I mean that what you hear on records today is impossible. . . . They have no idea how this music goes. It was really a one-time experience, and who can imagine having eight rehearsals for a relatively short and simple work today. The Chamber Symphony is not such an impossible work, and that was just what was wonderful—that Schoenberg could hold eight full rehearsals and always be able to say something new about the work, about how it sounded as a whole. Then single voices were rehearsed, then a couple taken together, until finally everyone played together, and in that you first heard each voice singly, you acquired a totally different understanding of the whole sound. First the single voices, then the phrasing and—well, what should I add—in the last rehearsals, the entire work was played through twice. . . .

SMITH: I'd like to ask you further about Schoenberg's technique in these rehearsals, for instance, what he talked about. Did he talk about analysis or about formal matters?

RATZ: Only the purely musical interpretations, such as *accelerando, crescendo, decrescendo*—so purely musical, no formal analysis; moreover the work is formally so simple and clear. There was also the analysis by Berg already—Alban Berg wrote an analysis of the Chamber Symphony. Therefore, formally, there was no problem. Tempo was always important—to decide about it correctly.

SMITH: Was he a good conductor?

MAX DEUTSCH: The first time, he conducted his own works very slow. My tempi, now I am conducting Opus 16, the Orchestral Pieces, are often much faster than Schoenberg. He needed very, very—a big number of rehearsals. That is the contrary from me.

SMITH: Do you think that Schoenberg felt that there was only one right tempo for his music?

DEUTSCH: For Schoenberg, the tempo was very important, very important. When he conducted, he was at the point—his music was too modern, he had not the energy to impose himself to the orchestra, because in this time, the orchestra was not able to play very, very quickly, very fast, these tremendous things you can find in the works of Schoenberg. But I can tell you that Schoenberg's writing for orchestra is absolutely *exemplaire.*

(Alban Berg)

13 June 1918

. . . Must give you a report on yesterday's concert (9th Rehearsal). It was wonderful. In the small Konzerthaussaal (where of course the acoustics are disadvantageous). The hall very full. First a quarter of an hour rehearsing a few passages, then play-through. Then an interval. . . . Before the second play-through started, Loos went up on the platform and read a short essay, "Beethoven's Disease of the Ear": . . .

* * * * * * * *

At the turn of the eighteenth century, a musician named Beethoven lived in Vienna. People laughed at him because he had his quirks, a small stature and a comical head. The bourgeoisie were offended by his compositions "because," so they said, "unfortunately, the man has sick ears. His brain brews terrible dissonances. He, however, maintains that they are glorious harmonies so his ears, as is evident to us who possess healthy ones, are sick. What a pity!"

The aristocracy, however, which thanks to privileges bestowed upon it by the world, also knew its responsibilities and gave him the necessary money in order for him to perform his music. The aristocracy also had the power to bring to production an opera of Beethoven's at the Kaiser's opera house. However, the bourgeoisie, who filled the theatre, gave the work such a poor reception that a second performance could not be risked.

A hundred years have gone by since then and the bourgeoisie are moved as they listen to the work of the sick, lunatic musician. Have they become aristocrats, as the nobles of 1819, and acquired respect for the inclinations of the genius? No, they have all become sick. They all have Beethoven's ear disease. Through a century, the dissonances of the holy Ludwig have mistreated their ears. This their ears could not endure. All anatomical details, all ossicles, sinuosities, eardrums, and Eustachian tubes have acquired the abnormal form exhibited by Beethoven's ear. And the funny face upon which the urchins have heaped ridicule, the people would have as the spiritual countenance of the world.

It is the spirit which furnished its own embodiment.[10]

* * * * * * * *

This message, full of irony and passion, was greeted with hearty applause. Then came the second play-through. It went superbly. A storm of clapping and cheering at the end, the performers and Schoenberg were called on again and again, and it was a long time indeed before the hall emptied. I was absolutely "shattered" by listening to the work twice—without following the score! I felt ten years younger, and as if, say, I'd been present at the first performance of Mahler's Third. Although I went to bed at 11:15, I couldn't get to sleep till two. . . . It really was so glorious. *You should have been there.* An irreparable loss for you, and for me as well, that you weren't.[11]

Notes

1. Egon Wellesz, *Arnold Schönberg,* trans. W. H. Kerridge (London: J. M. Dent and Sons, 1925; reprint ed., New York: Da Capo Press, 1969), p. 35.

2. Ibid., pp. 6–7.

3. It is not appropriate in this work to make a detailed analytical study of atonal music. Fortunately, several excellent studies are available. These include Mark DeVoto, "Some Notes on the Unknown *Altenberg Lieder,*" *Perspectives of New Music* 5 (Fall–Winter 1966):37–74; Allen Forte, *The Structure of Atonal Music* (New Haven: Yale University Press, 1973); and George Perle, *Serial Composition and Atonality: An Introduction to the Music of Schoenberg, Berg, and Webern,* 5th ed. (Berkeley: University of California Press, 1981).

4. Arnold Schoenberg, "A Legal Question," in *Style and Idea,* ed. Leonard Stein, trans. Leo Black (London: Faber and Faber, 1975), pp. 185–189.

5. Quoted in Ernst Hilmar, ed., *Arnold Schönberg, Gedenkausstellung 1974* (Vienna: Universal Edition, 1974), pp. 197–198.

6. Arnold Schoenberg, "An Artistic Impression," in *Style and Idea,* pp. 190–191.

7. According to Edward Steuermann in Gunther Schuller, "A Conversation with Steuermann," *Perspectives of New Music* 3 (Fall–Winter 1964):23–24.

8. For a more complete list of those attending the rehearsals, see Alban Berg, *Briefe an seine Frau* (Munich: Albert Langen and Georg Müller Verlag, 1965), pp. 345–355.

9. For an account by one reviewer, see Willi Reich, *Schoen-berg, A Critical Biography*, trans. Leo Black (London: Longman Group, 1971), pp. 113–115.

10. Adolf Loos, *Trotzdem: 1900–1930*, ed. Adolf Opel (Vienna: Georg Prachner Verlag, 1982), p. 118.

11. Alban Berg, *Letters to His Wife*, ed. and trans. Bernard Grun (London: Faber and Faber, 1971), p. 220.

~ 4 ~

Verein für Musikalische Privataufführungen

The success of the Chamber Symphony rehearsals encouraged Schoenberg to further efforts in public performance. Only a month after the rehearsals, on 1 July 1918, Berg wrote to his wife:

> Schoenberg has a marvelous idea, to start next season another society, setting out to perform musical works from the period "Mahler to the present" once a week for its members; perhaps, should the work be a difficult one, to perform it more than once. Performers to be a string quartet specially selected, to rehearse very intensively, male and female singers, pianists, etc., not yet famous but good calibre. Hall, the one in the Schwarzwald School.[1]

This idea blossomed into the Verein für musikalische Privataufführungen (Society for Private Musical Performances) the following November. The Society became one of the major occupations of the Schoenberg circle for the next three years—seminal years for the development of the twelve-tone method—and provided the model for later contemporary music groups, such as the International Society for Contemporary Music (ISCM, 1922) and the League of Composers (1923).

The aims of the Society, as stated in the prospectus by Alban Berg, were

> ...to give artists and art-lovers a real and accurate knowledge of modern music.
>
> One circumstance, which contributes to a large extent to the relationship of the public to modern music, is that any impression they receive of it is inevitably one of unclarity.... The performances are for the most part unclear. And in particular the public's consciousness of its needs and desires is unclear....
>
> ...The desire to achieve clarity at last, and thus take into account such needs and desires as are justified, this was one of the reasons that moved Arnold Schoenberg to found the society.
>
> Three things are necessary for the achievement of this aim:
>
> 1. Clear, well-prepared performances.
> 2. Frequent repetitions.
> 3. The performances must be withdrawn from the corrupting influence of publicity....[2]

The first general meeting of the Society took place on 6 December 1918. The statutes, drawn up by Paul Pisk's father, a lawyer, were read out and approved.[3] Then the following executive committee, proposed by Schoenberg, was elected: Ernst Bachrich[B], Alban Berg, Otto and Hugo Breuer, Max Deutsch[B], Paul Pisk[B], Josef Polnauer[B], Dr. Arthur Prager, Karl Rankl[B], Erwin Ratz[B], Edward Steuermann[B], Josef Trauneck, Viktor Ullmann[B], Dr. Anton Webern, Roland Tenschert, Pauline Klarfeld, Marta Koref, Olga Novakovic, and Christine Wurst. The tasks of the committee members were assigned as follows:

Rehearsal Directors (Vortragsmeister): Webern, Berg, Steuermann (later Erwin Stein[B] and Benno Sachs)

Secretary: Pisk (later Josef Rufer[B], Rudolf Wenzel, and Felix Greissle)

Treasurer: Prager

Archivist: Polnauer

Secretaries (Schriftführer): Bachrich, Trauneck

Organizers (Ordner): Polnauer, Ratz, O. and H. Breuer, Deutsch, Trauneck, Ullmann

Executive members without special function: Klarfeld, Koref, Wurst, and Tenschert

Music Committee: Webern, Berg, Steuermann, Pisk, Novakovic, Bachrich, Deutsch, Rankl, Trauneck.

The performers, young and highly gifted players as well as members of Schoenberg's own circle,[4] were coached in the early rehearsals (ten to twenty for each concert) by one of the *Vortragsmeister* and in the final rehearsals by Schoenberg himself.

Tickets were sold by subscription at four prices. In order to prevent attendance by critics, each subscriber was issued a membership card with photograph which was checked by Polnauer at the door. Applause was not allowed, nor was public reporting of events. To insure equal attendance on all occasions, the program content remained secret until the concert was about to begin, and consequently programs were not printed. In February of 1919, Berg wrote to Erwin Stein that there were about 320 members.[5]

The season ran from mid-September to the end of June, usually with one concert per week. Monday evening concerts were held either in the Schwarzwald School or in the Society of Engineers and Architects (Eschenbachgasse 9, Vienna I). Those on Sunday mornings were either in the Brahmssaal of the Musikverein or the Schubertsaal of the Konzerthaus.[6] During the first season, forty-five works were performed in twenty-six concerts; by the time the Society disbanded in 1921, over two hundred works had been presented.[7]

Material chosen for performance was varied, and as Schoenberg was concerned that there be no suggestion of bias in the program selection, no Schoenberg work was performed during the first year-and-a-half of the Society's existence. The first concert, on 29 December 1918, included the following works: Scryabin Sonatas Nos. 4 and 7 (performed by Steuermann), Debussy's four *Proses Lyriques* (Felicie Mihacsek[B], soprano at the Vienna State Opera, and Bachrich), and Mahler's Seventh Symphony for piano four hands (Steuermann and Bachrich). Thereafter, works by well-known foreigners and local students were presented, the most frequently performed composers being Reger, Debussy, and Bartók.[8] There were, in addition, concerts with works by Mozart, Beethoven, and Brahms.

The large number of concerts and the care with which each was prepared involved a major commitment of time and energy for Schoenberg and perhaps especially for his more gifted followers. The resulting concerts were a marked addition to the musical lives of those involved, widening considerably their knowledge of contemporary repertoire outside that of their own circle. It is evident, from the amount of time invested in the Verein, that Schoenberg considered this project of major significance. The presence of traditional as well as modern repertory is indicative of Schoenberg's commitment to performance. Performers testify to the coaching ability of Schoenberg and to the similarity between his coaching methods in contemporary music and in more traditional works—evidence that Schoenberg viewed contemporary music as a logical continuation of the music of the past.

Since the financial and organizational resources of the Society were limited, most of the works presented were for small combinations of performers. In order to make possible hearings of works intended by Mahler and others for large groups, reductions were made for one or more pianos or for a small chamber ensemble consisting of some combination of several strings and winds, one or two pianos, harmonium, and percussion. In all, fifty-four arrangements were at least projected for performance in the Society's regular and special concerts. In the early concerts of the Society, piano tran-scriptions of orchestral works were common, gradually yielding to arrangements for chamber orchestra in the second and third seasons.[9]

The arrangers of these many works were Schoenberg and his pupils. Schoenberg believed that the presentation of large works in arrangements for reduced forces allowed for a clarity of presentation and a simplicity of formal enuncia-tion often not possible in a rendition obscured by the rich-ness of orchestration. The success of these reductions, which received the same careful coaching as any other work, is attested to by Erwin Ratz, a refined musician and an expert on the music of Mahler:

> The high point . . . was the performance of the Sixth and Seventh Symphonies by Gustav Mahler arranged for piano four hands. . . . The interpreters were Edward Steuermann and Ernst Bachrich, with whom Schoenberg worked with loving solicitude in around thirty rehearsals of both sym-phonies. . . . Schoenberg was an accomplished interpreter; this was apparent in the performance of his *Gurrelieder,* which he directed in the Staatsoper.[10]

Although the concerts were primarily attended by mem-bers of Schoenberg's immediate musical circle, others inter-ested in contemporary musical developments frequented them as well. Alma Mahler[B] was regularly in attendance and Adolf Loos was also often there. A member of the Society and a regular at its concerts was the philosopher Karl Pop-per[B]. Popper was not an intimate of the Schoenberg circle and perhaps attended its concerts more from curiosity than from appreciation. In his autobiography, *Unended Quest,* Popper describes his relationship to the Verein and the motives for his involvement:

> Under the influence of some of Mahler's music (an influ-ence that did not last), and of the fact that Mahler had defended Schönberg, I felt that I ought to make a real effort to get to know and to like contemporary music. So I

became a member of the Society for Private Performances ("Verein für musikalische Privataufführungen") pre-
sided over by Arnold Schönberg. . . . For a time I also
became a pupil of Schönberg's pupil Erwin Stein, but I had
scarcely any lessons with him: instead I helped him a little
with his rehearsals for the Society's performances. In this
way I got to know some of Schönberg's music intimately,
especially the *Kammersymphonie* and *Pierrot Lunaire.* I
also went to rehearsals of Webern, especially of his
Orchesterstücke, and of Berg.

After about two years I found I had succeeded in getting to know something—about a kind of music which
now I liked even less than I had to begin with.[11]

By 1921 severe inflation in Austria seriously threatened
the activities of the Society, and on 27 May a special concert
of waltzes was held in order to raise funds. For this occasion, four Strauss waltzes were orchestrated: "Rosen aus
dem Süden" and "Lagunenwalzer" (by Schoenberg), "Schatz-
walzer" from *Zigeunerbaron* (by Webern), and "Wein, Weib
und Gesang" (by Berg). Performers were Steuermann, piano;
Berg, harmonium; Kolisch and Schoenberg, first violin;
Rankl, second violin; Othmar Steinbauer, viola; and Webern,
cello. At the end of the evening, the manuscripts were auc-
tioned off.

The Society managed to continue functioning for several
months after this event, until the end of 1921. Erwin Stein,
who was by then acting as director of the Society, endeavored to maintain the solvency of the organization by
placing advertisements in the newspapers and by putting on
special events to which the public was invited. Both Schoenberg and Berg felt that these moves violated the original
private intent of the Society.

The second production of *Pierrot lunaire* was prepared
in the Verein in 1921 and taken on tour several times thereafter, with either Erwin Stein or Schoenberg conducting.
Stein, who was in charge of organizing the performances
and who had secured Schoenberg's permission to perform
this and other Schoenberg works in the Verein during

Schoenberg's absence from Vienna, experienced numerous difficulties from the beginning. Finding rehearsal times was problematic and tour scheduling was not as successful as anticipated.[12] Stein began rehearsals with the singer Marie Gutheil-Schoder[B], who had sung the premiere of Schoenberg's second string quartet and who was preferred by Schoenberg for the role of speaker. Soon difficulties arose in rehearsing with Gutheil-Schoder, and although Schoenberg disapproved angrily, Stein replaced her with Erika Stiedry-Wagner[B].[13] Wagner was carefully coached by Stein and later by Schoenberg. Eventually, *Pierrot* received four performances in Vienna in the spring of 1921 and was taken to Prague twice during the 1921–22 season. A final private Society performance on 5 December 1921 and a public concert on 30 October 1922 were the last Vienna performances offered by the Society.

The success of these performances of one of the finest and most representative works of Schoenberg's early period greatly enhanced Schoenberg's reputation abroad and led to performances of the piece by other conductors. The composer Darius Milhaud conducted the piece in Paris. Because of wartime bitterness against the Germans and the German language, the singer for this occasion, Marya Freund[B], retranslated the text back into French, having first tried unsuccessfully to use the original French text of Albert Giraud. The performance was successful. According to an account by Milhaud,[14] there were also later performances in Brussels, which received a mixed reception.

An exciting side effect of these performances occurred when Milhaud traveled to Vienna in 1921 to appear in concerts of French music with Marya Freund. Milhaud visited Schoenberg, told him of his Paris performances, and was invited by Schoenberg to present his interpretation alongside Schoenberg's own. Milhaud later recalled the event, which took place at Alma Mahler's house:

> I told Schoenberg of my experiences with *Pierrot Lunaire* and . . . he hit upon the idea of bringing the two interpretations into juxtaposition. Thus it was one afternoon,

in Mrs. Gustav Mahler's house, we had two performances of *Pierrot Lunaire*, one with Marya Freund, conducted by me, and the other with Erika Wagner, under the direction of Schoenberg. It was interesting to note the differences in atmosphere that were produced. Perhaps the French and German languages used by the singers determined the "colors" that were imposed upon the instruments. The piano was played by Steuermann, an admirable exponent of Schoenberg's art, and the other instrumentalists were members of the Vienna Philharmonic. The French language, being the softer, made all the delicate passages appear the more subtle; but in the German interpretation the dramatic passages seemed more powerful, while the delicate ones assumed more weight.[15]

Alma Mahler, in her diary, also recorded the evening. Her remarks on the performances suggest that the French singer sang the words rather than speaking them in the manner directed by Schoenberg.

The work was performed here two times in succession, first by the conductor Stein, who was a student and disciple of Schoenberg, then by Darius Milhaud. It was first spoken [gesprochen] by Erika Wagner, coached by Schoenberg himself—then sung [gesungen] by Maria Freund, coached by Milhaud. Schoenberg scarcely recognized his work—but the majority of those present were for Milhaud's interpretation. Doubtless, it was more original in Schoenberg's more rhythmical style of accented speaking than in the song, where one noticed rather the similarity with Debussy. The authentic interpretation was naturally the one by Schoenberg-Stein.[16]

One of the most loyal organizers in the Verein was the composer and Schoenberg pupil Paul Amadeus Pisk. As its initial secretary, Pisk was responsible for many of the mundane arrangements of the Society. Later Felix Greissle took over many of these chores. Although Erna Gál played for Schoenberg on a number of occasions and was in addition a close friend of Kolisch, Stefan Askenase played only once.

Erika Stiedry-Wagner was involved in the Verein perfor-
mances of *Pierrot lunaire.* Clara Steuermann studied with
Schoenberg only after he moved to Los Angeles. She is
included in this study for the recollections of her husband,
Edward Steuermann, who was the primary interpreter of
Schoenberg's piano music.

CLARA STEUERMANN: I would say that Steuermann's qualities as an interpreter of music in the broadest range of
styles and so on were perhaps inhibited by the fact that
he became identified with Schoenberg at that time, but
you see, in the time of the Verein für Privataufführungen, his little society, he performed all sorts of music—
Russian, French—well, the Americans were scarcely in
evidence at that time—but the purpose of this Verein,
as Schoenberg established it, was, after the isolation of
the first world war, an attempt on Schoenberg's part to
acquaint the music public in Vienna with what had
been going on elsewhere in Europe during the years
that the war had cut them off. And so they brought first
performances of Ravel, Debussy, Milhaud, Scryabin, and
Prokofiev and all these things which were unknown to
them, as well as the works of German and Austrian
composers.* So Steuermann played all of that as well as
the entire classic literature. . . . This stems from the fact

*Schoenberg discussed his programming philosophy in a letter of 26
October 1922 to Alexander von Zemlinsky[B]:

> Now as to the "insignificant" Milhaud. I don't agree. Milhaud
> strikes me as the most important representative of the contem-
> porary movement in all Latin countries: polytonality. Whether I
> like him is not to the point. But I consider him very talented. But
> that is not a question for the Society, which sets out *only to
> inform.* It was actually primarily on your own account that I did
> Milhaud once again, hoping that he would interest you.—Reger
> must in my view be done often; 1. because he has written a lot; 2.
> because he is already dead and people are still not clear about
> him. (I consider him a genius.)

Arnold Schoenberg, *Letters,* ed. Erwin Stein, trans. Eithne Wilkins and
Ernst Kaiser (New York: St. Martin's Press, 1965), p. 80.

that Schoenberg also was a passionate musician altogether, and Schoenberg himself did not cut himself off
from the music of the past, and in later years, when his
eyes were not good and he was not well and he could
not work very well for himself, he listened to a great
deal of music. And I can remember still, in the time
when I was with him, his coming one day to class and
being suddenly terribly excited because he had heard
some Tchaikovsky symphony the night before, and he
said, "My God, what an incredible symphonist this
was—how he wrote for orchestra—how he made the
orchestra sound!" And he was enthusiastic in the same
way that any of us would have been discovering a piece
that we hadn't known before. And this capacity for passion and enthusiasm about music as music, never being
insular, never being narrow about its having to be I
don't know what level of special technique and so on, I
think this is very important to bring out about such a
person as Schoenberg. . . . I am not trying to whitewash
Schoenberg. He was a difficult person—an extremely
difficult person—and he was as much the victim of his
own reputation on the outside as anyone else would
be, but as far as music was concerned, he was a real
musician.

PAUL PISK: The three *Vortragsmeister* had to supervise the
rehearsals and then, when they were ready, then
Schoenberg took over and listened. See, now I wasn't
only the secretary but played quite a bit—I was a
pianist—and played for instance the famous first performance for the Webern *Passacaglia* for two pianos six
hands. I played one, Bachrich played one, and Steuermann. We three played this performance. . . . You know
they called the Schoenberg Verein "Reger-Debussy
Verein" because Schoenberg was so fond of Reger and
Debussy. . . . Anyway, so I became the secretary and I
had to get the rehearsals together and help the adminis-
tration, and of course, you can't imagine how wearing
it was for a normal human being to be with Schoen-

berg. Schoenberg was a most, I mean not only tem-
peramental, . . . but tyrannical. He didn't allow any
opposition.

The reductions used in the Verein, usually for piano four
or six hands, served as valuable learning experiences, both
for the students who made them and for the listeners, who
were able to hear complicated works clearly presented,
divorced from their coloristic properties. Schoenberg has
described the role of the piano reduction as follows:

> A sculpture can never be seen from all sides at once; de-
> spite this, all its sides are worked out to the same degree.
> Almost all composers proceed in the same way when han-
> dling the orchestra; they realize even details that are not
> under all circumstances going to be audible. Despite this,
> the piano reduction should only be like the view of a
> sculpture from *one* viewpoint.[17]

FELIX GREISSLE: Schoenberg had the Verein für Privataufführungen, you know. And we had to do a lot of tran-
scriptions there because we did not have the money to
have big orchestras; we still wanted to perform the
works and we made transcriptions. For instance, the
first concert—there I wasn't present; you see it was
before my time with him—was the Seventh Symphony
of Mahler for two pianos. And that—I don't know who
did the—it was probably a joint effort, everybody one
movement. . . . And he wanted to have the orchestra
pieces, the Five Orchestra Pieces, and I started out on it.
And I started out small, a few instruments only—much
less than later was. Then he put me to Mahler songs
which we needed very much. . . . And while I did that,
he needed the orchestra pieces, so he took what I had
done and added two or three instruments to it, and it
was performed this way. But then, it came back to me
afterwards, and I added still one more instrument, a
bassoon, to it. And . . . it is true that I had to show him
every movement; he said go back, take the time, some-

times, with something. It's just like Webern wrote the Passacaglia. The end result was this: it was basically done by me; there're a few corrections in German which he put in. With the Serenade, which I did for large orchestra, he only wrote the second violins in one place; he put three measures and that was all; the rest he left as it was. . . . The orchestra pieces, they are problematic. And there were questions, and I was very grateful. I had gotten a magnificent lesson in orchestration which he never gave. He never taught orchestration.

JOAN ALLEN SMITH: I'm interested in how Schoenberg, Webern, and Berg conducted rehearsals with you and what approaches they took to rehearsing their own music and that of others. I understand that Webern was quite picky about rehearsals. Is that true?

RUDOLF KOLISCH: No. You couldn't call him that. You couldn't term it "picky." He insisted on some kind of exactness which is necessary for this music.

SMITH: Would you say that this was more exactness than was possible or was he realistic about the possibilities of the group and so on?

KOLISCH: Oh yes. He made no, absolutely no unreasonable demands. Of course, sometimes it was difficult at this time; the music was new.

SMITH: Was Webern very detailed in his rehearsing?

ERNA GÁL: Yes, well everything was very emotional with him. And you see that these little piece fragments of melody which always come in his works—he used to then very expressively play them on the piano to show how to do it, and what started here finished there and all that. I liked his pieces [Four Pieces, Op. 7] after a while when I played them with Rudi [Kolisch]. I could not have played them otherwise if I hadn't.

SMITH: What about Berg—was his approach to rehearsing more—

GÁL: Berg was a little more cool than Webern and he was cooler than Webern towards other people. But very kind, very, very kind-hearted and noble—really very, very noble. . . . I liked Alban Berg very much. He was a wonderful, fine, aristocratic gentleman. Inside and outside. Really, he was a fine man. And Webern was so moving, always touching—really lovely.

SMITH: And how was Berg in rehearsals?

MARCEL DICK: Jovial as always, and just as exacting as Schoenberg but appreciative—much more congenial, much—he always gave one the feeling that one did better than he had expected, which was not so, because if it was not quite the way he wanted it, he then let us know. He was very, very pleasant to work with, and he would not have dared to take the attitudes of the master.

SMITH: I was wondering what your duties with the Society were. I understand that you were the secretary for a while.

GREISSLE: Oh, I was secretary, I was, what do you call it, *Vortragsmeister* and I had to do a lot. . . . Can you imagine—I had to orchestrate something, and I had to work with a singer who was a soloist for the next time, and I had to do—we all did that. Berg had to. I remember Berg had to see whether there were enough chairs in the hall, and that they were at a certain distance. Otherwise, if they were a little wider, there was not enough room; it was too small. And I remember Schoenberg coming and—horrible, you see. "The chairs are completely cockeyed. This is ridiculous. What did you do here?" So, Berg silently, without saying one word, took a measure, a tape measure, out of his pocket and measured and said, "You said that you wanted so and so many centimeter; it's really all right; it's a half centimeter more."

(Stefan Askenase)

27 July 1973

I was just back from the war (the first one) in which I have participated as an artillery officer, to continue my studies, interrupted during 3 years, when one day I received the visit of Eduard Steuermann, whom I knew almost since my childhood and highly admired. He was about 4 years older than I. . . .

It was in the early spring of 1919 that this visit took place and he told me that there was an association started by Schoenberg in view of giving on Sunday mornings concerts of contemporary music and invited me to participate in one of the concerts.

The piece chosen was the *Sinfonia Domestica* by Strauss to be performed on two pianos with a fellow student Miss Cesia Dische. Schoenberg's opinion was, that a work could be better judged without an orchestral decoration, that one could better find out what it really contained of musical quality.

So we did it and played the piece at a concert after many rehearsals under Steuermann's direction.*

It went probably quite well because I have been asked to play again, this time alone, a work by Viteslav Nowak, a Tcheque [sic] composer, intitled [sic] "Pan."

But this time the project ended with a debacle. When I had learned the piece, Steuermann came to my student's lodgings to hear it. He found it quite good, gave me a few advices. About a week later he came again for a second hearing, this time accompanied by Alban Berg and all went well. A few days before the concert, there was a third and final audition and I had to play it for Schoenberg in the house of one of his disciples. I think his name was [Max] Deutsch but I am not sure.

After one of the movements, Schoenberg made a witty remark, unhappily I do not remember what it was; any-

---

*Walter Szmolyan lists the pianists in the *Sinfonia Domestica* as Dische and Ernst Bachrich. Walter Szmolyan, "Die Konzerte des Wiener Schönberg-Vereins," *Oesterreichische Musikzeitschrift* 36 (February 1981):86.

how, I smiled. And this smile of mine made him furious. He said in a very disagreeable tone that I was arrogant, that I had no right to laugh at him (auslachen) and some more similar things. I had been rather shy and most respectful with him; meeting Schoenberg and playing for him was an event for me. Very surprised and shocked, I got up and went away without a word.

Later on I understood better how it happened. Berg and Steuermann, who were present at the scene, came to see me the following day, perhaps not to apologize but to explain the situation. Schoenberg was very poor in that time. When I saw him, he was still wearing military trousers (for he had been mobilised during the war), a coat that was much too large and certainly not made for him. He was suspicious of hostility with every person whom he met. There was a group of about 10 people, some of them of highest quality, who adored him and were strongly under his influence. Otherwise there was a number (a modest number) of music lovers who tried to penetrate into his music. But the official musical Vienna ignored him completely; he was not even offered a position as a professor at the Academy of Music; the press was of the sharpest hostility.

So I understood that one could not expect from him a friendly behavior as one expects it from ordinary people in a normal situation. Still, I confess, I never had the wish of meeting him again and I never met him since.[18]

SMITH: So when you started studying with Schoenberg, did you work with him first just in composition and then later did you start playing his music, or did you start as a performer?

KOLISCH: Well, I started playing not really his music at first. You know, he had this association for performance— ... Verein für musikalische Privataufführungen. I was immediately engaged in this activity. . . .

SMITH: And you studied composition with Schoenberg?

KOLISCH: Ja, ja. . . .

SMITH: How did you decide to form the Kolisch Quartet?* Were you encouraged by Schoenberg to do this?

KOLISCH: Yes. I mean more than encouraged. One could say that he gave me the order, you know, to form an ensemble which was needed for the performance of this music. . . .

SMITH: Do you think that the performance standards in Vienna were higher at that time than they are here today?

KOLISCH: Oh, no. I am sure that they weren't. . . . As a matter of fact, because of lowness of the standards, we embarked on this adventure of this society. That was the main idea of it—to raise the standard—set it, you know—set the standard, which really happened.

SMITH: So did you attempt to do better performances of more standard works as well?

KOLISCH: Of course, ja. Oh sure, we did not only perform contemporary pieces.

LONA TRUDING: I knew Kolisch very well. . . . I heard him as a soloist in the Schoenberg Verein . . . and then I heard his quartet. And of this I had a very high opinion, and I must say, they had absolutely that new interpretation of letting the music speak without any interference of personal emotions.

SMITH: Was this basically Schoenberg's idea?

TRUDING: Yes, it was Schoenberg's. That is what we actually attempted and strove for because I realized in time that, if I let the music speak, that *Enthusiasmus* which that language of the music brings about in me is of a

---

*The Kolisch Quartet was founded in 1922 as the Wiener Streichquartett. It toured extensively in Europe and in North and South America before disbanding in 1938, a casualty of emigration and the world situation. This group, which along with Edward Steuermann was primarily responsible for disseminating Schoenbergian performance ideals beyond Austrian borders, is discussed further in the following chapter.

different kind and of a different quality than if I would falsify the music, or the language of the music, by putting my own emotions or feelings about the music into it; so the process was reversed—I do not instill but I draw out. . . .

SMITH: And this was characteristic of all of the people who performed in the Verein?

TRUDING: Absolutely. . . . I think we learned that kind of interpretation through what we learned from Schoenberg, the organic way of musical analysis. I never played a sonata or any work before I had analyzed it. I sat with it, I read it like a book until the whole thing began to have a context—to have an organic development, to become an organic whole—before I realized that in the smallest detail of that sonata, the totality of that sonata is contained. . . . Now, actually, while you work at it and analyze it, you know exactly what happens, but when you play it, you forget. You don't play according to exactly what happens—you've forgotten that, but it still works in your subconscious where it has imprinted itself while you were consciously working at it. Therefore, the whole interpretation becomes different from anything which is entirely prompted by the mood in which you are.

SALKA VIERTEL: Schoenberg was very demanding and very possessive, as far as Edward [Steuermann] was concerned, because very often he had to sacrifice some concert with lucrative possibilities and let it go because he had to study with Schoenberg on some new piano piece or something. He was always working for Schoenberg. Edward was a very loyal and very idealistic person. And it was a very, very deep relationship, and Schoenberg was . . . like an octopus. My mother was sometimes very indignant about his egoism, Schoenberg's egoism, but Edward was so fascinated by him and they all were. They all were like little boys with Schoenberg. . . . My brother was interpreting Schoenberg and understanding Schoenberg to such an extreme that Schoenberg didn't want anybody else to play him.

SMITH: Did this limit your brother's career as a pianist?

VIERTEL: It affected his career because he would have made a greater career as a pianist if he wouldn't have devoted himself completely to Schoenberg.

SMITH: Did this bother him?

VIERTEL: No. . . . He thought it through.

SMITH: Do you think that being so involved with Schoenberg was limiting to Steuermann's career as a pianist?

STEFAN ASKENASE: Well, I don't think so. Well, if you mean that it prevented him, some way perhaps but some way to the contrary—made him well-known as a specialist of this type. No, I think the career he made corresponded to his taste. It wouldn't have been his ideal to give a concert every night and so, and travel every day and to play Beethoven and Brahms. . . . But he played extremely well—more than well, you know, it was very, very superior, but it was never nice. It was not agreeable to listen to. It was something else, but one felt that it is somebody very important. It was very serious. It was very hard—there was no charm, and I think even that he avoided it, that it was not that it was his nature to play like that, only that it was his taste.

SMITH: Was this typical of players in the Schoenberg circle or was this peculiar to Steuermann?

ASKENASE: I think it was peculiar.

SMITH: Did you not feel the same way about Kolisch?

ASKENASE: You know what? When Kolisch started, he played about the same way. Maybe it was the influence of the circle. Music—*Ewigkeitswerte* was every second word—the values of eternity. And, it was never a game, an amusement. It had to be always very dignified, very important, very, very, very serious. But Kolisch changed very much his playing when he had his quartet, and he brought Benar Heifetz, the cellist Heifetz, into this quartet, who was a Russian—full of musicianship in the normal way—full of soul, full of heart, and full of tone, and that influenced Kolisch very much because he played very—a lot of Mozart and Schubert and he played beautifully. . . . But he would not have been able to do this before he was influenced by Heifetz.

ERIKA STIEDRY-WAGNER: And then it was in Vienna was a Schoenberg Verein. . . . And there they made concerts. And there they wanted to make the *Pierrot lunaire*. And they wanted first Mrs. Gutheil-Schoder to do it—a singer, a very famous singer. But it is a thing you have to talk, to speak, not to sing. And so, she found it for her too difficult, and then they were thinking, "Whom could we ask?" And then Alban said, "Why don't you ask Erika Wagner? She's an actress and she's a singer," because I sang also. I had *Liederabende* and I sang operettas. And so it happened that I did the *Pierrot*. I studied it with Erwin Stein. . . . But with Erwin Stein I was working hard, oh very hard. Because you know it's very difficult to speak in rhythm—strong rhythm. And then the *Sprechmelodie*, you know. . . . He wants a certain line to speak, with low tones and with high tones, and that is very difficult to keep the tone if you have to speak a word through one whole measure—a long time. It's very difficult to keep it without singing. Singing is easy but to speak this way is very difficult. And so, I think I did it then quite well, and I liked the music, and I felt it, you know. And so, we had concerts, three first in Vienna in the Schoenberg Verein, and Erwin Stein conducted and Schoenberg was there for the rehearsals and so on. . . . Once I made a tour with Schoenberg himself conducting in Italy. . . . We had thirty rehearsals. I mean, first I had to learn it, of course, and it took me a long time and then we had thirty rehearsals.

SMITH: Did you go through bar by bar in the rehearsals or did you rehearse in larger sections?

WAGNER: No, not in larger sections. Eins nach dem andern. Some took longer time, some took—but we had very, very many—too many. . . . First, I learned it with Stein until I knew the part by myself. And then we started to rehearse with the musicians. . . . They didn't need the rehearsals with him solo. I was not a musician but they were musicians. They knew it of course. But I was not a musician, theoretically. I had really to feel it. I had to learn it, you know, so in my body I was, wie man sagt, in Fleisch und Blut übergegangen. I was then so connected with this and I knew every shade of my voice and I know it now and I couldn't do it otherwise. . . . But you need a very, very big *Skala*—deep and high and you have to be a *Sprecher*—you have to know how to speak, not how to sing, and that's the main thing. And it's very wrong—Schoenberg always told me it's wrong— to sing. . . . And this is really very difficult. So it was a *Spezialität*—a specialty for me. . . .

SMITH: What did Schoenberg say to you then about the *Sprechstimme?*

WAGNER: . . . He always said, "Always speaking but in a certain line and then some notes have to be sounded, but very little, only once, and otherwise, only *Sprechton.* But it is absolutely wrong if you sing the notes. It is not meant this way." He always said that to me. And he was satisfied because I was—I mean I am not a musician, but I was quite musical and I could speak and I could give the expression. . . . Some people, of course, it's strange for them; they laughed, of course. . . . Nobody laughed at me—nobody. Sometimes, if you hear recordings and they play it and they start this way to speak, then to myself or maybe not to myself [I] and the other people laugh and that is *komisch*, das ist sehr komisch! You have to make it very strong and very suggestive and then nobody laughs. You have to have the expression for it. . . . But if you know it, you know it for your life. . . .

SMITH: When you think back to the Verein concerts, who do you remember as having been in the audience?

WAGNER: My dear! In Vienna, you know, they were not really for the modern music.

SMITH: So the audience was small?

WAGNER: Ja. Young people, of course, and then old; you know, the Schoenberg *Kreis* had a lot of pupils and so on. Alma Mahler was there, of course. I don't know the names of the people but it was a big audience. Vienna was not so very enthusiastic about atonal music. But they did classics too. . . . The Schoenberg Verein, they did not only modern music, they did older music too—*Kammermusik.* But it was wonderful studied, you know, and they were . . . very strong, very strict about it—that we rehearse and rehearse, and they were so very, very, very good everything.

Notes

1. Alban Berg, *Letters to His Wife,* ed. and trans. Bernard Grun (London: Faber and Faber, 1971), p. 225.

2. Willi Reich, *Schoenberg, A Critical Biography,* trans. Leo Black (London: Longman Group, 1971), p. 120. In Reich, the prospectus is abridged. The complete prospectus appears in Appendix 1 of this book.

3. See Appendix 2.

4. For a list of Verein performers, see Walter Szmolyan, "Die Konzerte des Wiener Schönberg-Vereins," *Oesterreichische Musikzeitschrift* 36 (February 1981):101–102.

5. Reich, *Schoenberg,* p. 122.

6. Ibid., p. 121.

7. Leonard Stein, "The Privataufführungen Revisited," in *Paul A. Pisk: Essays in His Honor,* ed. John Glowacki (Austin: College of Fine Arts, University of Texas, 1966), p. 204.

8. For a more complete listing, see Appendix 3.

9. For a more detailed discussion of these arrangements, see Bryan R. Simms, "The Society for Private Musical Performances:

Resources and Documents," *Journal of the Arnold Schoenberg Institute* 3 (October 1979):142–148.

10. Erwin Ratz, "Die zehn öffentlichen Proben zur Kammer-symphonie im Juni 1918 und der 'Verein für musikalische Privat-aufführungen,'" in *Arnold Schönberg, Gedenkausstellung 1974*, ed. Ernst Hilmar (Vienna: Universal Edition, 1974), pp. 69–70.

11. Karl Popper, *Unended Quest: An Intellectual Autobiography* (La Salle, Ill.: Open Court, 1976), p. 54.

12. For details of these negotiations, see Simms, "Society," pp. 135–142.

13. Documents concerning this replacement appear in Simms, "Society for Private Musical Performances," pp. 138–139.

14. Darius Milhaud, "To Arnold Schoenberg on His Seventieth Birthday: Personal Recollections," *Musical Quarterly* 30 (October 1944):382.

15. Ibid., p. 383.

16. Alma Mahler-Werfel, *Mein Leben* (Frankfurt am Main: Fischer Taschenbuch Verlag, 1963), p. 128.

17. Arnold Schoenberg, *Style and Idea*, ed. Leonard Stein, trans. Leo Black (London: Faber and Faber, 1975), p. 349.

18. Personal correspondence from Stefan Askenase, 27 July 1973.

~ 5 ~

Performance Practices

Although the Verein concerts themselves were discontinued, the performance ideals of the Society were advanced and disseminated through the increasing reputation of some of its key performers. The pianist Edward Steuermann[B] traveled widely, giving many well-attended concerts of modern works and many first performances.[*] The Kolisch Quartet, formed as the Wiener Streichquartett in the Verein in 1922, gained an international reputation for its performances of standard repertoire, as well as for its commitment to the works of Schoenberg, Berg, Webern, Bartók, and others.[†] Throughout his life, Schoenberg maintained a lively interest in these performers and coached them extensively on many occasions, not only on his own works but on those of past masters—Beethoven, Mozart, and Schubert. Their

---

[*]Among Steuermann's first performances were Schoenberg's *Pierrot lunaire, Ode to Napoleon,* and the Concerto for Piano and Orchestra.

[†]Early permanent members of the Wiener Streichquartett were Kolisch, Fritz Rothschild, Marcel Dick, and Joachim Stutchewsky.[B] (There were other players as well in the early days.) Rothschild was later replaced by Felix Khuner, Dick by Eugen Lehner, and Stutchewsky by Benar Heifetz. First performances by the Kolisch Quartet included Schoenberg's Third and Fourth Quartets, Berg's *Lyric Suite,* Webern's String Trio and String Quartet, and the Third and Fifth Quartets of Bartók.

recollections of these coaching sessions provide insights into Schoenberg's theoretical views not available in his own writings. When these accounts are taken together with written descriptions of Schoenberg's performance ideas, there emerges a picture of a man with a highly acute ear for detail who wished to hear every minutia of the score without destroying a large-scale formal linear structure. By spending many long hours in these coaching sessions, Schoenberg showed that his musical concerns were practical as well as theoretical. This is understandable when viewed in the tradition of Bach, Mozart, Beethoven, and Mahler, all composers who had successful performance careers.

That Schoenberg was more coach than performer did not diminish his enthusiasm. He was an avid chamber music player, performing with apparently limited capabilities upon the cello, violin, and viola. Although he had had some violin instruction from the physician Oskar Adler[B], as a cellist he was entirely self-taught. His marathon Sunday chamber music sessions were attended by many professional players as well as by members of his own circle. During these day-long meetings, pontificating by Schoenberg alternated with renditions of the classics by players of widely diverse skills. Rather than an attempt to produce technically skilled performances, these meetings seemed an opportunity to clarify philosophical concepts and to try out interpretive ideas in an experimental environment.

As Schoenberg was heavily involved in performance questions during the years immediately preceding the emergence of the twelve-tone method, it is worthwhile to examine briefly how his views on performance may have influenced the form that the method was to take. Schoenberg's primary goal in performance appears to have been a clear and uncluttered presentation of the score, unfettered by emotionalism or catering to instrumental eccentricities. His belief in the importance of every note and the worthiness of every line to be heard is totally in keeping with the contrapuntal emphasis of the twelve-tone method:

The highest principle for all reproduction of music would have to be that what the composer has written is made to sound in such a way that every note is really heard, and that all the sounds, whether successive or simultaneous, are in such relationship to each other that no part at any moment obscures another, but, on the contrary, makes its contribution towards ensuring that they all stand out clearly from one another.[1]

The Kolisch Quartet performances of Schoenberg works are characterized by this fundamental principle of clarity.

This approach was later further developed by Rudolf Kolisch, who attempted to place the theory of performance upon a firm epistemological basis by eliminating from performance considerations such subjective categories as instinct, taste, and good sound. Eventually Kolisch developed what he termed a methodology of performance involving extensive study of the score before realization could be attempted. He outlined this procedure as follows:

1. *Study of the score*
   Macro-structure
   Retrace every thought process
   Motif vocabulary
2. *Mental concept*
3. *Instrumental preparation independently*
   Formation of "raw material"
   Realization
4. *Confrontation with concept*
5. *Act of performance: Subconscious re-creation*
   Objective vs. Romantic[2]

Thus study of the score, in Kolisch's view,

> . . . has to reach much further than usual structural analysis. It has to penetrate so deeply, that we are finally able to

retrace every thought process of the composer. Only such a thorough examination will enable us to read the signs to their full extent and meaning and to define the objective performance elements, especially those referring to phrasing, punctuation and inflection, the speechlike elements.

After such study, one forms a very precise concept of the piece, and only when one has reached the point where one feels completely certain of how the piece must go should the realization process commence.* Performance decisions thus are determined by the necessities of the mental concept rather than by accommodation to instrumental or personal idiosyncrasies. Kolisch goes on:

> The instrumental machinery must always be subjected to and be at the service of the idea, no matter how many conventions and conveniences have to be sacrificed. The instrumental preparation has to proceed independently, until full possession of the "raw material" is reached, which means playing the text with exact fulfillment of the precisely defined elements of pitch, duration-proportion, tempo and intensity. This "raw material" is then shaped into performance by confronting it with our mental concept, until full congruence is reached. The sum of these operations should lead to such a complete incorporation of the work into our consciousness, to such complete identification with it, that at the actual act of performance all conscious thoughts have sunk to a subconscious level and it becomes entirely spontaneous. When we have reached this stage, performance is what it should be, *re-creation*.

This subordination of the performer's conscious thoughts and feelings leads ideally to a performance which, although

---

*Kolisch's sense of the importance of exactly realizing the graphemic aspects of the score led him to feel great concern for accuracy of pitch. He favored the use by string players of equal temperament, the tuning system routinely employed for the piano. His concern for accuracy of tempo realization resulted in a large and important article on tempo in Beethoven's music. Rudolf Kolisch, "Tempo and Character in Beethoven's Music," *Musical Quarterly* 29 (April; July 1943):169–187; 291–312.

not at all devoid of emotional content, contains only that inspired by the piece itself and therefore related to its deeper structural essence.*

It must be stressed here that, although Kolisch's theories of performance arose from his association with Schoenberg and his concern for the performance of new music, he in no way envisaged his methodological contributions as being limited to music in that sphere. In fact, as the philosopher Theodor Adorno[B] states in the following passage, and as Schoenberg himself said many times, new music of the Schoenberg circle was seen by its members as being a natural perpetuation and continuing chapter of the Viennese musical tradition. Therefore performance techniques, although of necessity extended for this music, remained fundamentally unchanged. The alterations of performance practice advocated by Kolisch thus represented a rejection of nineteenth-century techniques for all music in the Viennese tradition—Mozart as well as Schoenberg—as Adorno, whose writings were greatly admired by Kolisch, makes clear:

> Nothing would be more inaccurate than to tag Kolisch's enterprise with the dreadful notion of the "champion" of new music. . . . What he in truth achieved is no less than the realization of a concept of musical interpretation, which the best musicians have always wished to have, but which he for the first time formulated and carried out in full consciousness to its fullest extent. This concept is not to be separated from the compositional principles of Arnold Schoenberg. . . . The idea of integral composition, of a technique in which each note is thematic, answering to its function in the whole, was taken over by Kolisch into

*This desire for "subconscious" performance explains the Kolisch Quartet's habit of performing from memory. In Kolisch's view, not only the music itself but the stand as well serves as a concrete distraction at the conscious level. The concept of totally subconscious performance in all probability represents an ideal rather than an achievable reality. It is also not at all certain that a subconscious performance such as Kolisch envisions would be totally devoid of egocentric emotional content. Perhaps "selfless" or "uninvolved" would better express Kolisch's ideals than "subconscious," which carries with it specific psychological implications.

the realm of musical presentation (performance). One becomes able to speak of an "integral interpretation." This integral interpretation sets itself the task, not to somehow reflect the work in mere pleasant sounds and smooth outlines, but to realize its structure completely in its own terms, to produce an X-ray of the work. This ideal of interpretation does not proceed from the sonic facade, but specifically from the functional, from the many-sided, pregnant musical events. The most exact analysis of the work, the precise experience of its "subcutaneous" elements is thus revealed.[3]

This view of performance recalls clearly the voice of Karl Kraus. As Kraus occupied himself with the exact placement of each comma and felt the importance of the smallest detail to the integrity of the thought expressed, so the involvement of the Schoenberg circle performers with the clarity and audibility of every note reflects this same concern. Indeed, there is a superficial similarity between the flowery and contrived articles that graced the *Neue Freie Presse* of the day and the overlay of sentimentality characteristic of many contemporary performances. The activities of these latter performers even seem in some respects more comparable to the work of Kraus and Adolf Loos than do the compositional activities of the Schoenberg circle. (It is somehow easier to equate the removal of window borders with the elimination of audible string shifts than with the death of tonality.) However, while it is tempting to imagine a Kolisch Quartet performance occurring in a Loos house, it would be simplistic to equate the two events with the elimination of ornament. If such comparisons must be made, it is rather more exact to consider both activities as expressing a devotion to the clear, integral expression of structure—architectural or musical—characterized by a constant uncompromising integrity.

It is difficult to evaluate Kolisch's performance theory from today's perspective of performance practice, as both Kolisch and Schoenberg were reacting to an ideal of performance which has since all but disappeared.[4] This previous practice, still noticeable on old recordings, superimposed a superficial and emotive style—characterized in string playing by heavy rubato, audible shifts, and wide, slow vibrato—onto any and all music of the Viennese classical tradition. This approach, vestiges of which remained in especially the early performances of the Kolisch Quartet, largely faded during World War II, when European concert life was seriously disrupted by strife and emigration.*

The principal realizers of Schoenbergian performance practice were of course Steuermann and Kolisch, and Kolisch's writings are a fascinating record of his own as well as Schoenberg's performance theories. Because of the Verein concerts and the Sunday chamber music sessions,

---

*The practice of performance advocated by the Schoenberg circle should not be confused with the more sterile approach that became prevalent following the second world war. Schoenberg was well aware of this change and wrote the following:

> Today's manner of performing classical music of the so-called "romantic" type, suppressing all emotional qualities and all unnotated changes of tempo and expression, . . . came to Europe by way of America, where no old culture regulated presentation, but where a certain frigidity of feeling reduced all musical expression. Thus almost everywhere in Europe music is played in a stiff, inflexible metre—not in a tempo, i.e. according to a yardstick of freely measured quantities. . . . It must be admitted that in the period around 1900 many artists overdid themselves in exhibiting the power of the emotion they were capable of feeling; artists who considered works of art to have been created only to secure opportunities for them to expose themselves to their audiences; artists who believed themselves to be more important than the work—or at least than the composer. Nothing can be more wrong than both these extremes.

Arnold Schoenberg, "Today's Manner of Performing Classical Music," in *Style and Idea*, ed. Leonard Stein, trans. Leo Black (London: Faber and Faber, 1975), pp. 320–322. As a goalless precision came to be substituted for the focused and flexible clarity of the Schoenberg circle performances, the more profound intentions of this latter group were lost. Perhaps the composer to suffer most from this transformation was Webern, whose works took on an aridity and remoteness in performance which this finely tuned and emotionally sensitive musician cannot have wanted.

many others were involved in some aspect of Schoenberg's performance activities. The members of the Kolisch Quartet and its predecessor the Wiener Streichquartett who were interviewed (Kolisch, Dick, Lehner, and Heifetz) had many opportunities to observe Schoenberg's coaching methods. Benar Heifetz, a warm, openhearted soul, loved his instrument, which he played for me when I interviewed him. A spontaneous player, largely undisturbed by theoretical deliberation, his recollections of Schoenberg were not altogether positive. A more natural musician physically than Kolisch, he lent his expertise to the quartet without becoming intimately involved with what he saw as intellectual speculation. From a performance view, however, Schoenberg was not interested in how a piece was put together but in what it was. It is clear in the interview material that some of his followers recognized this distinction while others did not.

LONA TRUDING: That was the time we definitely turned our backs on the nineteenth century, more or less half-heartedly because, at heart, we were all romantics but we never would have admitted it. And we were the new intelligentsia and we were really out to know things, to understand things, not just to feel, and that is very important for the new interpretation of music.

JOAN ALLEN SMITH: Can you describe what Schoenberg did in rehearsals with the quartet?

BENAR HEIFETZ: In our case, we were so prepared and Kolisch knew so well the composition—he is a scholar, Kolisch is really a scholar—so he didn't have to say much, and maybe he didn't know what to say, I don't know.

SMITH: When Schoenberg was leading rehearsals when you were playing, did he have the same sort of approach to Mozart and Beethoven that he would have had to his own work?

EUGEN LEHNER: Of course. More, much more even, because this music he understood. And so everything was
creating a certain problem, you know, either in the construction, in the harmony, or how to place it in anything.

SMITH: In the rehearsals, did Schoenberg ever discuss
more structural aspects of his pieces?

MARCEL DICK: No.... What happened in his workshop,
that was something that belonged to the workshop....

SMITH: Did he make many changes in his works during
rehearsals?

DICK: Very seldom. In his mind, the first idea has to be
right.

LEHNER: What I wanted to tell you about the rehearsals.... We started out always to rehearse his music,
but very soon, his eagerness abated and [he] less and
less interrupted us, and finally, I noticed from the
corner of my eye he wasn't even turning the page anymore in the score and then, we finished the movement
and he [said], "Do you, do you understand this music?"
"Yes." "Do you like this music?" "It's beautiful." "Huh.
Play something. Why don't you play a Mozart quartet?"
Well then he learned the fact that we—it was in the
summer, and that probably means that we were about
to play in New York the Beethoven cycle, so of course
that was without any Schoenberg music that we sat
down and rehearsed with him Beethoven quartets.

PAUL PISK: Rehearsals from nine to one and two to five
and at five o'clock, Schoenberg says, "What's the matter, are you tired?"

SMITH: Did these people ever rehearse with you?

FELIX GALIMIR: No matter what we played. Yes, no matter what we played, even music of their enemies,
you know, because we played just anything in the
modern [repertory]... —whatever there was. They al-

ways came, they listened, we rehearsed together. They had the score, said, ". . . should hear this voice a little, you know, and this"—and they discussed things—Webern, Jalowetz[B], Steuermann, they were terribly interested and they had time. It's fantastic when you think today that they all came at any moment when there was a rehearsal, not only ours—everybody's. They came, they were sitting there studying scores. It's unthinkable today that you would invite Stravinsky to come to listen—impossible!

SMITH: Did they ever discuss the structural aspects of pieces with you?

GALIMIR: Oh, very much so. Enormously!

SMITH: What did they discuss?

GALIMIR: Oh, well, structure, the form of the piece, the variation and so on, whatever there was to discuss, very much so. Very intensive, oh yes. Also, the harmonic things. No matter how it was with twelve-tone, but that, suddenly, this C-sharp comes in, and you know, there are functions of notes, special functions, which were very important.

SMITH: Do you mean largely in terms of voice-leading?

GALIMIR: . . . Melodic. There was one thing that was always in rehearsals. They were terribly meticulous about rhythms, and you know, that these sixteenths or the triplet comes after the second sixteenth, and you played and you finally could make it just right, and that was it. And when you finally got it and he says, "Yes, but it sounds stiff and . . . it has to be free," and that was really very important that one does play the music although very correct but with a certain freedom and not in a strait jacket because of the complications or the expression. I think the paramount thing was that one should not, especially because of the row and the intonation and dissonances, overlook the expressional aspect of the piece. And you know that Schoenberg's or Webern's music is so terribly expressive. It doesn't look

Karl Kraus, photo by D'Ora-Benda, Vienna, 1908 *(Bild-Archiv der Oesterreichischen Nationalbibliothek, Vienna)*

Karl Kraus reading *(Bild-Archiv der Oesterreichischen Nationalbibliothek, Vienna)*

Oskar Kokoschka, *Portrait of Karl Kraus,* 1925 *(Museum Moderner Kunst, Vienna; © ADAGP, Paris/VAGA, New York, 1985)*

Adolf Loos, photo by Otto Mayer, Dresden, March 1903(?) *(Bild-Archiv der Oesterreichischen Nationalbibliothek, Vienna)*

Oskar Kokoschka, *Portrait of Adolf Loos*, 1909 *(Staatliche Museen Preussischer Kulturbesitz, Nationalgalerie, Berlin [West]; © ADAGP, Paris/VAGA, New York, 1985)*

Josef Maria Olbrich, Secession Building, ca. 1930 *(Bild-Archiv der Oesterreichischen Nationalbibliothek, Vienna)*

Oskar Kokoschka, Drawing of Adolf Loos, 1910 (Bild-Archiv der Oesterreichischen Nationalbibliothek, Vienna; © *ADAGP, Paris/VAGA, New York, 1985)*

Adolf Loos, Apartment of Emile Löwenbach, 1914. Dining Room *(Bild-Archiv der Oesterreichischen Nationalbibliothek, Vienna)*

Adolf Loos, Building on the Michaelerplatz, 1920 *(Bild-Archiv der Oesterreichischen Nationalbibliothek, Vienna)*

Nr. 2 WIEN, 15. OKTOBER 1903 Preis 20 h

DAS ANDERE

EIN BLATT ZUR EINFUEHRUNG ABENDLAENDISCHER KULTUR IN OESTERREICH: GESCHRIEBEN VON ADOLF LOOS I. JAHR

Adolf Loos, *Das Andere*

Oskar Kokoschka (*Bild-Archiv der Oesterreichischen Nationalbibliothek, Vienna*)

Oskar Kokoschka, *Portrait of August Forel*, 1910 (*Mannheim, Städtische Kunsthalle; © ADAGP, Paris/VAGA, New York, 1985*)

Oskar Kokoschka *Self-Portrait, pointing to the Breast*, 1913, oil on canvas, 32⅛" x 19½" (*Collection, The Museum of Modern Art, New York; © ADAGP, Paris/VAGA, New York, 1985*)

Alban Berg, 1909 (Bild-Archiv der Oesterreichischen Nationalbibliothek, Vienna)

Anton Webern, 1932 *(Bild-Archiv der Oesterreichischen Nationalbibliothek, Vienna)*

Oskar Kokoschka, *Portrait of Arnold Schoenberg*, 1924, oil on canvas, 37¾" x 29⅛" *(Courtesy Galerie St. Etienne, New York;* © *ADAGP, Paris/VAGA, New York, 1985)*

Arnold Schoenberg *(Courtesy of the Arnold Schoenberg Institute, Los Angeles)*

Concert-Bureau Alexander Rosé
I. Kärntnerring 11.

Kleiner Musikvereins-Saal.

Dienstag den 18. März 1902
abends halb 8 Uhr

VI. (letzter) Kammermusik-Abend
Quartett Rosé

Arnold Rosé
(1. Violine)

Anton Ruzitska
(Viola)

Albert Bachrich
(2. Violine)

Friedrich Buxbaum
(Violoncell)

Programm:

1. HERMANN GRÄDENER Quartett D-moll, op 33.
   Allegro con brio.
   Adagio (im Balladenton).
   Scherzo.
   Rondo. Finale (Allegro moderato).

2. ARNOLD SCHÖNBERG Sextett nach **Richard Dehmels** Gedicht
   ›Die verklärte Nacht‹.
   (Manuscript, erste Aufführung.)
   2. Viola: Herr **Franz Jelinek** ⎫ Mitglieder des k. k. Hof-
   2. Cello: Herr **Franz Schmidt** ⎬ Opernorchesters.

3. JOHANNES BRAHMS Quintett F-dur, op. 88.
   Allegro non troppo ma con brio.
   Grave ed appassionato.
   Allegretto vivace.
   Allegro energico.
   2. Viola: Herr **Franz Jelinek.**

Während der Vorträge bleiben die Saalthüren geschlossen.

K. k. Hoftheater-Druckerei, IX, Berggasse 7.

Program, Quartett Rosé

Konzertdirektion Hugo Heller, Wien, I., Bauernmarkt Nr. 3.

Karte Nr. 13   Kleiner Musikvereinssaal

Zehn öffentliche Proben zur Kammersymphonie von

Arnold Schönberg.

Giltig für die   Preis K 3.50
2. Probe   **5.—8. Reihe**

Die Daten der Proben werden rechtzeitig in der Zeitung
und durch Plakate bekanntgegeben.

Kontroll-Coupon.

Ticket to Open Rehearsal of
Schoenberg's Chamber Symphony

(Right) Rudolf Kolisch, 1915
(Reproduced with permission of
Lorna Kolisch)

Erwin Ratz (Bild-Archiv der
Oesterreichischen
Nationalbibliothek, Vienna)

PRIVATAUFFÜHRUNGEN MODERNER MUSIK

LEITUNG: ARNOLD SCHÖNBERG

JEDEN FREITAG ABEND IM KLEINEN KONZERTHAUS-SAAL IM VEREIN FÜR MUSIKALISCHE PRIVATAUFFÜHRUNGEN. KANZLEI WIEN IX. TÜRKENSTRASSE 17. PROSPEKTE AN DER KONZERTHAUS-KASSE. EINTRITT NUR FÜR MITGLIEDER.

PROSPEKTE AUCH HIER.

Poster for the Verein für musikalische Privataufführungen
(Courtesy of the Arnold Schoenberg Institute, Los Angeles)

Kolisch Quartett (Reproduced with permission of Lorna Kolisch

Paul Amadeus Pisk, 1930 *(Bild-Archiv der Oesterreichischen Nationalbibliothek, Vienna)*

KLEINER MUSIKVEREINSSAAL

Samstag, den 14. April 1923,
7 Uhr abends.

Rudolf Kolisch

(Violine)

Mitwirkend: **ein Streich-Orchester**

Dirigent: **Anton Webern**

Erna Gál (Klavier)

PROGRAMM:

1. **Joseph Haydn:**   Konzert für Violine mit Orchester, Nr. 2, G-Dur
   Neu aufgefunden — Erste Aufführung
   Allegro moderato
   Adagio
   Allegro

2. **Franz Schubert:**   Rondo A-Dur für Violine mit Orchester

3. **Karol Szymanowski:** Mythes (für Violine und Klavier)
   a) La Fontaine d'Arethuse
   b) Narcisse
   c) Dryades et Pan

4. **C. Saint-Saëns:**   Introduction et Rondo Capriccioso

5. **Sarasate:**   Carmen — Fantasie

KLAVIER BÖSENDORFER

Karten an der Musikvereinskassa

Program, Rudolf
Kolisch and Erna Gál

Erna Gál and Rudolf
Kolisch *(Reproduced
with permission of
Lorna Kolisch)*

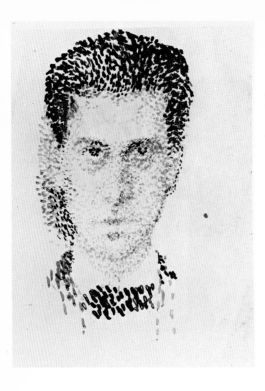

Richard Gerstl, *Self-Portrait,* 1906 *(Courtesy Galerie St. Etienne, New York)*

Richard Gerstl, *Portrait of Arnold Schoenberg,* 1906 *(Historisches Museum der Stadt Wien)*

Arnold Schoenberg, *Vision of Christ (Courtesy of the Arnold Schoenberg Institute, Los Angeles)*

Arnold Schoenberg, 1951
*(Bild-Archiv der
Oesterreichischen
Nationalbibliothek, Vienna)*

Alban Berg, photo by D'Ora-
Benda, 1924 *(Bild-Archiv der
Oesterreichischen
Nationalbibliothek, Vienna)*

Adolf Loos, 1920 *(Bild-Archiv der
Oesterreichischen
Nationalbibliothek, Vienna)*

Rudolf Kolisch *(Reproduced with permission of Lorna Kolisch)*

Oskar Kokoschka *(© ADAGP, Paris/VAGA, New York, 1985)*

like it because what you can do with one little note, and still that one little note has to go ahhhhhh—has to do that; otherwise, it doesn't make any sense musically.

FELIX GREISSLE: New ideas? He didn't come to discuss new ideas. The new ideas he discussed on Sunday around noon; we came to him and played chamber music until about two or three o'clock in the morning. And there, in the intervals which we had to put in, because you can't play through the entire—instruments get out of tune, so he started talking about music and about his own ideas. But there's one thing I must say, he talked about something new, and then, when he wrote it, it was still much farther advanced. You didn't recognize it. . . . He did not like to talk about it; he tried out, once in a while, he tried out the Serenade, for instance. When I came to him, he'd just composed one or two movements of the Serenade. . . . It was my first encounter with his music.

SMITH: Did you go to the Sunday chamber music sessions that he held?

ERNA GÁL: Oh, yes, sometimes, yes. The Sunday chamber music sessions, oh my God. Well, nobody said much to him, because you couldn't tell him that he was playing wrong. I can't remember any special details. Because they were all great players who came down to play there. Rudi [Kolisch] usually played first violin. He [Schoenberg] usually played second violin or viola.

SMITH: Who played cello?

GÁL: Who played cello? Stutchewsky I think played—[Wilhelm] Winkler. Rudi's partners usually went down to play, I think.

SMITH: Did Schoenberg play well? He played the cello, didn't he? And he also must have played the violin somewhat.

RUDOLF KOLISCH: No. He had never really studied. He

played, you know, without any idiomatic technique. He had . . . a little bit of study for violin but never for cello.

SMITH: Did he play the violin better than the cello?

KOLISCH: No.

SMITH: How about Webern, did he play better?

KOLISCH: Webern played a little better, he played viola.

SMITH: Viola? I thought he played the cello.

KOLISCH: Well, in our ensemble, he played viola.

SMITH: Berg played the harmonium, didn't he? Could he play well?

KOLISCH: No. Also not. No instrument, but Schoenberg had a passion for string quartet playing.

PISK: [About Schoenberg's cello playing] I said to Kolisch, I said, "Rudi, you can't tell me that that was wonderful cello playing." "No, but when Schoenberg makes a mistake, he shows by the mistake how to play right." You couldn't say a thing. That was the reason I wasn't in the inner circle.

LEHNER: All that I remember is the essence—so that I would say that he was very instrumental in my relationship to music; that is very much created by him. But I couldn't put my finger on one single technical fact that I ever got from him, except one word which was constantly repeated by him—clarity, clarity, clarity. For him, that was the alpha and omega of music making. His dictum was that you must play music so that the last person in the hall should be able to write up in the score what you do. So that's how he expected music should be played.

Although Schoenberg, Berg, and Webern were all known to conduct on occasion, Berg did so extremely rarely, and Schoenberg conducted primarily his own works. Webern, however, had an active career as a conductor both in

Vienna and abroad.[5] His major orchestral commitment was to the Arbeiter-Symphonie, a group founded by his friend Dr. David Josef Bach[B] in 1905 and sponsored by the Social Democratic Party. Webern conducted this orchestra and its vocal equivalent the Arbeitersingverein from the early twenties until they were disbanded by the Dollfuss regime in 1934. Under Webern's leadership, the Arbeiter-Symphonie presented modern and rarely performed works, providing both an opportunity for younger, more progressive composers to hear their own works and an educational experience for the largely working-class audience.

Webern's conducting style, which has been compared to Mahler's,[6] appears to have been modest, unassuming, and concentrated:

> No threatening fists and wild rubato, rather an intimacy of expression and a sensitivity which remains unforgettably as the basic principle of his interpretation. . . . Webern's secret lay in the intensity of the vocal line—but not in the sense of Wagnerian *Gestenmusik* and accentuated declamation. To the contrary, we experience the true, often moving, unpretentious representation of the union between word and sound.[7]

His total concentration and involvement with even the smallest details caused him difficulties in rehearsals, his painstaking technique often requiring more rehearsal time than was at his disposal. He conducted from score and studied assiduously.[8] The results were often exciting but meant for Webern great spiritual and physical strain.[9]

Berg had of necessity to be more practical. The premiere of his opera *Wozzeck* by Erich Kleiber at the Berlin State Opera on 14 December 1925 led to a series of successful productions of that work. Essentially overnight, Berg was transformed from an obscure Viennese composer into a European celebrity. During this period, from 1925 until the rise of Hitler, Berg traveled extensively to assist in the rehearsals for these performances. The coaching experience that he had gained in his work with the Verein für musikalische Privataufführungen must have been invaluable to him in his preparation of such a complicated work with performers often inexperienced in contemporary music.

The rehearsal techniques of Berg and Webern derived from those of their teacher. Both students had more opportunity than Schoenberg to put their performance ideas into practice, and for this reason interview material concerning their performance experiences is included. Berg was usually in the position of arriving for the final rehearsals of an opera performance, and he thus of necessity had to compromise. Webern, however, with his orchestral experience, was able to apply Schoenbergian ideals subject only to rehearsal limitations. The recollections of Wolfgang Ploderer are those of childhood. Those of Kolisch, Lehner, and especially Marcel Dick show an intimate acquaintance with Webern's rehearsal techniques.

JOAN ALLEN SMITH: What did Berg talk about [at the rehearsals for *Wozzeck* in Brussels]?

STEFAN ASKENASE: Sometimes about the tempo, sometimes about the intensity of playing; there were things like that. Oh, he said one very wise thing. He said, "When I heard the rehearsals of the first performances of *Wozzeck*, when it started, I tried to correct everything, to change everything and to get to the ideal performance, and now I have the experience that that is not possible. I must take the things as they are and just correct the most—anyway the most important things."

SMITH: Was he unhappy with this performance?

ASKENASE: No, he wasn't unhappy but it wasn't good. . . .

SMITH: During this week, Berg stayed at your house?

ASKENASE: No, he stayed at a hotel. He stayed in the hotel, but he went very much to our house. A pupil of mine played for him his sonata. And we had almost all meals together, either in my house or in town. Oh, that was something—now I remember a very nice thing. He invited us to dinner. He had a very fine restaurant recommended to him. . . . And we went to that restaurant, and he looked at the menu, and he found . . . Ris de Veau. You know what that is. It is not meat, it is one of the inner [organs]. It's a very fine dish. And there was Ris de Veau Santrène. Santrène was the name of the owner of the restaurant. And he ordered that veal. And the maître d'hôtel came and prepared it—brought the veal—and he prepared the sauce in our presence, and he did it in a very clever way, and then quickly he knew exactly what to do and how much to give of every little thing that he added to the sauce and mixed it. And Berg, whose way of composing was very slow and hard, and to take a decision was a matter of long reflection, he admired very much everything that was spontaneous. I remember, for instance, having played in Vienna in the radio a piece by Darius Milhaud called *Carnaval d'Aix*. It's a suite for piano and orchestra of twelve little pieces from a ballet—a ballet called *Salade*. Out of these, he made the piece of twelve very short and very gay pieces—very spontaneous and very light—and I played it on the radio in Vienna and Berg heard it. And . . . he liked it. You know the light—the things that he—throw them away like that! I remember, when he came to my house in Brussels, it was perhaps a year later, I had to play it to him, every piece three or four times, from this suite, because he—and he admired as well this maître d'hôtel who prepared the sauce in such a way. And he had been recognized in the restaurant because his picture was in the newspapers of this day. I think it was a day or two before the premiere. And so Monsieur Santrène brought the golden book of his place, of his restaurant, and asked him to write something. And so he wrote—he says, "Weiter zur Bereitung des Ris de Veau Santrène: *so* muss ich komponieren können." You know, "Looking at the preparation of Ris de Veau, that's the way how I should like to compose—to be able to compose."

SMITH: You say that he composed very slowly. Did you ever see any of his sketch materials?

ASKENASE: No, I don't believe so. I don't think I saw it but I knew it because everybody knew it. He talked of it himself.

SMITH: Berg would have died when you were about twenty, so your relationship with him was not a musical one?

WOLFGANG PLODERER: My relationship wasn't a personal one, as well as the relationship with Webern, of course, but only behind my father. My parents were living in Hietzing not far from Alban Berg, . . . and my father took me—for instance, on a Sunday morning, we went for a walk, and then we made a visit to Berg or we met Alban Berg; we made a walk together in the street. This time, you must remember, there was really no automobile circulation, and therefore, one could in this part of Hietzing, which you have seen perhaps in Schönbrunn Gardens, make very nice walks. And then my father discussed with Alban Berg; this partly I didn't understand and I walked along as children do. And of course children are not very interested generally in the conversations of the grown-up. But he was always very kind with me.

SMITH: When your father went on these walks with Berg, did they talk mainly about music or do you think that Berg liked to talk about many other things as well?

PLODERER: Many other things too, but one thing which is still amazing to me is that I remember that he was very interested in football [soccer] and the results of big football games. Football was very popular then in Vienna; it is still today, but it was much more in these times because, in these times, the national football team was very good. And I remember my father never went to football matches, but Alban Berg went to these big football matches in the stadium, and he could get very excited about that. A very funny thing that. . . . I don't

think it was so much the play as such, but it was perhaps the mass—the feeling of this enormous mass going
with it. As far as I have heard from my father, who
spoke about it, I think this mass suggestion was taking
him always. It's a funny thing, I'm not at all interested in
football, and I don't know anything about it, but I have
met several times very spiritual people who are very
interested in that. It is a very funny thing. . . .

SMITH: So you went to rehearsals with your father. What
did you think of them at the time?

PLODERER: Of course I found it very interesting as a small
boy. What I remember most are the Webern concerts—
orchestral concerts which make much more impression
on the children of course than chamber music and solo
music in small homes. That is natural. These were the
symphony concerts by the Vienna Arbeiter-Symphonie
Orchestra under David Bach.

SMITH: And you went to rehearsals and to concerts?

PLODERER: To rehearsals and to concerts, yes, and not only
was it the music from the Vienna School they were
playing there; they were playing Schubert and Beethoven and Bach and everything.

SMITH: What do you remember about Webern in rehearsals?

PLODERER: He was very impressive. He was a very good
conductor. I think that it is unfortunate that there are
not very many people who are still living who could
appreciate Webern as a conductor. . . . His personal
relation with the orchestra was very good, and when
one saw him work, one had really the feeling how it is a
great conductor. . . . And it is a pity that he died so
early, because I am certain that he would have had a
great future as a conductor too after the last war. If you
see the photographs, you think he is quite a small, slight,
tender man. He was quite nervous. He had a very firm
body, and when he made the rehearsals . . . —he was
conducting in shirt sleeves only—and then he sweated

so much and you could see by his trousers that he was very muscular and very, very manly I must say. It was a very great impression to me which nevertheless remains till today, which means that there must have been something in it.

MARCEL DICK: In 1931, I was in Vienna. . . . I had so much to do with Webern at that time. We worked on all kinds of performances, among them, the first performance of Milhaud's Viola Concerto. That, in the truest sense, the fullest sense, we did together. . . . Some time ago, I was searching for the part from which we worked and I couldn't find it. . . . I would have liked to show that to you—how almost every sixteenth note, you will find a crescendo, a diminuendo at the same time; a stretch, a staccato, but a tenuto at the same time, but all made sense. Because, coming from here and going there, this sixteenth note has all kinds of different connotations in relation to this and other things surrounding it, and in this relation, its meaning is this goes to there, but from that direction, it comes from there. . . . As a matter of fact, he did not conduct the concert. Twenty minutes before the concert started, . . . an alarm was sounded, I should come immediately; somebody else had to take over, he got sick. And why did he get sick? Again, two rehearsals that he spent with the orchestra on the Milhaud concerto, which he worked out to perfection, but he had no time for the others—the rest of the program.

SMITH: That seems to have happened very often with Webern.

DICK: Yes. He just could not organize his—and it didn't matter to him, what mattered [was] that everything . . . should have been absolute perfection, a perfection that is unobtainable. The Schoenbergian perfection was obtainable by those people who dedicated themselves to it. Webern went beyond that. . . . Webern's . . . rehearsal technique and, more, the rehearsal was Schoenberg on the nth power. And that was not always meaningful.

.... Everything that he could hear—that Webern could hear—was already too much. That offended his ear— then it wasn't delicate enough. He rehearsed the orchestra for the program the same way as he would have rehearsed with us who were his colleagues and who understood what he meant and not only were willing but eager to do everything fully the way he would have liked it to be done. . . . An orchestra does not have such ideas. An orchestra has two rehearsals for a difficult program and wants to get through. And time and again it happened that Webern was supposed to conduct a concert with two rehearsals—that was standard with the Vienna Symphony—you could play anything with anyone in the manner in which it was conducted. That was its great quality. For instance, on one such program was the [*Begleitmusik*] *zu einer Lichtspielszene,* . . . a Schoenberg composition. . . . Well anyway, that was new—it was supposed to be the first performance of it—and . . . so Webern comes to the first of the two rehearsals at half past nine—the rehearsal stops at twelve o'clock. At twelve o'clock, the orchestra manager says, "Time is up," and he was still on the second measure. "See, that clarinet, that wasn't quite—this staccato was too short—was too long. The clarinet was louder than the second bassoon. Now it was softer," . . . with the result that as usual he got sick. Somebody else took over—in this instance it was Erwin Stein[B]—and he had to do it with the one remaining rehearsal, the two works. So that did not always make quite as much sense. . . .

SMITH: He probably was as exacting in his composition too.

DICK: Yes. And that's why perhaps so few of his earliest pupils or early pupils became real composers, because he stifled them. He was so exacting, so demanding, that one didn't dare to write down a single note any more. "Is it really correct? Is it really—Did you hear that, did you really hear that, or just write it? Did you hear that?" Now only a few could get over that and free themselves from the superego that he imposed on one.

SMITH: I've been told that Webern would spend much, much time on single measures, when he was conducting a piece, and that, sometimes by the end of a rehearsal, he would have covered only a few bars.

FELIX GREISSLE: In conducting? No. He overstudied one movement and had to neglect the others because he didn't have enough time. That is true. But it was only lack of economy because he didn't conduct so frequently, and he probably didn't think it over or he knew too much to say. There was too much to say and there was no time for it, you see. He was a very good conductor.

SMITH: Was he generally satisfied with his performance afterwards?

GREISSLE: Ja, usually was. Sometimes he was not so much. He was an excellent conductor. It is too bad that he didn't conduct because Webern had too many difficulties. He was a very nervous person. At the Vienna Konzertverein, where he was engaged as a conductor, second conductor, but he didn't conduct anyway. He had a fight with them and quit. It's just when he came to the office to apologize, he had already resigned. It was very wrong to do that, resign, because he needed the money very much at that time. He had nothing, no job, nothing. And he quit there because they had made a stupid remark in the rehearsal.

SMITH: I have understood from several people that Webern's rehearsal techniques were so exacting that he would get through very few bars in one rehearsal. Consequently, he never had enough rehearsal time to prepare the piece and someone would have to come in at the last minute to rescue the performance.

RUDOLF KOLISCH: That's right—that is true.

SMITH: Was he unrealistic or were the performers not good enough?

KOLISCH: Both, ja. He was very uncompromising, no? He

had really this idea of an adequate performance, not compromise, so it's very true that very often he quit before the performance. Only, but when he reached the performance, it was an extraordinary performance.

(Alban Berg):

Undated (28. May 1922)

. . . Last night we had Mahler's Third, and you just can't imagine it. Without exaggeration: Webern is the greatest conductor since Mahler himself, in every respect. After the first and last movement I felt just as I feel after an Adrenalin injection, I simply couldn't stand on my feet. In the evening I nearly forgot to eat, only remembered in bed, so I got some bread and a tin of sardines. I'm almost frightened to hear the performance again tomorrow, that's how shattering it was. I was sitting with Stein, and was glad that this assorted audience should be seeing and hearing what our music-making is like. They were all bowled over. If only you'd been here, how thrilled you'd have been.[10]

EUGEN LEHNER: All the conducting that I experienced from Webern, that was when he was conducting us in the rehearsals. . . . I don't think that ever a musician lived with such incredible ears like his were and such an incredible musical sensitivity as his was. In fact, he was through several years the conductor of the Wiener Arbeiter-Symphonie Orchestra. But . . . it was always a disaster because, when it came to the dress rehearsal, he never came farther than the exposition of the first in a Haydn symphony or something, because he still was not satisfied and he still had something to say.

(Hans Csap) This work [*Friede auf Erden*], studied under the brilliant conductor Anton Webern, was, for those of us taking part at that time, an unforgettable experience. Anton Webern was able with true mastery and loving, sympathetic understanding to bring us workers closer to Schoenberg.

The most important thing for us worker-singers was that we, through this music, first learned to hear correctly, and that was the greatest contribution of Anton Webern. Indeed a long and steep path! I don't know where there is today a choir director . . . who regards it his duty to make some artistic progress.[11]

LEHNER: You must know something. At the time, for example, Webern—Webern was absolutely nobody. Webern was a freak in the eyes of everybody. Nobody took Webern halfway seriously. And the funny part is that the man who spoke the softest language . . . his voice carried the farthest—that's out now—in the second half of the twentieth century.

Notes

1. Arnold Schoenberg, "For a Treatise on Performance," in *Style and Idea,* ed. Leonard Stein (London: Faber and Faber, 1975), p. 319.

2. This and the material which follows is quoted from documents in the Kolisch Collection at Harvard University.

3. Theodor Adorno, "Kolisch und die neue Interpretation," *Frankfurter Allgemeine Zeitung,* 20 June 1956.

4. Schoenberg describes his view of more recent performance trends in "Today's Manner of Performing Classical Music," in *Style and Idea,* pp. 320–322.

5. Webern's conducting career has been extensively documented in Hans Moldenhauer and Rosaleen Moldenhauer, *Anton von Webern: A Chronicle of His Life and Work* (New York: Alfred A. Knopf, 1979).

6. Heinrich Strobel, "So sehe ich Webern," *Melos* 32 (September 1965):286.

7. Frederick Deutsch Dorian, "Webern als Lehrer," *Melos* 27 (April 1960):102.

8. For a further discussion of Webern's conducting techniques and rehearsal practices, see Moldenhauer and Moldenhauer, *Anton von Webern;* or Friedrich Wildgans, *Anton Webern,* trans. Edith Temple Roberts and Humphrey Searle (New York: October House, 1967), pp. 82–87.

9. Amalie Waller, "Mein Vater Anton von Webern," *Oesterrei-chische Musikzeitschrift* 23 (1968):331.

10. Alban Berg, *Letters to His Wife*, ed. and trans. Bernard Grun (London: Faber and Faber, 1971), p. 301.

11. Hans Csap, "Leserzuschrift an das 'Tagebuch,' Wien, 2. Juli 1955 (Auszug)," quoted in Werner Hofmann, ed., *Schönberg-Webern-Berg: Bilder-Partituren-Dokumente* (Vienna: Museum des 20. Jahrhunderts, May–July 1969), p. 67.

≈ PART III ≈

Teaching

They should be there as the painting students were once at home in the painter's studio, when, through their talent for this art and out of respect of the Master, they endeavored to gain admission to his studio.

Arnold Schoenberg

~ 6 ~

Schoenberg's Teaching

Others, too, have their indissoluble links with their teachers—some universal panacea to do with fingering, perhaps, or a new thorough-bass figuring. However, we want to emphasize something quite different by calling ourselves "Schoenberg-pupils." We know, rather, that the essence of the man has affected the thoughts and feelings of all those who call themselves his pupils, and, because of this, we feel a certain spiritual bond between all of us. For anyone who has been his pupil, his name is no mere reminder of student days: it is one's artistic and human conscience.[1]

Heinrich Jalowetz[B], 1912

Schoenberg began his teaching career around 1904. At first, he taught classes in the school of Dr. Eugenie Schwarzwald[B]. Most of the pupils who attended were sent to him by Guido Adler[B], an eminent musicologist at the University of Vienna and a friend of Mahler. Schoenberg found this arrangement unsatisfactory, apparently because of the quality of students available, and discontinued the class after only one year. Some of the more talented of these pupils then came to him as private students.

The year 1904 marked the beginning of Schoenberg's association with his two most famous students—Anton Webern and Alban Berg. Webern had been sent to him, as were Heinrich Jalowetz, Erwin Stein[B], and later Egon Wellesz[B], by Guido Adler. Berg's brother Charly answered an advertisement that Schoenberg had placed in the newspaper. After seeing some of Berg's early songs, Schoenberg invited him to his house and accepted him as a pupil.

From the beginning, Schoenberg was an outstanding and prophetic teacher. His students did not merely study with him but became his disciples. For his part, he endeavored to discover the inner personalities of his students and to help them all find their own way in music. As Erwin Stein described it:

> Schoenberg teaches one to think. He prompts his pupil to open his eyes and see for himself, as if he were the first person ever to examine the phenomenon in question. Whatever has been thought so far is not to be the norm. Even if our way of thinking is not better than others', what matters is not absolute truth, but the search for truth.[2]

Schoenberg encouraged performances of his students' works. These performances, however, often accompanied by extreme audience disruption, caused Schoenberg much loss of support and resultant financial hardship. To alleviate this problem, he applied in 1910 for permission to teach at the Academy of Music and Fine Arts.[*] He did not apply to be

---

[*]In his quest for this position, Schoenberg was in competition with another teacher and well-known musical figure, Heinrich Schenker[B], who was to become one of the most influential music theorists of all time. Schenker's fully-developed theories of tonal music, including his concepts of hierarchization of musical structure, large-scale harmonic prolongation, and a structural descent common to all tonal pieces, have earned for him an enduring place in the history of music theory. His reputation dur-

a member of the Academy but only to teach peripherally as a *Privatdozent*.† In a letter to the president of the Academy, of 19 February 1910, Schoenberg set out to answer possible objections and to define somewhat his teaching methods:

> I assume your only reason for hesitating to appoint me to the Academy staff is that you are, understandably, afraid

---

ing his own lifetime, however, was limited, despite his publication of a journal (*Der Tonwille*) and several books, the most significant being his monumental *Neue musikalische Theorien und Phantasien* (vol. 1, *Harmonielehre*, 1906; vol. 2, *Kontrapunkt*, 1910, 1920; vol. 3, *Der freie Satz*, 1935).

Schoenberg and Schenker had certainly met by 1903, when Schoenberg, apparently at the instigation of Busoni, orchestrated a piece by Schenker entitled *Syrian Dances*. The relationship remained cordial if not close until around 1910, when they attacked each other in print over major differences regarding the nature and theoretical significance of dissonance. (See Carl Dahlhaus, "Schoenberg and Schenker," *Proceedings of the Royal Music Association* 100 [1973–74]: 209–215.) After this time, relations were strained, although Schoenberg's attitude seems to have mellowed in later years. Schenker's theories were firmly grounded in tonal music, endowing him with a prejudice in favor of that music over more contemporary developments. Schoenberg was critical of Schenker's lack of interest in non-tonal music while appreciating his refined views of music from the past. Marginalia in works of Schenker owned by Schoenberg suggest that Schoenberg read Schenker's writings extensively in 1922 and 1923. (See Jonathan M. Dunsby, "Schoenberg and the Writings of Schenker," *Journal of the Arnold Schoenberg Institute* 2 [October 1977]: 26–33.) There is, however, no evidence that Schoenberg read any of Schenker's later and most significant work, including *Der Freie Satz* (1935) and the literature leading up to it after 1930.[3]

†Ernest Jones, in his book *The Life and Work of Sigmund Freud*, ed. Lionel Trilling and Steven Marcus (Garden City, N.Y.: Anchor Books, 1963), pp. 44–45, describes the position of *Privatdozent* as follows:

> This rank, so important in Austria and Germany, has no exact counterpart in American or British Medical Schools. A *Privatdocent* [*sic*] has not the right to attend faculty meetings, nor does he receive any salary, but he is permitted to hold a certain number of classes, usually on topics outside the regular curriculum. . . . It is a necessary condition for any university advancement, and it enjoys high prestige with the general public, since it is an assurance of special competence.

Freud was granted the position of *Privatdozent* in Neuropathology in 1885.

of protests from that section of the public which keeps on forgetting, despite everything, *who* I am and what abilities I have, and this although I have proved it a hundred times. This although I have so often shown both what people can learn from me and what people do learn from me, namely how to develop one's own talent in the way most suited to it. I do not force anyone to compose in the modern manner if he does not feel in a modern way; but he will learn to understand classical music more thoroughly than he would if taught by the dyed-in-the-wool academicians. On the other hand: anyone who wants to study modern music will learn from me all that can be learnt: based on a solid classical foundation, right up to the latest achievements in our art.[4]

Mahler, Karl Goldmark, Felix von Weingartner, and Ferdinand Löwe were approached for their opinions. The application was accepted and Schoenberg taught at the Academy from the fall of 1910 to the summer of 1911.

When this period ended and the possibility arose of appointing Schoenberg as a regular member of the Academy, there was organized opposition. Discouraged by these protests, his lack of recognition, and perpetual insolvency, Schoenberg moved to Berlin in the fall of 1911.

In Berlin, his financial situation worsened and finally became so acute that Alban Berg, without Schoenberg's knowledge, mounted a campaign to provide him with an immediate transfusion of funds.[5] Schoenberg was then living on the outskirts of Berlin in Zehlendorf, working on *Die glückliche Hand* and holding courses at the Stern Conservatory. For a while, however, he had no students there. By the time Berg's appeal produced results, the situation had improved.

In 1912 Schoenberg was offered the post at the Academy in Vienna but declined. His letter to the Academy of 29 June 1912 is remarkably open:

My main reason is: for the present, I could not live in Vienna. I have not yet got over the things done to me there, I am not yet reconciled. . . .

There are other reasons besides: the position you offered me is not the one I wished for. It would mean spending my whole life, up to my 64th year, droning over harmony and counterpoint. And that I cannot do. Since I am incapable of repeating myself without blushing for shame and since teaching year in year out makes it impossible to produce something entirely new each year, I could scarcely escape the petrification inherent in the situation. . . . What I had in mind was that I would organize the harm. and cpt. teaching according to my own ideas and then hand it over to one of my pupils, so I should be free to devote myself exclusively to teaching composition. But your intention is to engage two other teachers of composition besides myself, as a result of which all three would have to teach harmony and counterpoint. To all eternity, until the arteries are quite hardened.[6]

In September of 1912 the premiere of *Pierrot lunaire* took place in Berlin. Schoenberg completed *Die glückliche Hand* and worked on the Four Orchestral Songs, Op. 22, remaining in Berlin until 1915, when he returned to Vienna to report for military service. Although his own service was short and interrupted, most of his students were also in uniform and his teaching slacked off until the war was over.

After the war, Schoenberg did not lack for pupils, and his reputation became firmly established. His private pupils in Vienna included Max Deutsch, Hanns Eisler[B], Rudolf Kolisch, Karl Rankl[B], Erwin Ratz, Edward Steuermann[B], and many others, and he taught as well a seminar in composition at the Schwarzwald School for several years.

One of Schoenberg's pupils of the period, Josef Trauneck, described his first encounter with Schoenberg.[7] Having been impressed by Schoenberg's piano pieces, which he found in a secondhand shop, Trauneck, at the age of nineteen, decided to take his own composition seriously. Without any introduction, he rang Schoenberg's doorbell and asked to study. He showed Schoenberg a piece he had written which he called a sonata and played five or six minutes of it on the piano. When he had finished, Schoenberg pointed out to him that he had plagiarized *Der Rosenkava-*

lier of Strauss. Trauneck was naturally embarrassed by this revelation, but Schoenberg accepted him as a student anyway and directed him to study first the *Harmonielehre* and then Bellermann's *Contrapunkt.*[*][8]

In the fall of 1920, Schoenberg went to Amsterdam, where he remained until the spring of 1921. He conducted a number of concerts of his works and even considered making his home there but eventually decided against it. A few students who could afford the fare went to Holland with him; those who remained behind were turned over to Berg and Webern, whose teaching methods, although not their personalities, were closely modeled on Schoenberg's own.

Schoenberg's relationship with his students was more that of master–apprentice than of teacher–pupil. He felt strongly that students should be guided to discover the truth in themselves and disdained purely academic restrictions. His teaching technique was founded upon a firm and lively knowledge of the classical repertory. He made frequent reference to works of the classical and romantic composers but as sources for examples of problems solved and possibilities fulfilled rather than as models to be emulated. He was often able to show a student how a particular problem might be handled by resorting to examples from the literature. These examples were not to be strictly imitated, however; as much as possible, Schoenberg desired his pupils to be able to find their own solutions to compositional problems. He expected the technical exercises of his students to be creative efforts: "It is said of many an author that he may have technique but no invention. That is wrong; he has no technique either, or he has invention too. You don't have technique when you can neatly imitate something; technique has you."[9] One of Schoenberg's early pupils, Egon Wellesz, described Schoenberg's teaching methods as follows:

---

[*]Schoenberg often used Bellermann's book, a strict text based on the work of Johann Joseph Fux. As late as 1938, he recommended it in a letter to Hugo Leichtentritt. This letter appears in Arnold Schoenberg, *Letters*, ed. Erwin Stein, trans. Eithne Wilkins and Ernst Kaiser (New York: St. Martin's Press, 1965), pp. 206–207.

Every good teacher is able to discover and correct the faults in the exercises of his pupils. Most teachers would point out the place and say to the pupil, "There is a mistake." Some might take the trouble to show the pupil how he should have done it. It was Schoenberg's habit to write down three or four variants of the faulty passage to demonstrate to the pupil not merely how he might have worked correctly, but to point out to him a number of possibilities according to which he might have avoided the error. . . . In this way, he communicated to his pupils the utmost fluency in the technical handling of their musical material and great ease in surmounting the difficulties that arose from the nature of this material.[10]

One of the major drawing cards for Schoenberg's teaching ventures was his harmony book, the *Harmonielehre*, published in 1911. A highly unusual blend of conventional harmonic principles and practice with his own philosophical ideas, this book, more than any of Schoenberg's later pedagogical works, reveals both his charisma as a teacher and his greatness and uniqueness as a musical thinker. Full of musical ideas on the highest level and yet possessing a clarity of intent unusual in treatises of its type, this book contributed substantially to Schoenberg's international reputation and brought him many pupils from both Vienna and abroad. For many years, Schoenberg used this book for all of his students who did not already know it. In the preface, he outlined his teaching aims:

This book I have learned from my pupils.

In my teaching I never sought merely "to tell the pupil what I know." Better to tell him what *he* did not know. Yet that was not my chief aim either, although it was reason enough for me to devise something new for each pupil. I labored rather to show him the nature of the matter from the ground up. Hence, I never imposed those fixed rules with which a pupil's brain is so carefully tied up in knots. Everything was formulated as instructions that were no more binding upon the pupil than upon the teacher. . . . Had I told them merely what I know, then they would

have known just that and nothing more. As it is, they know
perhaps even less. But they do know what matters: *the
search itself!*[11]

Although he allowed a student's progress to germinate
from his own work without plethoric rules and guidelines, in
certain matters Schoenberg as a teacher was very strict.
These included nontheoretical, practical areas such as the
study of counterpoint. His standard text was the counterpoint book of Bellermann, which he used for many years,
and his students received extensive practice in eighteenth-
century contrapuntal techniques.*

In class, Schoenberg was fluent. He worked quickly and
easily and often wrote out whole pieces in front of his students. He was skilled at getting into a student's work and at
showing him many different ways in which a given passage
could be improved. He rarely discussed the music of his
contemporaries in class and referred to his own music
almost never. His examples were drawn nearly exclusively
from the classical repertoire—from Bach, Beethoven, Mozart, and Brahms. He felt a strong bond with the classical
tradition and saw his own music as a part of historical
continuity.

His commitment to his students was personal as well as
professional. He was nonetheless a terrifying personality who
often intimidated his students into inactivity. He demanded
total devotion from even his most famous students and was
highly suspicious of the most innocent remarks. The many
unreasonable demands that Schoenberg's personality placed

*Schoenberg's teaching methods in the United States were geared to
classroom rather than individual instruction. However, his several text-
books written during his American years are revealing of his musical
views. These books include *Models for Beginners in Composition* (New
York: G. Schirmer, 1943); *Structural Functions of Harmony*, ed. Leonard
Stein (New York: W. W. Norton, 1954); *Preliminary Exercises in Counterpoint*, ed. Leonard Stein (New York: St. Martin's Press, 1964); *Fundamentals of Musical Composition*, ed. Gerald Strang and Leonard Stein
(London: Faber and Faber, 1967); and *Style and Idea* (New York: Philosophical Library, 1950; enlarged edition, ed. Leonard Stein, trans. Leo Black,
London: Faber and Faber, 1975).

upon his students seem to have caused surprisingly little dissension among them, and many of them continued a meek and dependent attitude toward Schoenberg long into adulthood. One of the most remarkable characteristics of Schoenberg as a teacher was his ability, despite this overpowering personality, to identify and value the appropriate individual path for each student. It is one of the ambiguities of Schoenberg's nature that he should be sensitive to the inner direction of his students and yet dictatorial about their work and lives to the point that even his closest disciples felt the need to escape him in order to complete their work free of his influence. This conflict became even more apparent with the announcement of the twelve-tone method. Schoenberg wanted to take total credit for the method but expected even Berg and Webern, now mature composers, to adopt it. That these composers were willing and able to do so without violence to their own creative needs is tribute both to their admiration for Schoenberg and the excellence of the training that they received from him. Schoenberg is unusual among modern composers in having had himself great composers as pupils, and these pupils never became carbon copies of their master.

The students of Schoenberg who were interviewed for this study worked with him during various stages of his career. In his early years he had few pupils, primarily Berg, Webern, and Erwin Stein, who were close to him in age. At that time his teaching had a quality of mutual discovery that was lacking in his later work. Max Deutsch, one of Schoenberg's most intelligent and accomplished pupils, and the pianist Edward Steuermann belonged to the next generation. After World War I, Ratz, Kolisch, Greissle, and Karl Rankl began study. By this time Schoenberg was no longer working on the *Harmonielehre* and was instead occupied with performance. This concern led to an emphasis in his teaching upon arrangements that could be used in the Verein concerts. Soma Morgenstern, a writer for the *Frankfurter Zeitung* and a friend of Berg, had a broad view of the Schoenberg circle and its place in Viennese culture.

CLARA STEUERMANN: [About Steuermann] It was I think 1912 that he met Schoenberg and began to study with him and began going regularly to Mödling, and then the first world war started, so I think that it was hardly more than a year or a year-and-a-half, and because he was a very promising young pianist, Schoenberg very soon began to make use of him as a performer, and I think that the formal teaching sort of went by the way-side, and from what my husband told me, the teaching was never as thorough-going, let's say, as the teaching that Berg and Webern had. Steuermann always said that he came at a bad time, because when he came to Schoenberg, Schoenberg had just finished the first version of the *Harmonielehre* and was a little bit tired of this preoccupation with organizing the traditional harmonic ideas and so on, and so he did not work as systematically with Steuermann as he may have with others. Nevertheless, the procedure was that Steuermann would bring compositions and Schoenberg would look at them and make suggestions and so on. At that time, it was still before the whole beginning of twelve-tone so that the idiom was a kind of superchromatic almost on the verge of atonal writing. . . . The style of his teaching, at least as far as my husband was concerned, was very often not even at all directly related with music.

(Edward Steuermann) Schoenberg turned out to be the first person who did not just compliment my music. But he did not teach me in the orthodox manner at all. He seemed at this time uninterested in teaching counterpoint and thought that I didn't need any further harmony instruction. I simply started to compose; he corrected what I brought and gave me advice—sometimes very much in the "grand manner." You see, he never taught me as he had taught Webern and Berg, and later Eisler and others. Once, for instance, I brought him the beginning of a string quartet, and the introduction was a little too long. He went to his bookshelf, took out Schopenhauer's *Parerga und*

Paralipomena, showed me the first sentence which describes the contents of the work, and said, *"That* is an introduction!"[12]

CLARA STEUERMANN: Now of course this kind of teaching is very provocative and very stimulating, and it doesn't necessarily help in the moment that it is said, and so it was only some time later that Steuermann, after chewing all this through, came to realize what the point of this actually very perceptive observation was. But I think that, with Berg and Webern, he worked in a much more matter-of-fact way.

SALKA VIERTEL: [About Steuermann] He was studying with Busoni in Berlin. He was very young—sixteen years old or seventeen years old*—and Busoni asked him if he also composed and he said yes and showed Busoni some of his compositions, and Busoni [said] . . . "You must study. You must study counterpoint—" and whatever one has to study to compose, and Edward said, "That's what I am doing," and he was at the music academy in Berlin. . . . One of these famous German composers was teaching there and Edward came in and he asks him, "How do you want to compose, like Wagner or like Humperdinck?" And Edward said neither, nor—like myself. And so he studied there two months and then he couldn't stand it, it was so stuffy and so banal, and complained to Busoni, and Busoni told him, "Now there is a man who has arrived here in Berlin who is a marvelous teacher and is a genius composer and go to him," and arranged the meeting in Zehlendorf—that was a suburb of Berlin. . . . I remember I lived at that time with Edward—I was a young actress at Reinhardt's,[B] and he came home absolutely drunk with admiration. And then Schoenberg invited me too and I went, we went every Sunday—I couldn't go every Sunday because I had mati-

---

*Steuermann must actually have been at least nineteen years old at this time.

nees, but very often we went. It was a very hospitable house. He was married to Mathilde Zemlinsky who, always wrapped in a shawl, sat in the corner of the sofa freezing, and he was doing everything in the house; he was carrying the potatoes in and buying this—it was war. It was during the war. . . . I saw him in Mödling several times during the war, but at that time, it must have been '16 or '17—I know it was during the time when there was such a scarcity of food, and we were always so cold and hungry that, when we visited each other, one talked about nothing else except where can one get some potatoes and where can one get—especially with people who were not professional musicians and I wasn't. . . .

JOAN ALLEN SMITH: What else did you discuss at these Sunday meetings besides music?

VIERTEL: Well, the children were running around and the dog was there, and Schoenberg was mostly talking about . . . music, and I don't remember any more because I was not as interested in that time as I was later. But it was not like a lesson. Sometimes, if they discussed some phrase, some musical phrase, Edward would go to the piano and Schoenberg would ask him to play something . . . but it was not a professional gathering. . . . You want the atmosphere of the time. Well, as I told you, in my youth, being preoccupied with my work, then married and having children; the time I was more exposed, going out and living, I always was very close to my brother. We saw each other only when I came to Vienna or at home in summer, and then of course he was talking a lot about Schoenberg. But everything was overshadowed by the war—the war and the difficulties of getting food, and so this also showed in our relationship to others. One had to listen to the complaints—with Webern, for example, I remember we talked only about food, how to get something to eat. . . . When the war broke out, he had to enlist, Edward. They were all in uniform. They were all soldiers. And as he was in Austria, he was an Austrian soldier. And Eisler was an Austrian soldier, and Schoenberg himself offered his blood for the fatherland. They were all privates.

MAX DEUTSCH: The story is I came to Schoenberg in 1913. In this moment, he was just at the point to go to Berlin and the next year was the war, the first war, so I was an injured soldier. I had at the time to find my health, and I had to finish my studies at the university. . . . Schoenberg himself was a soldier. So, the start about 1918, the end of the war. So I was then in '18, '19, '20—'22, I was his assistant in Amsterdam when he replaced Mengelberg to conduct the Concertgebouw Orchestra. My time with Schoenberg was not really like Webern and like Berg. Webern and Berg came in to Schoenberg in 1904, and this kind of teaching was to end. You have to understand, that was only two people, Webern and Berg in 1904, and Schoenberg was already thirty years old in this moment and Webern and Berg twenty. So when I came to Schoenberg later, Schoenberg was about forty and this young enthusiastic time to be together with his students was to end. It was another aspect of teaching. . . .

SMITH: In the *Harmonielehre*, which things are really new from Schoenberg?

DEUTSCH: From the first sentence to the last! All is new. "This book, I learned by my students!" Now who before Schoenberg told that? "When a student makes a mistake, that's my fault. My explanations have not been right. So I have to change my explanation, not only my explanation, I have to change my view for this problem.". . . Of course, the most important thing, when he starts to speak about the chords in *Quarte* [fourths]— speaking from his own Chamber Symphony and coming back in the same way to Beethoven's *Pastoral,* you remember, and he said the *Thema* comes only in the second beat. He said the fact that Beethoven starts in this tremendous finale of the *Pastoral* at the second beat not the first is the proof of the importance of harmony. And, immediately after, he speaks from *Tristan,* the six horns—that means that the introduction for the chords in *Quarte.* And a little bit later, he is speaking . . . from his own orchestral pieces, from the third of the Five Orchestral Pieces, and the last sentence—melody in colors! I mean like painting. Who can speak here from theory? Who is able to explain that in theory? That is the highest point in his *Harmonielehre.* Of course, somebody who learned by *Harmonielehre* can learn his material in the professional way, absolute perfect. You need nothing at all. You'll be a perfect musician. That's what I think.

SMITH: How did you first decide to study with Schoenberg?

RUDOLF KOLISCH: Well, I really was prompted through the *Harmonielehre,* you know. I read it and it attracted me. And then I also had some connection with Berg and he advised me to go to Schoenberg. . . .

SMITH: Do you remember when you started studying with Schoenberg, what year?

KOLISCH: Well, oh ja. It was after I came back from the war—it was the first world war—it was in 1919.

SMITH: And you had known Berg before the war . . . ?

KOLISCH: Let me see, how did I know him? I believe that my father* knew him already before that.

SMITH: Your father knew Kraus quite well, didn't he?

KOLISCH: Ja. . . . He was a very good friend of Kraus and I was of course much younger.

FELIX GREISSLE: You came to Schoenberg, you showed him something . . . of what you had done. He started teaching you. . . . Sometimes he had groups—four or five—especially in composition, he liked to do that, because he liked everybody to play what he taught and

---

*Kolisch's father was a well-known physician in Vienna.

then the mistakes—teach the mistakes. And ja, he was boring three times; the fourth time he would get up and tell you things you'd never heard before. It was fascinating. And then he lapsed back again and was very theoretical. He had an enormous knowledge of technique. What he wanted to do, and what he actually always did, was that he sat down and he worked in front of us before our, rather than say eyes, before our ears. And he talked all the time: "See, I have done this now. This was not so good, for such and such a reason. But I've tried to correct it by doing that or that." Or, "I throw the whole thing away and start out new." He was never ashamed, he was very fast. But of course, in the first throw, sometimes something doesn't do anything but we learned the process of working much better. It's absolutely impossible to give someone a theoretical idea of what to do. But if you do it this way, you learn. It's like the old masters, the painters. They had their students around them and worked with them together. He did that, and then we had to work very hard, outside of that. If someone didn't work hard, he threw him out. But it's the way he taught. He was very systematic. I know that in counterpoint he was . . . unbelievable. He was in harmony too. Every problem that came up was analyzed thoroughly with so and so many examples. And I haven't seen this anywhere else.

SMITH: Do you know if Karl Rankl had much opportunity to see how Schoenberg himself composed?

KRISTINA RANKL: Oh, yes. He said that he would—that he was the fastest composer that he has ever—. There was another boy in the class, and Schoenberg said, "I'll give you a theme—. You give us a theme and we'll all sit down and write a set of six variations on that theme. And I don't just want a melodic line, I want a whole thing set for strings." And he finished in twenty minutes. And he hadn't invented the theme. . . . He asked somebody else for the theme. The others were still busy two hours later. He said it was quite incredible. He said for a moment there would be nothing. He would just sit and concentrate. And then he would write and that was it.

GREISSLE: [Except in performances] he never touched otherwise contemporary music. He talked . . . mostly about Beethoven, very much about Bach, little about Mozart or about Haydn. . . . About Mozart he didn't talk because he found him too complicated, invariably too complicated, because too irregular. Beethoven was in the beginning much more regular. But Mozart's very irregular—seven measure phrases and so on . . . but the main things were Bach, Beethoven.

SMITH: Did he talk much about composers after Beethoven—Brahms and Mahler?

GREISSLE: Ja, Brahms, very much about Brahms. He was very highly respectful of Brahms. . . . Some about Wagner—not too much.

SMITH: Mahler?

GREISSLE: Ja, very much about Mahler because Mahler—after all, he was befriended with Mahler. He knew Mahler; he obviously was very sorry, because when he came to Mahler, he was a young man and Mahler was already a very experienced musician, and he had many arguments with him. And he was sorry because he was wrong; he shouldn't have argued because Mahler knew much better about the problem.

SMITH: When Schoenberg himself was doing analysis, what did he pick out as being important?

DEUTSCH: With us, in the teaching, you mean. First, Schoenberg's teaching was more synthesis than analysis. Synthesis of course. For example, we had to do the *Kunst der Fuge*, the *Art of the Fugue*, and each one—Eisler, Edward Steuermann, me, and Kolisch, and even Webern, and even Berg—each had one fugue to do. And Schoenberg heard what we had to say, so finally he spoke, but not, "That's the *Thema*, and that's the *Dux*, and that's the *Comes*, and that—" in this way. Very modern view!—Bach, a modern composer; Brahms, a progressive composer; Mozart, the most modern of all! You know the word of Schoenberg, "I am that pupil of Mozart"—not one, *that*—the only! He told it. I heard it there.

SMITH: When Schoenberg would work in front of you, was this on improvement of something that you had brought him?

GREISSLE: No. Sometimes, yes, he improved them, but sometimes what he did, he did himself. A Scherzo—he'd write the whole Scherzo. He'd invent it himself. . . . He invented the theme in front of us and he worked on it. And he gave us sometimes several versions of this. He continued the one and he took another piece of paper and continued it another way. Whatever was possible, you see, whatever was indicated. He sometimes said, "I'm doing this now; I can't explain to you why but remember it. I'll tell you in the end why I've done it, in anticipation of what it becomes." It was very complicated. It was in fact very complicated.

ERWIN RATZ: Schoenberg never spoke about modern music to any student who was not able to, let's say, write a string quartet in Brahms' style well. He said, "If he can't do that, I will not talk to him about new music under any circumstances, because—he doesn't look at the composition at all." He said we can only judge what we want to say about new things by what we have learned by doing the same with classical music. With classical music, we are in a rather good position to say how something is new and what is great. Whereas, with new things, we must rely on instinct—this is both right and wrong—and we can only develop this instinct through the classics. This is why he placed so much value on really understanding classical composition.

DEUTSCH: Schoenberg was himself a battlefield, and that is what I learned from him—never to abandon. That's what I learned from him. For instance, one time, . . . I will tell you [about] a class of counterpoint. . . . We are twenty people around him—Webern, Berg, . . . in Mödling one time—and suddenly he asked us a question of Opus 16, the Five Orchestral Pieces. And nobody answered, and Schoenberg told us, "I know, my students, my pupils, my disciples, don't know my music." And he added, "This third orchestra piece is a *fuga*." Nobody batted an eyelash. They go, "Huh? How can that be?" How to find out the fugue. Two weeks after, the same people around him, and he stops. He starts to speak again from this third piece. The same phrase, the same sentence, "Nobody knows my music, of my students." "Master, I know it! This is a *fuga*." "How do you know it?" Well, for one second, I had the choice, to be a liar, to tell him, "I find it out for myself," or to tell the truth, "You told me." So, for one second, two seconds, I told him, "You told it." At this moment, Schoenberg, a little smile comes to him. That is historical!

SMITH: Did you find Schoenberg intimidating?

KOLISCH: Ja.

SMITH: Did he have close friends? . . . Even though he was intimidating, would you say that he was close to his friends?

KOLISCH: Very, very complex. And it is not easy to grasp. He had very close friends. Ja. Of course, my relationship to him then maybe transcended . . . later on when I became also closer to him.* But as a young man, as a student, yes. I will admit that he did intimidate me. No, he was just dominating.

MARCEL DICK: Schoenberg talked and you listened. There was no conversation on an equal level.

---

*Kolisch's sister Gertrud became Schoenberg's second wife on 18 August 1924.

SMITH: Did he have conversation with anyone on an equal level or was this true of everybody?

DICK: No, with everyone—with Webern, with Berg. . . . He acknowledged Webern and Berg as full-fledged composers of great importance, . . . but Berg and Webern did not feel that they can talk to the master as one would talk to you and you to me. They were always at a distance.

SMITH: Do you think that Berg was overly influenced by Schoenberg?

SOMA MORGENSTERN: I don't think that he was overly influenced by Schoenberg, I think that he was influenced by Mahler too. And I think that he loved and admired Mahler as much as Schoenberg, if not even more, because there was not this relation master–pupil with Mahler and Alban. Alban, he was an admiring young man—pupil of Schoenberg—who admired Mahler as Schoenberg himself. He had a great admiration of Mahler without any reserves. He was just in love with him. . . . Mahler was loved by Alban I think with all his heart. He talked about nobody with such love as he talked about Mahler. . . . With Schoenberg, it's a different story. Schoenberg wasn't as lovable a man as Mahler was. Schoenberg was a person which was, I would say—he was a little tyrannical! Schoenberg was very stubborn and he was the master, of course. All of them had the same relation to Schoenberg. The only one with whom I could talk about Schoenberg without risking something was Steuermann, rather. Because Steuermann was a very, very educated . . . man, and he was a strong character himself. Of course he admired Schoenberg as a composer and as his teacher, but . . . he was too tyrannical. Mahler wasn't a soft guy either, but it was a different thing in his being director of the opera. It's a different story.

DEUTSCH: So when you see also a big man like Schoenberg—a small guy but a big man, a tremendous man, but his eyes—Schoenberg's eyes at you. His face was eyes, and Schoenberg's eyes at you, you disappeared.*

SMITH: You didn't find Schoenberg intimidating then?

VIERTEL: I found him always very funny, gay, very witty, very sharp. I never agreed with his political views. He was such a mixture of dictator and a very advanced man, but it was very difficult to agree with him, for me, at that time. Now that I am older, I would like to talk to him.

GREISSLE: Schoenberg was very reluctant to talk to other people about more than conventional matters. He didn't want to talk about himself and about his music and about music in general anyway. It's very difficult. I have seen two or three people become very friendly with him because he liked them.

DICK: There was a graphologist in Vienna, a handwriting expert, not a fake and so on; he was a court-appointed handwriting expert, fashionable and quite fabulous. But, outside of court, he did private consultations and would read your character. So, one day, unknown to Schoenberg and very much behind his back, Webern and Steuermann I think was the other perpetrator took an envelope that had an address on it in Schoenberg's handwriting . . . to give to Mr. Schermann the handwriting expert. . . . He had no idea whose handwriting it was, but he told them the most amazingly clever things—described completely what kind of a person he was in amazing detail and accuracy. And then, when he

---

*Others' interest in Schoenberg's eyes is mirrored by his own preoccupation with those organs in his paintings. Most of his self-portraits are frontal views, the eyes prominent, and in his more visionary works, the eyes are often the only strongly articulated facial feature. See especially *Gaze* (1910), *Gaze, Vision* (1910), and *Red Gaze* (1910) reproduced in "Arnold Schoenberg: Paintings—Drawings—Sketches," *Journal of the Arnold Schoenberg Institute* 2 (June 1978): 185–231 (nos. 124, 128, 242, and 246).

ended his presentation, he said, "And anyway, this man thinks he's the emperor of China." That was in the early twenties. In California, . . . Schoenberg celebrated his seventieth birthday and many of the old guard were there—Steuermann was there, Kolisch, of course, and others from this era. And then, Schoenberg noticed that a group of his old friends were whispering around in a corner and laughing and smiling, and Schoenberg could not tolerate that anything should happen in his surroundings that he didn't know about and had no control of. So, he said, "You, over there! What's that? What are you laughing at?" And so, finally, one of them took the courage and—after so many years they were all grandfathers and what have you, but still, hesitantly, one of them took the courage and told him the story of Schermann the graphologist and what he said and that he said that the man thinks he's the emperor of China. "What, what? Well, didn't you tell him that I am?" So this was Schoenberg. Of course he was!*

---

*In an article following the publication of Karl Kraus's letters to Sidonie von Nádherný, Elias Canetti relates another story about this same graphologist: "The clairvoyant and graphologist Raphael Schermann, who was creating a sensation in Vienna, had written an analysis of Kraus's hand, writing without knowing him personally and with no clue as to his identity. Kraus found this analysis to be so phenomenal that he copied it down for Sidi. Since it showed him as he wanted to be seen (he dispatched it to Sidi to influence her), I would like to quote the most important parts:

A rare mind; a writer who writes dreadfully grippingly. . . . When he commits himself to a cause, he pursues it until death. His language and his tongue are like a 42-centimeter mortar. . . . When he faces an enemy, he will not budge until the enemy is on the ground. He is afraid of nothing, *and if a thousand people are present*, he advocates his cause so vociferously and grippingly that everyone collapses virtually hypnotized. . . . He must have fought enormous fights in his life. He is always ready for an attack, holds his weapon in hand ready to fire so that no attack can catch him unprepared. The impact is so strong that I cannot get away from it. A dreadfully sharp observer, even sharper in criticizing. No mere mortal can approach him. . . . His work has brought him many insults and persecutions, but he has

During the years when Schoenberg was in Holland and Berlin, Webern and Berg took over the pupils left behind. Berg never taught as much as Webern, who had a number of pupils and continued his teaching activities until his death.

Berg's early responsibilities for the running of his family estate in Carinthia and his later successes with *Wozzeck* took him often away from Vienna and also secured his income so that extensive teaching commitments were rarely necessary. Still, he was greatly admired as a teacher and as a person, for his kindness and generosity as well as for his knowledge of music and literature. An attractive man, he was considered charming and highly cultured by those who knew him. Stefan Askenase, in a letter dated 27 July 1973, recalled Berg's fine qualities: "He was one of the most charming men I ever met. Of great intelligence, full of wit and irony, he loved life and company. Still with all familiarity, he commanded respect."[13]

According to people who studied both with Schoenberg and with Webern or Berg, the teaching techniques of the three composers were essentially the same, Webern being more scrupulously attentive to detail and Berg more kindly and less authoritarian than Schoenberg.

Theodor Wiesengrund-Adorno[B] (1903–1969), eminent philosopher of the Frankfurt School, was intimately associated with the Schoenberg circle in the twenties and thirties. In 1925, shortly before Schoenberg left for Berlin, he began compositional studies with Berg, and from 1928 until 1932 he was editor of *Musikblätter des Anbruch*, the maga-

---

always carried the day. . . . No vanity whatsoever, not even personally. . . . His nerves are overstrained. He allows himself no relaxation. . . . He understands more about the war than some people running it, *but he can say nothing.*"

Elias Canetti, *The Conscience of Words,* trans. Joachim Neugroschel (New York: Seabury Press, 1979), p. 231. The complete letter of 20 July 1915 from Karl Kraus to Sidonie von Nádherný is found in Karl Kraus, *Briefe an Sidonie Nádherný von Borutin 1913–1936,* vol. 1, ed. Heinrich Fischer and Michael Lazarus (Munich: Kösel-Verlag, 1974), pp. 169–174.

zine that Berg himself had edited from 1920 to 1921. In 1931 he joined the philosophy faculty of the University of Frankfurt, where he remained until he was expelled by the National Socialists in 1933. In addition to significant philosophical writings, he was the author of numerous musical articles, a book on Berg, and an important work, *Philosophie der neuen Musik*, containing an extended discussion of the twelve-tone method.

In his musical writings he adhered to a Marxist view of twentieth-century composition, which ascribes fervid ideological construction to the musical tenets of its antipodal principals, Schoenberg and Stravinsky. Although revered by many of Schoenberg's younger pupils, including most importantly Rudolf Kolisch, Adorno was not close to Schoenberg.* Some of Schoenberg's aloofness may have stemmed from Adorno's independence of thought, a characteristic he never tolerated easily in anyone; Schoenberg also found Adorno's obscure writing style antagonistic to his own ideas of clarity, which dated back to his association with Karl Kraus. Of the *Philosophie der neuen Musik*, he wrote to Josef Rufer:

> The book is very difficult to read, for it uses this quasi-philosophical jargon in which modern professors of philosophy hide the absence of an idea. They think it is profound when they produce lack of clarity by undefined new expressions . . . naturally he knows all about twelve-tone music, but he has no idea of the creative process.[14]

---

*SMITH: Who was the most important philosopher to you?

KOLISCH: For us, it was probably Hegel, and still Kant also. But to me personally, the most important philosopher was a friend, Theodor Adorno.

SMITH: Was Adorno respected as a philosopher by the Schoenberg circle?

GREISSLE: Schoenberg didn't get along with him very well. . . . He did not like people to talk too much about music, . . . and Teddy Adorno used to talk too much.

Adorno is important as one of the most articulate and intelligent of Schoenberg's followers. Adorno was much more closely associated with Berg than with Schoenberg, but his real influence was with the younger pupils, and then only after 1925, when the twelve-tone method had already been in existence for at least two years. Adorno's description of his pedagogical experiences is valuable nonetheless for its detailed account of Schoenbergian teaching methods as practiced by Berg:

> In order to give an idea of studying with him, one has to imagine his particular musicality. Also, as teacher, he reacted slowly, almost broodingly; his strength was one of spiritual imagination and of the greatest conscious mastery of the possibilities, and a strong and original fantasy in all compositional dimensions. None among the newer composers, including Schoenberg and Webern, was so much the opposite of the then ideologically puffed-up concept of musicians as he. Generally, he looked for a long time at what I brought him, and proceeded above all with places that didn't work out, with attempted solutions for them. . . . He developed my feeling for a high standard of musical form, inoculated me against the unclearly articulated, the vacuous, and above all against mechanical and monotonous rudiments in the midst of worked out compositional material. Whatever he exemplified in individual cases was of such potency that it was imprinted forever. . . . All of his corrections had an unmistakably Bergian character. He was, as a composer, much too distinctive to be able to empathize, as the phrase goes. . . . The main principle that he conveyed to me was that of variation; everything should properly be developed out of something else and at the same time differ in itself.[15]

Berg and Webern learned their teaching technique from Schoenberg. Felix Greissle, who studied with both Schoenberg and Berg, was able to compare their pedagogical styles. The pianist Bruno Seidlhofer studied harmony with Berg. His attitude is that of a performer, and his interest in contemporary composition, especially the twelve-tone method, was slight. Webern, who had more pupils than Berg, was highly respected as a teacher, and his lectures, published as *The Path to the New Music*, stand as one of the principal statements on atonal and twelve-tone theory.

SMITH: So Rankl went to Schoenberg in 1918?

KRISTINA RANKL: '17. He was very ill when he came out and he was there until Schoenberg went to Berlin. Schoenberg went to Holland and then went to Berlin. But of course they kept in touch all the time.

SMITH: Did your husband study with Webern also?

RANKL: Yes. You see, when Schoenberg went to Holland, my husband was handed on to Webern, who was then getting into the age group where he could teach. So, he went to Webern and knew Berg very well. But Berg did not teach. . . . Berg was busy and lived mainly in Carinthia. . . . But Webern lived in Mödling, which was very near where my husband came from, so he went and had lessons there.

BRUNO SEIDLHOFER: But, for instance, what happened before I had lessons with Berg, which were very interesting—he was a very intelligent and charming man, Berg; he also liked us very much and drank coffee with us, which he ground himself with his little Turkish machine. He had these lessons mostly after lunch and then ground coffee. . . .

SMITH: I am rather curious to know why you went to study with Berg. . . .

SEIDLHOFER: All young people are curious. I had flipped through the book by Schoenberg also, the *Harmonielehre*. That is very interesting, that book. It was at that time still more interesting than it is today. And then, I knew Berg. I knew his music—the songs, the early songs—about which I was enthusiastic. I think I learned very much from Berg. He told me a great deal.

SMITH: Was Berg a good teacher then?

SEIDLHOFER: Yes, one profited very much. He was very open; he knew literature also very well.

SMITH: What did you do in your lessons?

SEIDLHOFER: Harmony above all. I composed also at that time and showed him a couple of things. Of my things, he said that one could improve them, by doing such and such. . . .

SMITH: I wonder if you could describe exactly what would go on at one of your lessons. Were you alone with Berg? How would the lesson proceed?

SEIDLHOFER: Ja, ja. Now, I did the exercises which he gave me, also from the Schoenberg book and so forth; I did them and he corrected them. He sat at the piano with me and showed me this and that. . . .

SMITH: Did Berg ever talk about his own compositions in your lessons?

SEIDLHOFER: Yes, certainly. When I was his student, *Wozzeck* had just appeared in print. He showed me several things and he also explained the forms and so on, which one could not see immediately, in individual acts and so forth. I had asked him for that; he wouldn't have done so on his own. I was interested in it.

SMITH: Do you remember much about what Berg was interested in besides music?

STEFAN ASKENASE: I think more or less in everything. . . . He was very *gebildet*—of much knowledge, you know. He knew literature very well and—yes, I think he had many interests. . . . I think musically he was interested— it was very, at the end, it was very narrowed to one chord and that was the first chord of *Tristan*. He was fascinated by it. And you know that he quoted it in the *Lyric Suite* in the last movement. But when he saw a piano, he always played that. But he knew music extremely well, all sides.

SMITH: How would Schoenberg's methods of analysis have differed from those of Berg and Webern?

ERWIN RATZ: I never got to know Berg as a teacher. Schoenberg was freer than Webern. Webern was, I might say, more orthodox; but in other respects, there wasn't much difference.

SMITH: Would you say that Schoenberg's approach to analysis was different from Berg's?

FELIX GREISSLE: No. That is to say, Berg had learned it from Schoenberg actually. How can I describe the analysis? It was not an analysis, it was a synthesis, actually, that he did. He composed or recomposed the work before your eyes. And Berg did the same thing. What Berg did in the few essays Berg wrote on that, it came even out better and more clear. Pfitzner[B], you know Pfitzner, he had at one time written a pamphlet, a little book, you see—a very stupid one against contemporary music.[16] And then, he had juxtaposed Schumann, how wonderful this is, and you take, for instance, the "Träumerei." What can you say about it? And, as he expressed it, "in the air," you cannot say anything except that the melody goes up through the triad and comes down again. And still it is so beautiful, you cannot touch it. And Berg took this melody and replied in an essay.[17] . . . And he said, "I have a little more to say about this." And he analyzed "Träumerei" very well—different. There were strong harmonies. It was very beautifully done. And this was the form Schoenberg—he composed it before your ears, or eyes or what you say, and then, you see, he was very sarcastic and Pfitzner's music is not important.

EUGEN LEHNER: But the three persons—Webern, Schoenberg, Berg—were three completely different personalities. Berg was a typical aristocrat, Austrian aristocrat—a certain nonchalance, great charm, and a certain very man-of-the-world and so on—incredibly handsome, very warm. And Schoenberg was absolutely the fire ball—just [full] of ideas but incredibly warm.

Notes

1. Willi Reich, *Schoenberg: A Critical Biography*, trans. Leo Black (London: Longman Group, 1971), p. 29.

2. Ibid., p. 27.

3. For more on the relationship between Schoenberg and Schenker, including their correspondence, see Charlotte E. Erwin and Bryan R. Simms. "Schoenberg's correspondence with Heinrich Schenker," *Journal of the Arnold Schoenberg Institute* 5 (June 1981):23–43; Bryan Simms, "New Documents in the Schoenberg-Schenker Polemic," *Perspectives of New Music* 16 (Fall–Winter 1977):110–124; and Helmut Federhofer, *Heinrich Schenker: Nach Tagebüchern und Briefen in der Oswald Jonas Memorial Collection, University of California, Riverside*, Studien zur Musikwissenschaft, vol. 3 (Hildesheim: Georg Olms Verlag, 1985), pp. 210–211.

4. Arnold Schoenberg, *Letters*, ed. Erwin Stein, trans. Eithne Wilkins and Ernst Kaiser (New York: St. Martin's Press, 1965), p. 27.

5. Quoted in Reich, *Schoenberg*, p. 60.

6. Schoenberg, *Letters*, pp. 32–33.

7. Interview with Josef Trauneck, Vienna, summer 1974.

8. Heinrich Bellermann, *Der Contrapunkt* (Berlin: Verlag von Julius Springer, 1901).

9. Arnold Schoenberg, *Style and Idea*, ed. Leonard Stein, trans. Leo Black (London: Faber and Faber, 1975), p. 366.

10. Egon Wellesz, "Schönberg and Beyond," *Musical Quarterly* 2 (January 1916):79. For another view, see Paul A. Pisk, "Memories of Arnold Schoenberg," *Journal of the Arnold Schoenberg Institute* 1 (October 1976):39–40.

11. Arnold Schoenberg, *Theory of Harmony*, trans. Roy E. Carter (Berkeley: University of California Press, 1978), p. 1.

12. Gunther Schuller, "A Conversation with Steuermann," *Perspectives of New Music* 3 (Fall–Winter 1964):22–23.

13. Personal correspondence from Stefan Askenase, 27 July 1973.

14. H. H. Stuckenschmidt, *Schoenberg: His Life, World and Work*, trans. Humphrey Searle (New York: Schirmer Books, 1978), p. 508.

15. Theodor Adorno, *Alban Berg: Der Meister des kleinsten Übergangs* (Vienna: Verlag Elisabeth Lafite; Oesterreichischer Bundesverlag, 1968), pp. 39–40.

16. Hans Pfitzner, *Die neue Aesthetik der musikalischen Impotenz: ein verwesungssymptom?* (Munich: Süddeutsche Monatshefte, 1920); reprinted in Hans Pfitzner, *Gesammelte Schriften*, vol. 2 (Augsburg: Dr. Benno Filser Verlag, 1926), pp. 99–281.

17. Alban Berg, "Die musikalische Impotenz der 'neuen Aesthetik' Hans Pfitzners," *Musikblätter des Anbruch* 2 (June 1920); reprinted in Willi Reich, *Alban Berg*, trans. C. Cardew (New York: Harcourt, Brace and World, 1965), pp. 205–218.

~ 7 ~

The Schwarzwald School

The generation gap was far more between us twentieth-century people and the nineteenth century because the young generation of today are twentieth century and so are we, but Schoenberg and all his old friends—and a that is also Webern and Berg, the younger ones and Erwin Stein [B]—all these people were for me a generation gap because the difference between the nineteenth and the twentieth century was terrific. You know, we really had done with it, us, really done with it. That is why we freely could adhere to Schoenberg. And it was only via Schoenberg that I learned to appreciate Mozart, that I learned to appreciate Wagner, and above all, I learned to appreciate Brahms—especially the chamber music.

Lona Truding

One of the most innovative institutions in World War I Vienna was the Schwarzwald School, a progressive school for girls* founded and directed by Dr. Eugenie Schwarzwald[B]. Dr. Schwarzwald was an active and concerned feminist. At a time when women were denied most opportunities outside of the home and expected to limit their educations to subjects suitable for ladies of fashion, the Schwarzwald School provided a unique environment in which young women could acquire the skills necessary for entrance to the university as well as test their minds against some of the outstanding creative forces of their time. Schoenberg, Loos, and Kokoschka all taught at the Schwarzwald School, and the house of Herr and Frau Dr. Schwarzwald, to which the educator often invited her students, was a meeting place for Vienna's cultural intelligentsia.† Loos and Kokoschka were familiar faces at these gatherings. Schoenberg, however, was more reclusive (perhaps for the personal reasons discussed in the following chapter), and although in his position as instructor at the Schwarzwald School he would have been included in the salons, there is no evidence that he socialized heavily at these affairs.

Dr. Schwarzwald had constantly to battle to maintain the standards of her institution against the stultifying effects of an official educational curriculum. For many years she attempted to obtain a license that would allow her to offer the courses necessary for university entrance. Without this, women students prepared with private tutors for the examination which was given at a boys' secondary school, a situation that placed women applicants at a disadvantage. In an attempt to give her students the best preparation possible for higher education or whatever else life had to offer, Dr. Schwarzwald engaged teachers who often were opposed to

*A few selected boys also attended the school, among them the pianist Rudolf Serkin.

†In the twenties, Webern offered a conducting course at the school that was attended largely by students from Schoenberg's composition seminar. For an account of this course, see Hans Moldenhauer and Rosaleen Moldenhauer, *Anton von Webern: A Chronicle of His Life and Work* (New York: Alfred A. Knopf, 1979), pp. 465–466.

the rigidities of a standard curriculum that stressed the events of the past at the expense of all current cultural activity. After meeting the Schwarzwalds through Loos in 1911, Kokoschka taught at the school during 1912 and 1913. He rejected the traditional pedagogical method of copying boxes and other stationary objects in favor of drawing from the imagination. In this, he gained the affection and praise of his students as he fell afoul of the education inspectors who ultimately forced Dr. Schwarzwald to dismiss him in order to save her license.[1]

In the fall of 1917, spurred on by financial hardship, Schoenberg announced a seminar in composition to be held in the Schwarzwald School, where he had taught many years before. The course prospectus, dated 1 September 1917, reveals Schoenberg's concern with the purposes and quality of education. Schoenberg shared with Kokoschka a strong feeling that the goal of art is to follow one's inner voice ("to paint what one sees"). Consequently, he never tried to force his own way upon his students but endeavored instead to help them find their own voice. Some of this purpose is expressed in the following document:

One learns perfectly only those things for which one has an aptitude. Then, no particular pedagogic discipline is needed: a model, provoking emulation, suffices; one learns as much as one's inborn aptitudes allow.

This carefree way of learning has to be helped out by pedagogic means only because the number of things to be learned is ever on the increase, and the amount of time available correspondingly smaller.

Now though it is astonishing how many people can in fact reach a "prescribed standard" in matters for which they have little aptitude, there is no denying that the results are but mediocre. This is particularly apparent in the artistic field. At one time, the difference between the very best amateur and the artist might lie not in their respective performances, but merely in the fact that the amateur did not earn his daily bread through art; nowadays, there are all too many artists whose performance is amateurish, the only difference being that their sole con-

cern is with bread-winning. The able amateur has, however, become relatively rare.

One main cause is teaching. It asks too much and too
little of artist and amateur alike; too little, since in bringing
him to the prescribed standard it gives him more than he
needs, and so relieves him of the need to find, within himself, the superabundant energy through which his natural
gifts can spread themselves and take on fullness; too
much, since by the same token it gives him less than he
needs, so paralysing whatever energies he has, and pre-
venting his becoming even the specialist his aptitude fits
him to be.

In art there is but one true teacher: inclination. And he
has but one usable assistant: imitation.

. . . There should be nothing missing in this seminar,
which a student can learn from a teacher: he will by no
means learn less—there will rather be more subjects. But
apart from selecting them according to his inclination and
gift, there should here take place what, according to my
experience in my private teaching, achieves the best
results: constant and unconstrained communication between me and my students. I will reserve certain regular
hours for them to discuss with them questions which they
may put before me. We will play, analyze, discuss, search,
and find. They will come if they feel like it and remain as
long as they wish. And it will be my concern to heighten
their inclination and thereby to encourage their talent.
They should not feel that they are learning; they will perhaps work, perhaps even toil, but not notice it. They should
be there as the painting students were once at home in the
painter's studio, when, through their talent for this art and
out of respect of the Master, they endeavored to gain
admission to his studio. . . .[2]

Shortly after publishing this announcement as a flier,
Schoenberg was redrafted into the army in which he served
until 5 December. Schoenberg was thus unable to begin the
course until early 1918. In April of that year, he moved to
Mödling, Bernhardgasse 6. The course continued until 1920
and some of his students visited him often in the Mödling
house.

According to an advertisement for the course of 1918, subjects taught included harmony, counterpoint, form, orchestration, and analysis for beginners and more advanced students. The meetings were generally held from four to eight o'clock in the evening, and according to Egon Wellesz[B,3] there were additional evening discussions of a less formal nature where Schoenberg answered questions and analyzed pieces as outlined in the above-quoted brochure. During his tenure at the Schwarzwald School, Schoenberg completed no new works.

The Schwarzwald School presented an unusual opportunity for female students, and Dr. Eugenie Schwarzwald provided a strong and fascinating role model for these students. Erna Gál and Lona Truding were both pupils of the school itself. In addition, Gál performed works of the Schoenberg circle as a pianist, while Truding was in Schoenberg's Schwarzwald School class. The students in this class were not all students from the school itself. Felix Greissle studied there before he became a private pupil of Schoenberg. Kokoschka's view of the school is as a teacher. His involvement appears to have been with the school directly, whereas Schoenberg taught in the building after school hours. Schoenberg doubtless viewed his teaching at the school primarily as a source of income. The school itself, however, was a unique institution which deserves mention in these pages because of the radical cultural atmosphere that Dr. Schwarzwald created around it.

JOAN ALLEN SMITH: When you went for your lessons, were there other people in the same class?

LONA TRUDING: Yes, it was a seminar. It was a group of, say, seven or eight.

SMITH: Was this at the Schwarzwald School?

TRUDING: Yes, that's right. And that was the first year and we had the advanced year and then we had private lessons. And only if you had private lessons with him were you allowed to call yourself a pupil of Schoenberg.

SMITH: . And you went for the entire course?

TRUDING: Yes, I did, and I did even counterpoint too. But I think I did it either with Rufer[B] or with Polnauer[B]. I did it only indirectly with Schoenberg. He might have looked occasionally at some of my work, but I think I did it with Rufer. And when Rufer was delayed or couldn't do it, then Polnauer took over.

SMITH: Who else was in your class?

TRUDING: All of those who are now famous and I'm not! Ja, Jalowetz[B], Polnauer, Rufer.

SMITH: Was Paul Pisk in your class?

TRUDING: Yes, of course, Paul Pisk, but I think he was a bit older than we were. I think he was in the second year.

SMITH: Were you at the Schwarzwald School . . . ?

ERNA GÁL: Yes, I was in the school. I made my humanistic gymnasium at the Schwarzwald. She had a four years course for people like me. I went there from fourteen to eighteen years and then I made my *Matura* in a boys' school, and it was awfully difficult. They didn't know me there and I had to do an exam on every little subject. But I passed somehow, and then I went to university only I didn't finish it, I didn't make my doctor. So, I studied for two years under Guido Adler[B] there and Rudi [Kolisch] did too, but he didn't finish it either. We kept on playing together so we had no time really to study.

SMITH: Was Kokoschka teaching at the school when you were there?

GÁL: Well he taught at the school but not me. I never went there. And he must have taught very much earlier than I came there actually because then, when I was at the school, he didn't teach. He was a very, very good friend of Frau Dr. Schwarzwald's—wonderful friend. I mean, he always was there when I came and so was Adolf Loos, of course, the great architect. . . . And then she had this country place in Grundlsee; she had this house, and all her friends came there and pupils from the school. I was still a pupil when I went there. And there came people like, well, Lotte Leonard[B] always came and gave concerts. Rudi Serkin came there quite a lot. He was a pupil at the school—Rudi and Rudi's sister. And actually, we took Rudi Serkin to Professor Robert, Richard Robert, who taught him the piano for his first ten years. And he was then ten years old—twelve years he was.... Of course George Szell was there too. George Szell never liked Schoenberg's compositions. He never performed them.

SMITH: Did Schoenberg go to these things too at the same time as Kokoschka did? I know that he taught at the school.

GÁL: Oh, yes, he had a course on composition at the school. I remember that very well because I often went there. But I cannot remember any details from that. It was on the second floor and the school was on the third, and he had a room in the afternoon from five on, and he taught his pupils there, and I often popped in sort of when I was at the school. But I can't remember any details.

SMITH: Was that while you were a student there?

GÁL: Yes. No. That was when I had already finished but I kept on going to the school for sort of social evenings and seeing Frau Dr. Schwarzwald and all that. I kept on going. We were like a big family, the Schwarzwald pupils, all of them. It was quite a modern circle.

SMITH: Did Schoenberg go to the social evenings too?

GÁL: No, he never did. No. And I don't know whether he knew Frau Dr. Schwarzwald very well, actually.... I never met him at her place.

SMITH: But Loos and Kokoschka—

GÁL: Oh Loos and Kokoschka, and there was this marvelous writer, what was his name [Egon Friedell[B]] who committed suicide when the Nazis came into his flat. He was a great friend of hers, an enormous fellow, very Jewish looking, and the first thing he did when they rung his bell, he jumped out of the window—But then there was this wonderful writer, Carl Zuckmayer[B], you have heard of him? He came along to Grundlsee—But Schoenberg never came there.

SMITH: And Karl Kraus?

GÁL: Oh, Kraus, yes, Kraus knew Frau Dr. Schwarzwald very well. I never met him personally. I went to his lectures a lot. . . . Kokoschka I met for the first time when I was twelve. I was, as I say, a pupil of Schwarzwald, and Eugenie Schwarzwald used to call me to play the piano in her home, and people were there, to accompany some singers. Lotte Leonard was very often there. . . . She was a very famous German singer in the early twenties and thirties—concert singer. Now then, Eugenie called me and I met Kokoschka there. And one day, he said that he wanted to draw me. And he did a very nice sketch half and he didn't finish it. And I had my hair awfully long then to the shoulders and the next day, I cut it without thinking and he said he wanted another session, and when I came, my hair was short, and he . . . called me a medieval knight's page or something like that.

SMITH: Do you remember the Schwarzwald School?

OSKAR KOKOSCHKA: Yes, of course. Now, when I was chased from all official schools where I wanted to be an assistant in the—make money with the—in tuition, again and again, the *Neue Freie Presse*—it was also against Schoenberg of course—the organ, the *Neue Freie Presse*, wrote something, "This degenerate man shouldn't be tolerated in the official job like a teacher in that and that and that school." I always got chased, and the director was coming and, "Look here, the *Neue Freie Presse*, so you're losing your job, no good." And finally, Frau Schwarzwald—she had a girls' school. Today, still, very old ladies write to me from when I was at that school.

OLDA KOKOSCHKA: Serkin was picked up by Eugenie Schwarzwald as a little boy and he played there. And that's where they first met.

OSKAR KOKOSCHKA: Yeh, that's our friendship. She was a great woman. Also a friend of Adolf Loos of course. . . .

OLDA KOKOSCHKA: . . . She had open house. Lots of people met there, I think, at the house.

OSKAR KOKOSCHKA: Whoever came through Austria. Or if he was worthwhile. You immediately had been discovered by Frau Schwarzwald and you were there. All over, from America, . . . from Italy, from everywhere. . . . She wrote a few nice—in the *Züricher Zeitung*. . . . She wrote about the impression that Karl Kraus shared with her and Adolf Loos that I was a fool, an innocent fool, but when I said something—usually I was very silent—but suddenly I made . . . a wisecrack as if something were to have been dropped from the moon.

OLDA KOKOSCHKA: Yes, but she decided—that was the famous thing that she decided—that his knowledge or his education was like the pagodas in the desert of Gobi, you see—nothing, and then occasionally—

GÁL: Oh, Eugenie was a wonderful person. And she did everything she could. After the war, she instituted . . . those cheap midday meals and evening meals. In going to Vienna, if you want to eat cheap and well, you go to the WÖK. . . . You get the cheapest, most wonderful meals there. . . . But the WÖK, Frau Dr. Schwarzwald instituted. After the first world war, everybody went to eat there and it's still going. And she was really a great philanthropist. . . . You haven't heard about . . . Frau Schwarzwald's home [in Grundlsee] where everybody went in the summer? . . . Loos was there too with his wife—his first wife, no it was his second wife—Else Altmann. She was a dancer—a great friend of mine—a lovely person, but they divorced after a few years.

TRUDING: ... You know that these people were—they were all oddities. They were really odd. For instance, you know Schwarzwald. I was in the private school of Schwarzwald. Well, we were on holiday ... and Adolf Loos came with us and he had constipation. And he said, "A human being must be able to bear everything." And, at breakfast, in front of all of us young girls, he used to pump out his stomach himself. He swallowed the tube and pumped out his stomach—vomited and we had to bear that without being sick. So that was the training he set. It was definitely not the "Oh, so flowery Romanticism!" No, on the other hand, we greatly admired his new technique of building and then this highly witty kind of conversation which people had in this time. I remember we used to meet at definite cafés in Vienna. And it was either the Herrenhof or it was in the Café Central. They were both one next to the other. Frankly speaking, I do not know how I managed to keep myself and my brother, to study at the university, to study with Schoenberg, and to sit half the days and afternoons and nights in these cafés with these new bohemians. That's how I grew up—most unbourgeois.

FELIX GALIMIR: I would say the prototype of Romanticism was Berg—as a person, you know, this dreamer type, a little sickish, never quite well—terribly tall—ideal romanticist. And his whole attitude was so romantic. I guess you feel it in the music too—Have you read the letters to his wife?

SMITH: Yes.

GALIMIR: This is not faked—that's exactly him. And in some way, he was a little bit out of context already then, because there were very few people left of this caliber romanticism as he was.

SMITH: What year was it that you came to Schoenberg?

FELIX GREISSLE: To Schoenberg? About 1920. ... I was at the University of Vienna and met Rudolf Kolisch there

... and Kolisch saw that I studied with Grädener. Grädener was a direct pupil of Brahms, a very good craftsman—but nothing much, and Kolisch said to me, "This is a ridiculous thing to study and why don't you go to Schoenberg." I said, "I don't know." You see, my family had lost their money during the world war, the first world war, and I didn't have enough money to study with Schoenberg, and Kolisch said to me, "So you go to the course." Yes. He had a course in a school, Schwarzwald School in Vienna, and I came there, and after the third or fourth time—he always had somebody else holding the course for him—Schoenberg came and he immediately started asking me, and then, eventually, he invited me to become his private pupil, and he didn't care whether I had money because, at that time, Schoenberg had a principle. He had close classes of three that had nothing to do with the course but they were really close pupils, and one of the three had to have money and he paid for the whole course. And the other two had no money but they were gifted. So, I was together with a man, Cort van der Linden[B], who came from Holland. He was very nice and he had a lot of money and no talent. . . . He was very generous but he knew what happened and he didn't mind at all. And the other two were, in the beginning, Serkin and I, and Serkin didn't stay too long.

SMITH: What did he do in an ordinary lesson? . . .

TRUDING: Right from the beginning, it had to be creative work. It was never a harmony exercise; it was right at the outset a little composition of sixteen bars. It usually was sixteen bars, because he gave us as the model examples of short and in every way excellent compositions, the dances by Schubert, and they were models for the right bass, the right harmony, and the right melody. . . .

SMITH: How long did you study with Schoenberg?

TRUDING: Until he left Vienna for Berlin.*

GREISSLE: This was one of the most important things to him—to hear something as he taught it—hear something out. And that is something which I only found in him. When you brought him something, he said, "My God, you didn't hear that right. Because, if you had heard it right, you would have gone that way or done this or that but you didn't."

TRUDING: This is a very important thing, what Schoenberg said: "Through studying composition, if you gain nothing else but a very acute hearing, a kind of good education for your ear, that is really all you need." So he considered this as a real ear-training and that is what it is.

Notes

1. Hedwig Schleiffer, "Kokoschka, Pioneer in Art Education," *School Arts* 59 (June 1960):29.
2. Arnold Schoenberg Institute. Partially quoted in Willi Reich, *Schoenberg: A Critical Biography*, trans. Leo Black (London: Longman Group, 1971), pp. 110–111.
3. Egon Wellesz, *Arnold Schönberg*, trans. W. H. Kerridge (London: J. M. Dent and Sons, 1925; reprint ed., New York: Da Capo Press, 1969), p. 45.

*Schoenberg moved to Berlin in 1926 to take up a position at the Prussian Academy of Fine Arts.

~ PART IV ~

The Twelve-Tone Method

Today I have discovered something which will insure the superiority of German music for the next hundred years.

Arnold Schoenberg

~ 8 ~

Interruptions

Between the years 1915 and 1923, Schoenberg published no new works. Since the works that followed this hiatus showed Schoenberg's preoccupation with his new twelve-tone method, it can be assumed that part of this time was taken up with theoretical speculations, as well as with work on the *Jakobsleiter*, which remained unfinished. Other projects as well as some personal difficulties also affected the composer's frame of mind.

Throughout the early years of this important period of his life, Schoenberg was involved in World War I, first as a soldier (from December 1915 to October 1916 and again in the fall of 1917), and later as a survivor. Along with most other Viennese, he was concerned with the problems of finding food and other necessities in a city impoverished by the collapse of the Austro-Hungarian economic network.

Immediately following the war, Schoenberg acquired more students, private as well as those connected with the Schwarzwald seminar. From 1918 until 1921, the Verein für musikalische Privataufführungen demanded vast amounts of both Schoenberg's time and that of others in his circle, so much, in fact, that for some it became a full-time occupation. From the fall of 1920 until the spring of 1921, Schoenberg was in Holland.

173

In addition to these activities, Schoenberg had certain domestic difficulties during this period which may have influenced his ability to work well. In 1906 his friend and teacher Alexander von Zemlinsky[B] introduced him to the painter Richard Gerstl[B]. Gerstl lived in the same house with the Schoenberg family during the summers of 1907 and 1908. It was probably Gerstl who aroused Schoenberg's interest in painting and who taught him the fundamentals of the art. Although Gerstl felt great affection for Schoenberg, he became romantically involved with Mathilde Schoenberg, Zemlinsky's sister and Schoenberg's wife since 1901. Mrs. Schoenberg moved out to live with the painter but was eventually convinced by friends of Schoenberg to return to her family. This painful affair ended with Gerstl's flamboyant suicide on 7 November 1908.[1]

Although Mathilde Schoenberg returned to Schoenberg, she is consistently described as silent and inactive by visitors to the Schoenberg house after that time. She died in 1923, following a long illness, in a sanatorium outside of Vienna.

It is easy to imagine that a man with Schoenberg's degree of self-absorption did not find his domestic difficulties easy to handle. The confirmed betrayal by two of those closest to him must have contributed, along with the violent rejection of his work, to the suspicious trait of character often remarked by his students and friends. In the years following Gerstl's suicide, Schoenberg at least once considered suicide himself. In a will that he wrote at that time, he described his regrets about his prospective suicide.

> I would have liked it if what I will leave behind appeared richer. Richer in number of works and achievements, more richly developed and deeper of meaning and intention. I would have liked to have left the world one or another additional idea; still more, I would have preferred to plead for it, to represent it, to fight for it. I would have liked to do myself what my disciples will do. I would also have liked—I cannot deny it—to have reaped the fame for it.[2]

After the death of Mathilde Schoenberg, Schoenberg's daughter Trudi and son-in-law Felix Greissle lived with him for a while. According to Eberhard Freitag, Schoenberg smoked sixty cigarettes a day, drank three liters of black coffee, much liquor, and took codeine and "pantopon."[*3] The situation became impossible for the Greissles who soon moved back to their own apartment.

(Felix Greissle) After his first wife died, and when he felt very lonely, my wife and I offered him to live with him, which we did, for a couple of months, you see; it was very, very difficult. We used to have fights almost every day about really minor matters, you see, and so one day, it was impossible to live further with him. We packed and moved out into our apartment which we still had, you see; so with the child, which was about 1½ year old, and which Schoenberg loved very much, but it was a boy, and we moved out, and it was . . . we didn't talk—nothing we left, you see, and said goodbye, and he nodded. . . . The same day, at night at nine o'clock—I lived on the second floor close to the street—somebody threw pebbles on my window. I opened the window and down there was Schoenberg. He said very meekly, "May I come up?" So I said, "Oh, please do come up by all means." And he came up, he apologized, and he said, "I'm sorry, you are of course absolutely right, you cannot live with me, that's impossible, the whole situation is impossible but, of course, we can come to each other, you see, and I'm over the worst."[4]

Schoenberg's mental outlook soon improved, and less than a year later, he married Rudolf Kolisch's sister Gertrud Kolisch.

Schoenberg's involvement with painting was greatest between the years 1907 and 1912, when eighty paintings were produced, although he continued a lively interest in graphic works until at least 1936. In October of 1910

[*]"Pantopon" is a purified, concentrated form of opium.

Schoenberg had an exhibit of his paintings at Hugo Heller's[B] Art Gallery and Bookshop. This exhibit included forty-one portraits and studies. At the opening, the Rosé Quartet played the first and second Schoenberg quartets. The critical response to Schoenberg the painter was similar to that of Schoenberg the composer, and the exhibit was not a public success. Although even some of Schoenberg's own associates were surprised that he would make a formal display of what had seemed to be a hobby, the quality and subject matter of Schoenberg's paintings, despite his primitive technique, are uniquely his and reveal an ambition of expression beyond that usually associated with the Sunday painter.

In Vienna, between 1904 and 1910, Schoenberg had the opportunity to view works by Van Gogh, Munch, and later Kokoschka, as well as those works produced in the Secession. In 1910 he met Kandinsky. He became involved in the *Blaue Reiter* group which was formed in Munich in December of 1911. Kandinsky was somewhat influenced by Schoenberg's theoretical writings and impressed by his paintings. Schoenberg exhibited in the *Blaue Reiter* exhibition which opened 18 December 1911. Two paintings, a song, and an article, together with songs by Berg and Webern, appeared in *Der Blaue Reiter,* an almanac published by the group in mid-May of 1912.[5] Schoenberg was later invited by Kandinsky to join the Bauhaus but declined. His reason was real or imagined anti-Semitism,[6] but it would be difficult to imagine Schoenberg abandoning his independence for an environment with a communal atmosphere.

Schoenberg's beliefs about painting corresponded closely to those of both Kandinsky and Kokoschka, although the styles of the three differed sharply. Kokoschka, in his portraits painted before World War I, painted not the physical resemblance of the sitter but the sitter's personality as experienced by the painter. Kokoschka and Schoenberg too valued the inner voice over the external reality, in sharp contrast to the highly decorative styles of Klimt[B] and the Secession or of the Jugendstil. In an article published in 1912, Kandinsky wrote about Schoenberg's painting:

First of all, we see immediately that Schoenberg paints not in order to paint something "beautiful" or "engaging," but that he paints without even thinking about the painting itself. Renouncing the objective result, he seeks to affix only his subjective feelings, and uses for that purpose only the means which seem to him indispensable at that moment. Not every professional artist can lay claim to this mode of creativity! . . .

We see that in every painting of Schoenberg, the inner wish of the artist speaks in the form which best befits it. Just as with his music, (inasmuch as I a layman may affirm), Schoenberg also in his painting renounces the superfluous, (therefore the harmful) and proceeds along a direct path to the essential, (therefore to the necessary). He leaves alone, unnoticed, all embellishments and artistic detail.[7]

Schoenberg himself took an independent view of his painting. Acknowledging himself an amateur technically, he nonetheless felt his painting to spring from the same source as his musical urges:

I planned to tell you what painting meant—means—to me. In fact, it was the same to me as making music. It was to me a way of expressing myself, of presenting emotions, ideas, and other feelings; and this is perhaps the way to understand these paintings—or not to understand them.[8]

Although in his later years Schoenberg seemed willing to recollect his discussions with Gerstl, with typical defensiveness, he denied any outside contemporary influence upon his work. In an essay of 1938, he made his position abundantly clear:

If one compares my pictures with those of Kokoschka one has to recognize forthwith their complete independence. I painted "Gazes," which I have already painted elsewhere. This is something which *only I* could have done, for it is out of my own nature and is completely contrary to the nature of a real painter. I never saw faces but, because I looked into peoples' eyes, only their "gazes." This is the reason why I can imitate the gaze of a person. A painter, however, grasps with one look the whole person—I, only his soul. . . .

However, if one thinks of this certain Mr. Gerstl then the matter stands thus. . . . In many conversations about art, music and sundry things I wasted many thoughts on him as on everybody else who wanted to listen. Probably this had confirmed him in his, at that time, rather tame radicalism to such a degree, that when he saw some quite miscarried attempts of mine, he took their miserable appearance to be *intentional* and exclaimed: "Now I have learned from you how one has to paint." I believe that Webern will be able to confirm this.[9]

These then are some things that affected Schoenberg's life during the years preceding the inception of the twelve-tone method. Although the method itself arose from a compositional necessity, it seems evident that the creative urge behind it for always greater clarity was related to Schoenberg's involvement in other areas—his painting, and especially his associations with Karl Kraus and Adolf Loos. Schoenberg's trip to Amsterdam and his preoccupation during this period first with painting, then the war, and later with the Society for Private Musical Performances would make a break in his compositional production not surprising. His ability to manage a major intellectual effort at this time sets him apart as a person of extraordinary energy and concentration.

Of the people who knew Schoenberg during the time of his friendship with Gerstl and afterward, Felix Greissle, the son-in-law of Schoenberg, was the most intimately knowledgeable about this period in Schoenberg's life. An intelligent man with a fine sense of humor, Greissle talked easily about his views of his famous relative, feeling it important that Schoenberg should be understood as a human being and not only as a great musical innovator. The other people interviewed saw Mathilde Schoenberg either in a more formal social setting, as did Kokoschka, or after this time, in the cases of Kolisch, Pisk, and Deutsch.

JOAN ALLEN SMITH: What did you think of Schoenberg's paintings?

OSKAR KOKOSCHKA: That was my influence of course. You knew that. He started after my exhibition and he'd seen it. It was good, it was true. Our opinion was that everybody could paint if he just—if he tried to produce what he sees. At that time, painting was quite different. It was like today—the school, you had to belong to a certain fashion. . . . I didn't belong. What I did at that time was so offensive because I painted what I saw, in my naïve way if you want. And Schoenberg, affected by it, did the same—what he saw.

SMITH: Why did Schoenberg paint? I know that he exhibited in the *Blaue Reiter* exhibit—did he consider his work worth exhibiting?

RUDOLF KOLISCH: Oh no. . . . I don't know how that came about. . . . The experts found it very interesting it seems. But he probably didn't expect that.

SMITH: Did he have much to do with Kokoschka?

KOLISCH: I don't think that one could say that he had much to do with any—no. But they did know each other.

SMITH: Was he closer to Loos than to Kokoschka?

KOLISCH: Oh, ja. Definitely so.

KOKOSCHKA: [About painting Schoenberg] And his wife, the Hungarian or whatever she was, sitting, and there was such a warm atmosphere. She was like a peasant woman. And I think very intelligent, although she didn't talk. And there was a—it was I think during winter. I remember it was very cold and I felt frozen, and I find his warm room there and the woman [Mathilde] not fat but . . . like an oven, expanding warmth to us. . . .

SMITH: When you painted Schoenberg, was he actually playing?

KOKOSCHKA: Yes, and like the painting of Casals here, also in that case, the cello was bigger than, taller than the man behind it.

FELIX GREISSLE: Schoenberg was not a painter. He painted for entirely different reasons. It's a very private matter. And when this didn't exist anymore, he didn't paint anymore. . . . I find that Schoenberg was very much overrated; he didn't have enough talent. I know it because I was a painter before I became a musician, and I knew very well all the things he was lacking. . . . This self-portrait where he was walking from behind is fantastic, because he really had exactly—he knew himself from behind. I don't know how he did it. If he would have been able to paint, this would have been an enormous painting. This way, it lacks a lot of things to bring the idea really out, you see. . . . Please don't misunderstand me. The ideas were enormous he had for painting; he didn't have the technique.

PAUL PISK: In his domestic habits, Schoenberg was so conservative—not the artistic temperament—regular meals, and his house cooled down, and the shoes off—not the artistic type but really like Richard Strauss. Schoenberg didn't play cards, but Strauss had to have his afternoon coffee and playing the cards or he wasn't happy.

GREISSLE: There was the Second Quartet, which was dedicated to his first wife,* and after she died—while she was very sick, we were outside Vienna. A friend of ours

---

*An interesting dedication since it was written around 1907 and 1908 during the Gerstl affair. Joan Peyser quotes Theodor Adorno as saying that the second quartet was an "echo of a crisis in personal life whose sorrow, hardly ever mastered, brought to Schoenberg's work its full creative weight." Joan Peyser, *The New Music: The Sense behind the Sound* (New York: Dell, 1971), p. 23.

had a house in Vienna, a big house, and invited the whole family to be near the sanatorium where Mrs. Schoenberg was. . . . So, we lived there really, you know. It became a home, a very sad home. And after she had died, Schoenberg in gratitude gave to the friend the manuscript of the second quartet.

MAX DEUTSCH: The point you want to know now, why Schoenberg did not publish between 1918, something like that, and 1923. But because he [had] too many things to do, it was not a possibility to have really an existence. Very poor—and Webern, very poor. Me, I was an Austrian official. I had my money paid by the government, so I was the most rich man of all.

SMITH: Do you have any idea why Schoenberg composed so little during the years 1918 to 1921?

MARCEL DICK: Yes. Well, working on the twelve-tone. He had difficulties making ends meet and all that, but that is not the reason why. They were perhaps the most productive years of his life.

SMITH: Did he say at this time that he was working on anything special or did he just more or less withdraw?

DICK: There was a mystery about him. He lived at that time in Mödling, and I always envisaged Schoenberg inside a house and there were the two sentinels Webern and Berg watching outside the house that nobody nears it. No, that was in his own privacy—completely withdrawn from everything, except he was interested in the preparation of performances—the Schoenberg Verein.

Notes

1. Joan Peyser, *The New Music: The Sense behind the Sound* (New York: Dell, 1971), pp. 23–25.
2. Quoted in Ernst Hilmar, ed., *Arnold Schönberg, Gedenkausstellung 1974* (Vienna: Universal Edition, 1974), p. 202.
3. Eberhard Freitag, *Arnold Schönberg, in Selbstzeugnissen*

und Bilddokumenten (Reinbeck bei Hamburg: Rowohlt Taschen-buch Verlag, 1973), p. 115.

4. Interview with Hans Keller for the BBC, 4 November 1965.

5. Wassily Kandinsky and Franz Marc, eds., *Der Blaue Reiter* (Munich: R. Piper und Co. Verlag, 1912; reprint ed., 1965). English edition, *The Blaue Reiter Almanac,* ed. Klaus Lankheit, trans. H. Falkenstein, M. Terzian, and G. Hinderlie (New York: Viking Press, 1974).

6. See letters from Schoenberg to Kandinsky of 20 April and 4 May 1923 in Arnold Schoenberg, *Letters,* ed. Erwin Stein, trans. Eithne Wilkins and Ernst Kaiser (New York: St. Martin's Press, 1965), pp. 88–93. Also Jelena Halh-Koch, ed., *Arnold Schönberg— Wassily Kandinsky: Briefe, Bilder und Dokumente einer aussergewöhnlichen Begegnung* (Salzburg: Residenz Verlag, 1980).

7. Wassily Kandinsky, "The Paintings of Schoenberg," trans. Barbara Zeisl, *Journal of the Arnold Schoenberg Institute* 2 (June 1978):182–184. The elimination of ornament was of course a common theme of the period. See Adolf Loos, "Ornament und verbrechen," in *Trotzdem: 1900–1930,* ed. Adolf Opel (Vienna: Georg Prachner Verlag, 1982), pp. 78–88.

8. "Schoenberg Interview with Halsey Stevens," Columbia Masterworks Recordings M2L 309/M2S 709. Text reprinted as "Schoenberg Talks about His Paintings," in Hilmar, ed., *Arnold Schönberg,* pp. 109–110; and as "A Conversation with Schoenberg about Painting," *Journal of the Arnold Schoenberg Institute* 2 (June 1978):179.

9. Arnold Schoenberg, "Painting Influences," trans. Gertrud Zeisl *Journal of the Arnold Schoenberg Institute* 2 (June 1978):237–238.

❧ 9 ❧

The Twelve-Tone Method

The method of composing with twelve tones
grew out of a necessity.

Arnold Schoenberg[1]

Several Viennese composers outside of the Schoenberg
circle were concerned with repeated pitch structures and
some even with the concept of chromatic completion (the
structurally geared use of all twelve pitch classes) coinci-
dentally with Schoenberg. However, the idea of an ordering
within the twelve-tone set, and the application of the four
systematic operations of transposition, inversion, retrogression, and retrograde-inversion, which brought about a musically constructive method for twelve-tone composition, were
Schoenberg's alone. They did not come to him in a single
insight but rather developed slowly over a number of years.[*]

---

[*]Technical discussion of the twelve-tone method is not within the scope
of this study. Modern twelve-tone theory has in its formulation of the
properties of the system gone far beyond Schoenberg's understanding

183

The composer probably most concerned, besides Schoenberg, with finding a substitute for the long-range structural functions of tonal harmony was Anton Webern. Of all of Schoenberg's pupils, he was the most noticeably experimental, and in many ways Webern seemed musically less tied to the past and more willing than Schoenberg himself to carry theoretical ideas to their logical extreme. However, it was always Schoenberg who saw the far-reaching implications of compositional trends, and it was Berg, of the three most closely tied to past ideas, who many years later performed the feat of adapting the twelve-tone method to his tonally oriented style while still expanding the limits of the method far beyond Webern's rather conventional serial techniques.

Recalling the developmental period, from about 1906 to 1923, Webern, in "The Path to Twelve-Note Composition,"[2] and Schoenberg, in various sources, remember many of the same points as being important.

> (Webern) In 1906, Schoenberg came back from a stay in the country, bringing the Chamber Symphony. It made a colossal impression. I'd been his pupil for three years, and immediately felt "You must write something like that, too!" Under the influence of the work I wrote a sonata movement the very next day. In that movement I reached the farthest limits of tonality.[3]

> (Schoenberg) Fall 1906 Webern returned from vacation, sees Chamber Symphony (written Rottach-Egern), says had thought about how modern music should look. Sees Chamber Symphony fulfills that idea.

> 1907 new style. Told Webern about short pieces. One of the piano pieces should consist of only 3–4 measures.

---

of its possibilities. This theoretical work, by Milton Babbitt, Allen Forte, and others, while of extreme importance for a clear understanding of set-theoretical properties, is not strictly relevant to a study of the twelve-tone method which aims to illuminate its historical development rather than its compositional possibilities. For those who wish to delve further into the truly fascinating properties of the twelve-tone method, a section dealing with such technical matters has been included in the bibliography.

Webern starts writing shorter and shorter pieces. Follows all my developments. Always tries to surpass everything (exaggerates).[4]

(Webern) What happened? I can only relate something from my own experience; about 1911 I wrote the "Bagatelles for String Quartet" (Opus 9), all very short pieces, lasting a couple of minutes—perhaps the shortest music so far. Here I had the feeling, "When all twelve notes have gone by, the piece is over." Much later I discovered that all this was a part of the necessary development.[5]

The Bagatelles for String Quartet, in common with other Webern works of the period, are significant in that they serve as a bridge between the earlier atonal music and that of the twelve-tone period. In these works, concern for a twelve-pitch organization is already evident. Many pieces (in the Bagatelles, all except the fifth piece) begin with a statement of the chromatic collection, without repetition of pitches. Although the remainder of the piece can often be divided into statements of this collection that roughly correspond to phrasing, these divisions contain numerous repeated pitches. The collection is always unordered, and most significant, it does not constitute the primary structural stratagem of the piece. This continues to focus upon the factors characteristic of earlier atonal works. As is interesting to note, with regard to Webern's feeling that "when all twelve notes have gone by, the piece is over," the introductory presentation of the chromatic collection is sometimes quite different from what follows; sometimes it is set off as an introduction, and often there is a quality of display about it. When the score reverts to the old motivic way of doing things, it is easy to speculate that Webern simply didn't know what else to do. Schoenberg described this and related problems in an essay, "Composition with Twelve Tones (1)":

The first compositions in this new style were written by me around 1908 and, soon afterwards, by my pupils, Anton von Webern and Alban Berg. From the very beginning such compositions differed from all preceding music, not only harmonically but also melodically, thematically, and motivally. But the foremost characteristics of these pieces *in statu nascendi* were their extreme brevity. At that time, neither I nor my pupils were conscious of the reasons for these features. Later I discovered that our sense of form was right when it forced us to counterbalance extreme emotionality with extraordinary shortness. Thus, subconsciously, consequences were drawn from an innovation which, like every innovation, destroys while it produces. New colourful harmony was offered; but much was lost.

Formerly the harmony had served not only as a source of beauty, but, more important, as a means of distinguishing the features of the form. For instance, only a consonance was considered suitable for an ending. Establishing functions demanded different successions of harmonies than roving functions; a bridge, a transition, demanded other successions than a codetta; harmonic variation could be executed intelligently and logically only with due consideration of the fundamental meaning of the harmonies. Fulfilment of all these functions—comparable to the effect of punctuation in the construction of sentences, of subdivision into paragraphs, and of fusion into chapters—could scarcely be assured with chords whose constructive values had not as yet been explored. Hence, it seemed at first impossible to compose pieces of complicated organization or of great length.

A little later I discovered how to construct larger forms by following a text or a poem.[6]

This problem was of course eventually solved by Schoenberg's four operations (transposition, inversion, retrograde, and retrograde-inversion). In fact, a principal contribution of these operations was that they allowed the piece to continue, and in so doing, made possible a revival of large-scale traditional forms.*

*Schoenberg, in his Wind Quintet, Op. 26 (1923–1924)—the first major twelve-tone work—employs the forms typical in the nineteenth century for large multimovement works: sonata, scherzo, ternary, and rondo. In other works of this period (the Piano Suite, Op. 25; and the Suite, Op. 29), however, he favors the dance and variation forms more characteristic of

In an essay published posthumously, Schoenberg relates his excitement about *Jakobsleiter:*

> Ever since 1906–8, when I had started writing composi-
> tions which led to the abandonment of tonality, I had been
> busy finding methods to replace the structural functions
> of harmony. Nevertheless, my first distinct step toward
> this goal occurred only in 1915. I had made plans for a
> great symphony of which *Die Jakobsleiter* should be the
> last movement. I had sketched many themes, among them
> one for a scherzo which consisted of all the twelve tones.†[7]

But in the manuscript notes, the competition with Webern comes through:

> 1914(15) I start a symphony. Wrote about it to Webern.
> Mention singing *without* words (Jakobsleiter). Mention
> Scherzo theme including all 12 tones. After 1915, Webern
> seems to have used 12 tones in some of his composi-
> tions,—*without telling me.*
>
> Webern jealous about Berg. Had suggested to me to
> tell Berg he (in about 1908 or 9) should not work in the
> new style—he has no right to do it—it does not fit to his
> style—but it fitted to Webern's!!!
>
> Webern commited at this period (1908–1918) many
> acts of infidelity with the intention of making himself the
> innovator.[8]

---

the Baroque period. Whereas these latter forms are well-suited to the
concept of perpetual variation embraced by Schoenberg, and compatible
with the quasi-ostinato character of the twelve-tone set, the use of classical sonata form, traditionally associated with specifically tonal activities,
in a nontonal context raises serious issues beyond the scope of this work.
For Adorno's views on this problem, see Theodor W. Adorno, *Philosophy
of Modern Music,* trans. Anne G. Mitchell and Wesley V. Blomster (New
York: Seabury Press, 1973), pp. 96–99.

†It is clear from the Webern-Berg correspondence that both composers
saw *Die Jakobsleiter* while Schoenberg was working on it. See especially letters from Webern to Berg of 1 July and 12 July 1917. Although
Webern was estranged from Schoenberg for three months during the fall
of 1918, prior to that time he saw Schoenberg frequently.

The gradual move toward a twelve-tone composition seems to have gone on steadily with both composers. Webern described one of his Goethe songs, "Gleich und Gleich," from 1916, as follows:

> My Goethe song, "Gleich und Gleich" (Four Songs Op. 12, No. 4, composed in 1917) begins as follows: G sharp–A–D sharp–G, then a chord E–C–B flat–D, then F sharp–B–F–C sharp. That makes twelve notes: none is repeated. At that time we were not conscious of the law, but had been sensing it for a long time. One day Schoenberg intuitively discovered the law that underlies twelve-note composition. An inevitable development of this law was that one gave the succession of twelve notes a *particular order.*[9]

Webern begins this piece, as he describes, with a statement of the chromatic collection partitioned into tetrachords. The remainder of the piece is divisible into sections in which the entire collection is in most cases represented. These sections correspond largely to the phrase divisions of the piece. It is the tetrachordal division, however, rather than the twelve-tone nature of it, that evokes the motivic material of the piece, and it is clear that at this point (1916) Webern had no idea of twelve-tone ordering as an organizational means for nontonal music.

Theodor Adorno suggests a problem of Webern's abbreviated works which begins to be solved in the Opus 12 songs:

> With the Songs Op. 12 an almost unnoticeable change begins. Webern's music secretly expands: in his own way he is mastering the solution which Schoenberg first displayed in *Pierrot lunaire* and the Songs Op. 22: that one cannot persist with the method of absolute purity [clarity] without music being spiritually reduced to physical deterioration. The new expansion is only hinted at; the first and last of the songs are still aphoristically short, but they do breathe a little, and the two middle songs . . . have well developed vocal lines, though certainly of a subtle character in which the earlier process of splitting-up is still maintained.[10]

This point is reminiscent of certain issues suggested by Adolf Loos:

> Twenty-six years ago I maintained that ornament would disappear from articles of use as man develops. . . . But I never meant that decoration should be ruthlessly and systematically done away with. . . . Only when time has made it disappear, can it never be applied again. Just as man will never go back to tattooing his face.[11]

Loos believed that absence of decoration was a sign of cultural advancement. A strong believer in the reflection by art of its time, he did not himself eliminate all decoration from his own work. Even in cases where the beauty of his materials was itself decorative, he employed carving to accent the line of a chest or friezes to outline the top of a wall. But for Webern, the situation was somewhat different. Music, unlike architecture, usually lacks external function, and Webern, in perhaps going too far in the direction of clarity, endangered that essential filigree which, although in the foreground of musical structure, is nonetheless an inherent, essential aspect of its character. There is a point at which, in music and the painterly arts, too much clarity jeopardizes depth of expression.

The law that until all twelve pitch classes have occurred none may be repeated—a law essential to twelve-tone structure in that it creates a contextual framework within which repetition may occur—is described by Schoenberg in his same manuscript notes:

> [1921] Found out that the greater distance between a tone and its repetition can be produced if 12 tones lie between. Started 12-tone composition. Told Erwin Stein[B] I had now a way I wanted to keep secret from all my imitators, because I am annoyed by them: I even do not know any more what is mine and what is their's [sic].[12]

Between 1920 and the meeting of 1923, in which he revealed the method to his students, Schoenberg worked out the several consequences of ordering all twelve pitch classes and incorporated his findings into several pieces.

In the Five Piano Pieces, Op. 23; the Serenade, Op. 24; and the Piano Suite, Op. 25, Schoenberg experimented with various aspects of what was to be the method long before the twelve-tone method itself crystallized. George Perle has succinctly described the complex interrelationships of these pieces:

> In Opus 23, No. 1, pitch or pitch-class order is exploited as a separable referential component, as it is to some degree in Schoenberg's earlier atonal compositions, but far more pronouncedly and extensively. The pitch and pitch-class order of the initial melodic figure in the second number of the same opus is so pervasive that one may already speak of it as an ordered set, but it is not the only source of pitch-class relations. Both movements were completed in July, 1920. Around the same time Schoenberg commenced the Variations movement of Opus 24, the earliest example of an entire movement exclusively based on a totally ordered—though not yet twelve-tone—series. The first consistently twelve-tone piece, Opus 25, No. 1, was composed in July of the following year.[13]

Perle goes on to call our attention to an important sketch for a twelve-tone "passacaglia," dated 5 March 1920, four months prior to any of the works described above, which already contains a chart from an all-combinatorial* twelve-tone set:

> In the compositional sketches the row does not serve merely as a special sort of "theme," as in the passacaglia on a twelve-tone row in the first act (completed in the previous summer) of *Wozzeck.* Every harmonic and melodic element participates in the unfolding of one or another serially generated hexachord. The idea of a twelve-tone

---

*A technical term referring to those sets in which, under some transposition and some inversion, the hexichordal pitch-class content of the original form of the set is preserved.

system, in which every pitch component is derived from an ordered twelve-tone series, was thus already formulated in these sketches, before Schoenberg had taken the first step along the irregular path he followed for almost three years before definitively arriving at the same result with his resumption of the composition of Opus 25.[14]

The first totally twelve-tone work of some length was the Wind Quintet, composed in 1923 and 1924. Schoenberg has described the freedom provided by his method:

> The construction of a basic set of twelve tones derives from the intention to postpone the repetition of every tone as long as possible. . . .
>
> The other function is the unifying effect of the set. Through the necessity of using besides the basic set, its retrograde, its inversion, and its retrograde inversion, the repetition of tones will occur oftener than expected. But every tone appears always in the neighbourhood of two other tones in an unchanging combination which produces an intimate relationship most similar to the relationship of a third and a fifth to its root. It is, of course, a mere relation, but its recurrence can produce psychological effects of a great resemblance to those closer relations.
>
> Such features will appear in every motif, in every theme, in every melody and, though rhythm and phrasing might make it distinctly another melody, it will still have some relationship with all the rest. The unification is here also the result of the relation to a common factor.[15]

The implications of the twelve-tone method were most completely understood by Schoenberg's more intellectual students. Max Deutsch and Felix Greissle, who both taught the method for many years, and Erwin Ratz, who was a scholar, all knew Schoenberg's music intimately and could follow his musical development in great detail. Their knowledge of the twelve-tone method is organic and invaluable. Humphrey Searle, a pupil of Webern rather than Schoenberg, came to Vienna after Schoenberg had already moved to the United States but had the opportunity to observe

Webern's compositional technique. Of the performers included in this chapter, those of the Kolisch Quartet, especially Rudolf Kolisch, engaged in exhaustive analytical
labors and therefore had an intimate acquaintance with the
method. Their concerns focus upon the interpretive problems of twelve-tone music.

EUGEN LEHNER: I don't know who coined the phrase "It's
not the answer that matters but the right question is
what matters." But I would really, if nobody else claims
the authorship, then I would rather attribute it to
Schoenberg. That was what Schoenberg was about—to
find the right question, not the answer. He was not
interested in the answer but the question he was interested in. And that's the reason he would not supply an
answer if somebody asked about something he did,
because, "That's your worry." So, I would say, I wish
nobody would claim it so that I can attribute it to
Schoenberg. . . . And that was the essence of Schoenberg as intellectual, as the egghead. And that's the reason, whatever he heard, whatever snatch remark, he
worked on it. It bothered him and occupied him until he
could formulate the right proof.

OSKAR KOKOSCHKA: Webern was an outspoken puritan. He
reduced even what he learned from Schoenberg.
Schoenberg was already reducing the material to the
essential, but he—in just five sounds, he wrote music.
He gave what Schoenberg wanted. . . . Schoenberg
wanted to reduce [to] the essentials.

MAX DEUTSCH: You have some pages in the *Harmonielehre*
where you can find he was under the impression to find
out something very exceptional. When he wrote *Jakobsleiter* . . . for the first time in the history of music, you
have a chord with twelve tones—all the twelve tones are
in it. . . . * That was the first moment he had the twelve

---

*Twelve-note chords were in fact written before *Die Jakobsleiter*. A
good example is the extended twelve-note chord with constantly varying
scoring that opens the third song of Berg's *Altenberg Lieder*.

tones together. You have a kind of discord in *Erwartung.* You have it too in *Glückliche Hand,* but not in this way. I mean, . . . without the octave and not doubled. For the first time in this place in *Jakobsleiter.*

LEHNER: *Pierrot lunaire* as a twelve-tone piece. In other words, it's so close to it—to total organization—that it is just one step off it, and why should we believe that Schoenberg, with his incredibly keen intellect and his superhuman sense of curiosity, was not aware of that? Certainly he formulated, "What makes music get away from a tonal center? Obviously, the equal importance of all the notes, so there is no tonal center and no more gravitating force.". . . Of course, if we could consciously force our whole musical thinking [so] that this balance is kept perfect, no predominance of any single note which could possibly exert a gravitation, then that would be the ideal of atonal music. . . . Then, of course, we must organize it so that there is a perfect balance— take care that no note happens more often before the other notes are out. So therefore,— . . . remember that's a conjecture on my part—the idea of the twelve-tone must have been born [at] this moment when he realized what makes music lose tonality, the tonal effects. And the next step was probably a conscious step: if the equality of the existing twelve notes in our Western system brings that, then we must organize it so that we make sure that there is no tonal center. And indeed, if I could accept my own supposition, and if you go through such a piece . . . like the Wind Quintet, then you will see how true it is. But then, fortunately for posterity, this phase didn't last, because Schoenberg was the same naïve, inspired artist like all the great composers were. So, fortunately, . . . no matter what his intention was, when he sat down and the inspiration came, he was just writing music, very much to his astonishment, because it always turned out differently than what he expected.*

---

*LEHNER: As I was saying, Christmas night celebration and we were everybody . . . terribly happy and rather alcoholized, and at one moment Kolisch's wife was teasing him [Schoenberg], "Ah, you with your big

Schoenberg might have continued to keep his secret had it not been for the publications of another composer, Josef Matthias Hauer[B]. Hauer, who began writing a kind of twelve-tone music around 1908, organized the possible combinations of the twelve pitch classes into groups, called *Tropen*, which formed the material for the composition. Hauer began publishing articles about this method in 1919.[16] Schoenberg did not like to read articles and seems not to have read these until several years later, although some of his students, including Kolisch, had seen the articles. He himself had met Hauer through Adolf Loos. It was the fear that he would be considered a follower of Hauer and not himself the originator of the twelve-tone method which prompted him to announce the method publicly. Schoenberg's attitude toward Hauer varied but was always formal and courteous.[17] Although Hauer was more a theoretic realizer than a composer, several of his pieces were performed in concerts of the Verein für musikalische Privataufführungen.

In June of 1921, the Verein held a competition for chamber music works. The judges for this event were listed as Schoenberg, Berg, Webern, Stein, and Steuermann, although it is doubtful that Schoenberg and Stein actually took part in the deliberations, being away from Vienna for the entire summer. Fritz Heinrich Klein[B], a pupil of Berg, entered under a pseudonym a piece entitled *Die Maschine: Eine extonale Selbstsatire*, a work that experimented with various unusual twentieth-century compositional techniques; these were itemized on the title page of the piece:

---

theories and the twelve-tone and so, you just write so because you couldn't write anything tonal—I bet you couldn't make a modulation even!" So Schoenberg, "Who says I could not modulate?" So we went to the piano. "Look, where shall I move and from where?" So I don't know what she thought up . . . and so Schoenberg made a few attempts and finally heated up, "How the hell shall I make a modulation if I am not inspired?"

This work contains:
1) A twelve-beat "rhythmic theme";
2) A twelve-different-note "pattern theme";
3) a twelve-different-interval "interval theme";
4) a "neutral scale" constructed from alternating minor and major seconds;
5) a "combination theme" constructed from nos. 2, 3, and 4;
6) the largest chord in music: the "mother chord" consisting of twelve different pitches and also twelve different intervals, derived from the "pyramid chord" (twelve intervals arranged according to size);
7) the "mirror construction" and the "clef register" of a theme, as well as its "systematic symmetry," and
8) the mathematical-contrapuntal development of ideas 1 to 7.[18]

This piece, which utilized a kind of chromatic completion including the all-interval set discovered by Klein and used by Berg in his first twelve-tone works, "Schliesse mir die Augen beide" and the *Lyric Suite*,[19] eventually won the competition. It thus seems unlikely that Schoenberg would not have seen the piece. A copy of the score containing the following inscription was found in Schoenberg's library:

It is the same Machine which found itself (as a score for chamber orchestra) in the summer of 1921 in your beloved hands, on the occasion of the competition of the Society f. P. M. P. . . .

Beneath this, Schoenberg added the following note:

Not correct. In Webern's hands, who told me about it but was not able to interest me in it. I doubt if I had this in my hands, but more especially that I looked at it, and certainly that I knew what it represented.

In any case, he has fundamentally nothing in common with twelve-tone composition: a compositional means

which had its discrete precursor in "working with tones,"[*]
which I used for two or three years without discovering
the twelve as the ultimate necessity.[20]

Schoenberg's concern to prove the twelve-tone method
entirely the necessary and inevitable consequence of his
own musical development[†] and so irrevocably tied to histori-

---

[*]In a letter in English to Nicolas Slonimsky dated 3 June 1937, Schoenberg described what he meant by "working [or "composing"] with tones":

> After that [1915] I was always occupied with the aim to base the
> structure of my music *consciously* on a unifying idea, which pro-
> duced not only all the other ideas but regulated also their
> accompaniment and the chords, the "harmonies." There were
> many attempts to achieve that. But very little of it was finished
> or published.
>   As an example of such attempts I may mention the piano
> pieces Op. 23. Here I arrived at a technique which I called (for
> myself) "composing with tones," a very vague term, but it meant
> something to me. Namely: in contrast to the ordinary way of
> using a motive, I used it already almost in the manner of a "basic
> set of twelve tones." I built other motives and themes from it, and
> also accompaniments and other chords—but the theme did not
> consist of twelve tones. Another example of this kind of aim for
> unity is my *Serenade.* In this work you can find many examples
> of this kind. But the best one is the "Variationen," the third
> movement. The theme consists of a succession of fourteen tones,
> but only eleven different ones, and these fourteen tones are per-
> manently used in the whole movement.

Willi Reich, *Schoenberg: A Critical Biography*, trans. Leo Black (London:
Longman Group, 1971), p. 131.

[†]Schoenberg's touchiness on the subject of Klein's piece is further revealed by mention of it in the notes cited earlier:

> About 1919 or 1920 Berg brought me a composition of Klein. I
> think it was called "Musical Machine" and dealt with twelve
> tones. I did not pay much attention to it. It did not impress me as
> music and probably I was still unconscious of where to my own
> attempts might lead me. So forgot entirely having seen some-
> thing in twelve tones.

H. H. Stuckenschmidt, *Arnold Schoenberg: His Life, World and Work*,
trans. Humphrey Searle (New York: Schirmer Books, 1978), p. 443.

cal·context is not evidence that he was uninfluenced by this and other early twelve-tone or serial experiments. Schoenberg's highly developed curiosity and his tendency to impose himself upon the activities of his students and associates would in fact suggest the opposite. There is no reason to believe that Schoenberg's own eventual method was not influenced by the work of those around him, although such influence may have been unconscious. Schoenberg preferred to consider himself influenced by Mozart and other great composers of the past, a view attributable to his own sense of uniqueness and a necessity to set himself apart. Whatever the effects of these other early ventures, Schoenberg's method does indeed possess important features that go far beyond the developments discussed above and that were for Schoenberg himself of basic importance.

The aspects of twelve-tone writing that Schoenberg took most seriously—the concept of chromatic completion and the ordering of pitch classes within the set—are missing in Hauer's method. As Schoenberg described it:

> In using Hauer's *Tropen*, one could not even postpone the reappearance of a tone for as long as possible. Hauer mixes *Tropen*, that is sets of six tones, according to his own taste or feeling of form (which only he himself possesses); there is certainly no such function of logic as in the method described here.[21]

Although Schoenberg himself was not fully aware of the totality of implications inherent in his method either at the time of its inception or later, it is nevertheless true that the Schoenbergian twelve-tone idea embodies a richness of combinational and derivational possibilities related to its special properties that is unavailable in other similar but less refined approaches.[22]

In February of 1923, after learning about Hauer's publications, Schoenberg called together about twenty of his students and friends and explained to them his method of twelve-tone composition. Felix Greissle, who was present at the meeting, recalled it as follows:

He all of a sudden called all of his students and friends together, you see, and we had a meeting at which there were present Alban Berg, Anton Webern, Egon Wellesz[B], Steuermann[B], Erwin Stein[B], and many others, and there he began to develop the twelve-tone theory; in other words, he explained to us the four forms of the row, and he also showed us certain fragments he had composed this way— a piano piece, I remember . . . —we all tried to understand and I think we came pretty close to what he meant except there was one person who resisted—who resisted more by being silent and not saying anything, and that was Anton Webern. He was the one who resisted most. At one point, when Schoenberg said, "There I used the row transposition and transposed it into the tritone," so Webern said, "Why?" Schoenberg looked at him and said, "I don't know," and then Webern burst out, "Ah, ah!," because Webern was waiting for some intuitive sign in the whole matter and this was it, you see.[23]

Considering that Webern undoubtedly was already very aware of the ramifications of eliminating tonal structure and even of the concept of chromatic completion (although probably not of the structural possibilities of chromatic ordering), it is interesting that, according to Greissle, he more than Berg had difficulty in accepting the twelve-tone method as outlined in this initial meeting. It seems likely that it was the very concept of ordering within the set, together with the seemingly mechanical operations implied by that ordering, that caused Webern some concern. Only with familiarity and practice would it have been possible for the operations of the twelve-tone method, which must first have seemed so mathematical and artificial, to have been handled with the ease and custom of the often equally mechanical operations (such as modulation, progression, and cadence) that long use of the tonal system had by then made second nature. This view is supported by Schoenberg's recollection of the meeting:

In 1924 [actually 1923] I had become aware that Hauer had also written 12 tone music. Up to this time I had kept it a secret that I do it. But in order to make clear that I had not been influenced by Hauer, but had gone my own way, I called a meeting of all my students and friends where I explained this new method and the way which I had gone.

Curiously, when I had shown the four basic forms, Webern confessed that he had written also something in 12 tones (probably suggested by the scherzo of my symphony of 1915) and he said: "I never knew, what to do after the 12 tones" meaning that the 3 inversions now could follow and the transpositions.* One thing had become clear to all of them:

That the permanent use of only *one* 12-tone set in one work was something quite different from everything else others might have attempted. My way meant: *Unity*. My way derived from compositional necessities.[24]

Although Schoenberg explained the method to his pupils in this meeting, he did not especially encourage them to use it in their own compositions. (At the same time, he expected it from Berg and Webern.) He mentioned it rarely in lessons with his students and resisted talking about either the method or about his own compositions in front of them. This reticence could be explained by his strong reluctance to interfere with the direction of his pupils and by his conviction that the twelve-tone method arose out of historical necessity:

In the last hundred years, the concept of harmony has changed tremendously through the development of chromaticism. The idea that one basic tone, the root, dominated the construction of chords and regulated their succession—the concept of *tonality*—had to develop first into the concept of *extended tonality*. Very soon it became doubtful whether such a root still remained the centre to which every harmony and harmonic succession must be referred. Furthermore, it became doubtful whether a tonic appearing at the beginning, at the end, or at any other

*This is the problem outlined by Webern with reference to his Bagatelles for String Quartet.

point really had a constructive meaning. Richard Wagner's harmony had promoted a change in the logic and constructive power of harmony. One of its consequences was the so-called *impressionistic* use of harmonies, especially practised by Debussy. His harmonies, without constructive meaning, often served the colouristic purpose of expressing moods and pictures. Moods and pictures, though extra-musical, thus became constructive elements, incorporated in the musical functions; they produced a sort of emotional comprehensibility. In this way, tonality was already dethroned in practice, if not in theory. This alone would perhaps not have caused a radical change in compositional technique. However, such a change became necessary when there occurred simultaneously a development which ended in what I call the *emancipation of the dissonance.*[25]

Although Berg appears to have been less concerned than either Schoenberg or Webern with the compositional problems leading to the development of the twelve-tone method, it is possible that he was more intimately involved than was Webern in its beginnings. This alternative is suggested in a letter from Berg to his wife, dated 1 April 1923:

Schoenberg was very nice and once more very friendly to me. But alas at the expense of other friends who (according to him) whenever he talked about his achievements in musical theory would always say: "Yes, I've done that too." As he doesn't expect this sort of thing from me, he wants to show me all his secrets in his new works.[26]

It is not conclusively established by any textual evidence in the work of Berg that he was familiar with the details of twelve-tone composition before Schoenberg explained it to his followers. Although many passages in *Wozzeck* suggest an awareness of the concept of twelve-tone completion albeit within an otherwise tonalistic context, there is no indication that Berg was consistently attempting a substitution for the articulative possibilities of the tonal center. His experiment with the abbreviated style of Schoenberg's Opus 19 and many of Webern's pre-twelve-tone works was confined to the Clarinet Pieces, Op. 5, and the *Altenberg Lieder.** Even after taking up the twelve-tone method, Berg never completely abandoned tonal concepts, preferring instead to suit the twelve-tone method to his own tonally-enhanced ideas in a way that went far beyond Schoenberg's adaption of tonally associated formal structures to twelve-tone composition. In his use of the twelve-tone idea, Berg never strictly adhered to the Schoenbergian method, using more than one set in a composition (something not done by Schoenberg) and, especially in the case of *Lulu*, interpolating passages of material that cannot strictly be termed twelve-tone at all.

Schoenberg accepted Berg's independent use of the method:

> I have to admit that Alban Berg, who was perhaps the least orthodox of us three—Webern, Berg and I—in his operas mixed pieces or parts of pieces of a distinct tonality with those which were distinctly non-tonal. He explained this, apologetically, by contending that as an opera composer he could not, for reasons of dramatic expression and characterization, renounce the contrast furnished by a change from major to minor.
>
> Though he was right as a composer, he was wrong theoretically. I have proved in my operas *Von Heute auf Morgen* and *Moses und Aron* that every expression and characterization can be produced with the style of free dissonance.[27]

Berg may not have understood fully or cared about the theories motivating the genesis of the twelve-tone idea but rather adhered to it in his position of Schoenberg disciple or

---

*Berg would have learned of the four operations (transposition, inversion, retrograde, retrograde-inversion) from the February meeting before his use of them as a part of the large-scale formal structure in the Chamber Concerto. The Chamber Concerto predates Berg's own first strict twelve-tone writing.

for other, also personal, reasons. His adoption of the twelve-tone method at a time when he was at the height of his success as a composer was made possible through his great originality and compositional flexibility. Although the twelve-tone method may not have been adopted with the same urgent necessity by Berg as by Schoenberg and Webern, it is perhaps in Berg's music that the twelve-tone method is used in the most refined and original manner, even if the composer himself may not have come to it spontaneously and from necessity. Certainly, as a composer, Berg was very conscious of the need to remain independent of the opinions of his mentor, as he stated repeatedly in his correspondence. It seems unlikely that he would have embraced the twelve-tone method purely from a loyalty to Schoenberg if he in fact failed to appreciate its possibilities.

MAX DEUTSCH: You know the score of *Glückliche Hand?* That is the most important work of our century. The row technique is in it. So, . . . in 1923, when he came back from Amsterdam, he called us for [an] appointment for a meeting in Mödling, . . . in the Bernhardgasse 6 in Mödling. And he spoke the first words, . . ."I finally have found out that the new technique is the completion with twelve tones of the chromatic scale, but these twelve tones in interdependence from what"—that is, those were Schoenberg's words, and he added, "And with that, our music," he means Austrian music, "they have for fifty years the leadership." That was the words of Schoenberg. . . .

JOAN ALLEN SMITH: Before this time, had he said anything to you about it?

DEUTSCH: Never! . . . Nothing! 1923, he told it and he wrote it down. That is the truth!

SMITH: Who was at the meeting where Schoenberg disclosed the twelve-tone method?

FELIX GREISSLE: . . . [People] close to Schoenberg like Wellesz, who had at one time studied a little with

Schoenberg but then was not so close any more. . . .
Then [Oskar] Adler[B] was there. He was a friend of Schoenberg's youth—a doctor, a medical doctor—played the
viola marvelously, and he was at the same time very
much occupied with theosophy and astrology. He was a
very unusual man. He was there. . . . George Szell composed at that time, but he was not there. Szell was in the
other camp. Ja, Hauer, he was not on that day there, but
a little later, he invited Hauer on one Sunday and again
a lot of friends, and he said, you know, he and Hauer
had found from another side almost the same thing,
and he was very—and he acknowledged it very much.
He did it also, you see—he wouldn't have done it, it
would have looked bad, but if he did it openly and
friendly, it looked much better. Hauer behaved badly,
very badly. I never understood why he gave Hauer so
much importance, because Hauer was a very bad
composer—he was a terrible composer. . . .

SMITH: But Hauer did get the idea first, didn't he?

GREISSLE: Ja, he did it but it was absolutely—the genesis
was so different. It was put together almost mechani-
cally, you see, and with Schoenberg it was the result of
coming to it through composition—Hauer through
speculation. There was an enormous difference between
the two. . . . Hauer was—I found him mediocre, really
very stupid. You know, there is an excellent portrait of
Hauer. There's a novel by Werfel, *Verdi*, and in there, I
think in the fourth or fifth chapter, comes a German
composer who befriends Verdi, and this is a portrait of
Hauer—an excellent portrait of Hauer. I was there
when Hauer was invited by Mrs. Mahler[B], who was
married to Werfel at that time, and Hauer . . . started
immediately talking about twelve tone and he never
stopped. He wore everybody out. And Werfel was there
and he listened. . . . And he wrote and the portrait is
very good—better than almost anything else Werfel
ever did.

SMITH: Did you have any idea that Schoenberg was work-ing on something new before this meeting with the students?

ERWIN RATZ: Oh yes, he entertained ideas of it for many years. We see it in the works—what is the oratorio called?

SMITH: *Jakobsleiter.*

RATZ: Yes, yes. These ideas were already in preparation for a long time. It didn't happen overnight. Schoen-berg had for many years—already during the war he was occupied with these ideas. The real revelation was . . . 1923. . . .

SMITH: I wonder if Schoenberg ever talked about this new thing to you while he was thinking about it.

RATZ: No, he spoke first about it after it was completely worked out. After he [had written] his first compo-sition—that was the Suite, the Piano Suite, then he showed us the thing.

SMITH: At this meeting with the students, was everyone enthusiastic about it or did it seem very difficult?

RATZ: They really weren't students. There were—yes, I was also studying at the university at that time, but it was a matter of people who had a private interest. They had heard nothing about twelve tone. There was then the later circle of students, to some extent the older ones— there were Berg, Webern, Polnauer, and so forth.

SMITH: So then did he present this to you as something he had already thought out completely?

RUDOLF KOLISCH: Ja.

SMITH: Do you think he ever discussed his ideas with anyone during this period? It was all by himself? Not with Berg or Webern?

KOLISCH: No. In fact, it was only as a *fait accompli.* It was even presented in a very strange and solemn way. He called us all together, you know. It was Mödling. And he told us that he—but I don't know whether he called it—

probably not discovery or invention, but he said he had found something which would assure the hegemony of German music for centuries. . . . Ja. That is true. That he really said, but . . . it's very strange, no? Don't you find it strange? . . . The particular perspective of assuring that the—

SMITH: How did people react? Was everyone very excited in a positive way?

KOLISCH: Well, there was only the small circle of his, you know. All of us were of course very excited about it. None of us had any idea what it really was.

SMITH: Did everyone accept it immediately and start working on his own piece or were there people who were skeptical?

KOLISCH: Well, there was no model yet at this time. There was no model which to follow. Of course I knew already. I had been thinking about it because I was in touch with Hauer. Hauer showed me his tropes, you know?

SMITH: And this was independently that you were in touch with Hauer? Did you perform his music?

KOLISCH: Also I did—as much as one could call it—. It was really more demonstrations of the principle than music.

SMITH: Did Hauer himself consider them mere demonstrations or did he consider them important pieces?

KOLISCH: That is hard to say. Certainly important. He considered it important—very—completely convinced of— the importance of himself and of—and, in a way, it was important. But, whereas Schoenberg always emphasized the—what happened apart from this category, Hauer was completely absorbed in it. . . . The principle is the same, only Schoenberg composed music and used this—ja?—as a method of composition, whereas Hauer composed tropes—twelve-tone rows.

SMITH: Was Hauer at this meeting?

KOLISCH: No.

SMITH: He did meet with Schoenberg several times, didn't he?

KOLISCH: Oh yes. They were friends. . . . And Schoenberg took him completely seriously.

HANS CURJEL: I was in Donaueschingen, the music festival, in '24; there Schoenberg was playing his Serenade and in the same program was Hauer—not the same evening. And they met at Donaueschingen, and I remember there was a big discussion in a café . . . with Schoenberg and Hauer, and the atmosphere was not too friendly—was not at all too friendly.

SMITH: Do you remember what was said?

CURJEL: It was a discussion about how near Hauer and Schoenberg were, and everybody—Hauer said, "I am the inventor" and Schoenberg said, "I am the inventor."

SMITH: And they argued there in the café?

CURJEL: Yes, it was very lively. There were Schoenberg, Hauer, Hindemith, and a few people—two or three—and I.

GREISSLE: I think he must have made up his mind not to tell anybody. He had a reason later to do it. And the reason was that he—I told you that he didn't read any books about music and so on. But he came across an article of Hauer, and then he saw all of a sudden. So he invited all his pupils and friends, and he told us what twelve tone was. He explained it. We were in part puzzled and part surprised. I was not because I knew already that there was something, and even that it was twelve tone. And there were degrees of acceptance, and there was one who couldn't accept it so easily. Guess who?

SMITH: Perhaps Berg?

GREISSLE: No. Berg didn't have a hard time at all. Berg accepted it only in part, huh? He had a twelve-tone row and he made a, as he called it, a palette of colors. And he used it in different combinations, but he was not twelve-tone. Almost never twelve-tone with him.* No, Webern had a hard time—terribly hard time. . . .

SMITH: Do you think he accepted it because he decided eventually that it was the right thing to do?

GREISSLE: Ja. That it was the right thing to do. Oh, yes, of course, yes. Naturally. The only thing is that Webern did nothing of which he wasn't sure that Schoenberg would approve of it. Webern was never independent—his whole life, he wasn't independent. Wait a minute, from 1933 to 1938, ja. In 1933, Schoenberg left Germany and came to this country, and I lived very close to Webern. So I saw him almost every day, and I saw the dependence. I don't blame him for it, you know. I mean, still he was a great composer. Well let's say—I don't like to use the word "great" easily. He used to write Schoenberg in Los Angeles, and Schoenberg never answered letters very frequently, and the longer Webern would have to wait for an answer the more angry he got and the more things he found that weren't so bad about the Nazis and so on. And Schoenberg wrote a letter and he got the letter and everything was all right. . . . Webern was sometimes towards friends very open and his innermost thoughts would just spill out. But between thought and action is an enormous difference. And that was there, you see; he never would have done anything against Schoenberg. But he was hurt if Schoenberg didn't write him—he was deeply hurt because everything—his belief in himself depended on how Schoenberg [saw him]. . . . And of course, when he said something uncontrolled, it didn't mean that he actually thought it.

SMITH: Well, do you think that it would have been possible for Webern to decide against writing twelve-tone?

*Perusal of the sketches reveals that Berg was both imaginative and strict in his use of the twelve-tone method. Greissle is, however, correct in that Berg's music is often not totally twelve-tone, and his use of the method is not Schoenbergian in all respects.

GREISSLE: No, no, impossible! Totally impossible.

SMITH: Webern seems very remote to me. Was he that way in person? Was he very restrained?

KOLISCH: Ja, ja, he was that. He was even inhibited. But enormously strong—very strong person. . . .

SMITH: One of the impressions that I have definitely received is that he changed his mind frequently.

KOLISCH: Entirely wrong. . . . I know no other person who—who changed his mind so little. . . .

SMITH: Did Schoenberg appreciate Webern's work?

KOLISCH: Oh, ja.

SMITH: But Schoenberg was never influenced by what other people were composing. Do you believe that Webern was himself influenced much by Schoenberg?

KOLISCH: Well, completely. . . .

SMITH: Then how can you say that he was a strong person when he was so completely influenced?

KOLISCH: You see, he established his own orbit—ja?—around the planet. The planet was still in the center.

SMITH: Did Schoenberg ever discuss twelve-tone music?

RATZ: Well, you see, I was there when he gave his first lecture on twelve-tone music. He called his group of students together and said he would like to talk about these new principles. . . . Schoenberg always refused to do twelve-tone analyses. He said it was a purely technical matter which isn't anyone's business, and it certainly has nothing to do with art; it's as if someone wanted to develop a philosophy of C-major.

CLARA STEUERMANN: My husband told me that when the first performances of *Gurrelieder* were being prepared and a whole group of them traveled together, I forget which city it was, but they went together to hear the performance and to hear the rehearsals. And at one of the rehearsals—they were having difficulty at the time because this chorus in the last part, the voices were not finding their pitches. And so there was Schoenberg sitting with—I don't know, Jalowetz[B], Erwin Stein, Steuermann, and whoever else was there, and Schoenberg was sort of thinking out loud and said, "I wonder what I could do, what instrument I could use to reinforce the voices to help them to find their pitches." And Steuermann, who was then a very young man, and who had not been with Schoenberg very long, sort of said under his breath "harp," because it occurred to him that after all the harp has a sort of indeterminate quality and would blend with the voices. Whereupon, Schoenberg turned around and said, "Why did you say that? How did you think of that? How did you know what was in my mind?" He was very disturbed because apparently he had also thought of using harp, so he was not at all charmed by the idea that someone else could have that idea also. So it seems scarcely possible to me that, with something like this twelve-tone idea, he would have discussed it *a priori* with any one of his students. Now, my husband did say that he had a feeling that Webern may have begun to sense certain implications of the consequences of atonal writing. But as far as I know from anyone connected with it, there is no question whatever that this was indeed Schoenberg's unique intellectual property at the time that he presented it.

BRUNO SEIDLHOFER: Berg was, in my opinion, by far the most musically gifted of the three. He obeyed; Schoenberg was a god to him. Even when one talked with him—ah, Schoenberg, ah, whatever Schoenberg said, that was it. . . . Also other people said that who knew Schoenberg—. He had an enormous will, had Schoenberg—influence! He was a great man. He was above all many-sided, I think; he painted fantastically well also, and he composed very well, but unfortunately, its grounding on a twelve-tone basis shifted everything off-balance. I don't think much of it.

SMITH: So you think that Berg really didn't want to do twelve-tone composition?

STEFAN ASKENASE: He would never have invented it. That is sure, because Schoenberg was a very strong personality and he was very much influenced by him. If he had not been influenced—let's say even if he had been living in the same period and had not met Schoenberg, I don't think he would have become a twelve-tone composer. That's my feeling.

SMITH: Do you think that this relationship with Schoenberg was a bad thing for Berg?

ASKENASE: As I said, . . . he could see that it was—well, I can't say a bad thing, but something—etwas was ihn belastete. He had the feeling of a weight—something that [weighed] on him.

SOMA MORGENSTERN: Alban usually—all of his life, most of his works he did on vacation in the country. He composed—very few things composed in Vienna. The most of the work he did on vacation.

SMITH: What did he do when he was in Vienna?

MORGENSTERN: Oh, he was teaching, he was working continuously, but he didn't do the first version, you know. But he worked in Vienna. But the very first composition, he always made on vacation.

SMITH: When you first began to play twelve-tone works, did you approach the music in the same way more or less that you would have approached a tonal work?

KOLISCH: Yes.

SMITH: And when Schoenberg would rehearse you, did he rehearse in the same way that he had rehearsed tonal music?

KOLISCH: Ja. He even refused to let us in on the secrets, you know? You already knew that. . . .

SMITH: Why do you think he had this attitude?

KOLISCH: Well, he had it mainly because this method for composing was so much misunderstood and taken as . . . a system and a recipe for composing. . . . It was not necessary with us, of course. It was an error, which he admitted. It was, you know, a principle which he really carried through. He did not talk about it—and much later, you know, and not very deeply. And you know he never taught it . . . never even wrote it.

SMITH: I understand that Schoenberg was very particular in his rehearsals.

EUGEN LEHNER: Very, ja. Especially when he was younger. And naturally, when he dealt with music which he understood. His later music, he obviously didn't understand.

SMITH: What do you mean by that?

LEHNER: . . . I maintain that all these things that Schoenberg did that were rationalized, it was only [ex] *post facto*, not before the fact. . . . I see an incredible resemblance between Bruckner and Schoenberg, even physical. . . . Both were the same naïve, inspired composers who, when the inspiration came, they just sat down and they were writing with an incredible speed music. But then, when the final double bar came, then the difference set in. The Austrian peasant, the Catholic Austrian peasant [Bruckner], when he finally did the final double bar, knelt down and thanked the Lord that he deemed his body right to be his mouthpiece. The intellectual Jewish Schoenberg did the same, but something else happened to it. He was too curious. When he, next day, when he surveyed what he did, he was astonished. "What the hell did I do here? What does it mean? That's not what I wanted to write. Why did I do it?". . . That's how I feel it must have happened. And then, out of his intellectualism, the rationalization and the theories, building theories, came into the picture. But [ex] *post facto*. And the more, I have an indirect indication of it when I see certain compositions. When I take a piece like the Wind Quintet. It's worthwhile studying this fact because you see that is a piece that I have the impression that was written with premeditation. Because that was just about when circumstances forced him to formulate, unfortunately much too prematurely, a theory about the twelve-tone. . . . Well anyway, when circumstances forced him, very, very prematurely, to formulate the theory of it, then I think the Wind Quintet must have been the piece to which he sat down with that in mind, you know, to prove it. Because, if you study it, you can see the really practically infantile simplicity and completely guileless proceeding—how he applied that.

SMITH: When you say, "forced by circumstances," are you speaking of Hauer's activities?

LEHNER: Partly that and partly also the interests of all his— don't forget that Schoenberg was a passionate teacher. Don't forget that Berg and Webern, they were more than pupils, they were absolutely dependent on Schoenberg. . . . Schoenberg was absolutely the most essential part of their lives. . . . So it's easy to imagine how such a person, when he hits upon a fascinating idea, that he was unable to keep it for himself and not theoreticize and talk about it endlessly and formulate it and so on.

SMITH: After he started writing twelve-tone music, was his approach to analysis of twelve-tone music very similar to his analysis of tonal music?

GREISSLE: . . . I can't tell you. First of all, you see, the analysis of a piece always depends upon what the piece is. So, if it is like other music, then it [the analysis] will be like [that] of other music. You mean, did he follow the same principles? Yes, of course. And always—it was frequently—almost always—the interaction between the theme or the melodic line of the harmony, you see, which in twelve-tone counterpoint didn't count so much any more, but all that was going on, what the events forced the composer to do.

SMITH: Have you seen many of Schoenberg's sketches?

DEUTSCH: Frankly, no. But I can tell you something which happened with me and him alone. One day, after the war—1918, 1919—I was very—because I was an injured soldier, he asked me to come to Mödling. I was alone with him. He had something to tell me concerning his son. I was the teacher of his son. But not a musical teacher—in Latin and Greek, in *mathematique* and so on. He chose me for his tutor. The other story! He was alone in his room, and suddenly, he rises up and goes to his armoire, took out a score. . . . I was the first man to see the score of the *Jakobsleiter*. . . . And I have seen, in this first page, corrections. I had not—I was not able—I was so emotional for that that I cannot ask him, so he told me, "Very good, huh?" That's all. I was so emotional. And that is what I have seen of his own works. Nothing—I am not Webern, and not Berg. And none of the others have seen it.

SMITH: Did Schoenberg ever discuss his sketches and unfinished pieces with other people or was he very private?

GREISSLE: Occasionally he did, yes. Occasionally he did and he even told us what he had done and why he had done it. I heard quite a lot about the Serenade. And—he showed us at one time the slow movement of the Suite for clarinets, strings, and piano. . . .

SMITH: Did you ever have a chance to find out how Schoenberg himself went about writing a piece?

GREISSLE: Ja, at one time, he said how he invented it. This was much later. At one time, there was a contract at Universal Edition that some of his works had to appear in transcriptions. And we all got it distributed among us, and Steuermann got *Die glückliche Hand* and *Erwartung*. Jalowetz got the *Pelleas und Melisande*, and I got . . . the Second String Quartet. The First String Quartet, nobody wanted it I think. And when I worked on it, I had to show him every movement, and when it came to the second movement, he looked and I said to him, "I don't know how you wrote this. . . ." So he said to me, "The first time I had in mind nothing but the motion. Something was moving in eighths, in fast eighths, and only out of this motion, the theme finally evolved, and when I had the theme, it was a regular composition." He said it's the piece that was one he always wanted to write and never succeeded. . . . I think that the work came to him as a whole concept, so that he didn't make any mistake when he worked on it because this was always in his mind somehow. But, it went from measure to measure. I never saw him. I lived in the house, and I saw how he worked for instance on the woodwind quintet, and it was from measure to measure. In the evening, he stopped and it continued there and he never—oh, he did a little erasing once in awhile when he wrote something down wrong but very little only—only when there was a slip of the pencil. Otherwise, it came out of his mind. He was at that time already—when he was at the last movement, he knew the row in all its forms by heart. He didn't have to write it down again. Webern never knew. Webern always had to write it down.

SMITH: Did Schoenberg make charts of the different set forms?

GREISSLE: In the beginning, he made a chart for himself. And then, when he started working he knew it by heart. Webern never knew it by heart. Webern used too many forms, too many forms—four or five transpositions and so on for one small piece. I always remember Webern's big boards on the piano. . . . And there were all the rows in all their forms. In the middle, was a small sheet of music paper. There were four notes, and it was the composition. And when I visited him three days later, there were two more notes. And, look, one shouldn't make any jokes about somebody. It is none of our business how he does it. The result is what counts.* And the

*SMITH: Did you ever have a chance to observe Webern composing?

HUMPHREY SEARLE: Well, yes. What I do know was that he had work on the piano—he certainly used the piano while he was composing, result was there, but it was very hard for Webern—very difficult. It was not difficult for Schoenberg. Schoenberg really wrote with comparative ease. When he had a problem, it was certainly not a problem because he was not able to put it down on paper. Never. This was never true. Schoenberg, of all the musicians I have met in my life, had the greatest technique—fantastic technique—with greatest ease! . . .

SMITH: I know that there are some sketches in the Schoenberg collection. Would you say that in these sketchbooks the materials are quite well developed when they are first written down.

GREISSLE: Sketches? Very little—almost immediately the whole piece. And I said because he had this idea in total of something—of a Gestalt of a whole piece—and he worked from there, the sketches were in his mind. . . . The image was there already. He didn't need to sketch.

LEHNER: Once, we spent a summer with Steuermann and Kolisch . . . down in the mountains in a village, and we analyzed the whole Third Quartet, bar by bar, note to note, and in these nearly thousand bars, to our great satisfaction, we found two places where there is a misprint or, if not a misprint, Schoenberg made a grave mistake. . . . So, no sooner we came to Berlin, the first time we went to Schoenberg, we . . . showed it to him. "Is that a misprint?". . . I don't know the notes; let's say it was an F-sharp into an F-natural and a B-flat instead of a B-natural. . . . And so he called his wife to bring the manuscript. So she found the manuscript. ". . . That's

---

and on the piano he had a large board which had all the different versions of the tone row on it, and I think he would choose by ear which one would sound best rather than working it out mathematically. He had an extremely acute ear. When I did these simple harmony exercises, which are from Schoenberg's harmony book, which are perfectly terrible things, and he used to go and play them on the piano, he didn't just look at them as some teachers do. He used to say to me quite often, "If it sounds wrong, then it must be wrong." That was his idea about the logic of harmony or the structure of music in general.

correct; it is F-sharp." "And this other place?" "No, no, that's correct." So, we said, "Oh, it's not a misprint, then it's a mistake, because it must be an F-natural and a B-flat." And then we explained to him and I don't know, that's the third transposition and that is the fifth note. . . . And Schoenberg gets mad—red in the face! "You want to say—if I hear an F-sharp, I will write an F-sharp. If I hear an F-natural, I will write an F-natural. Just because of your stupid . . . theory, are you telling to me what I should write?"

BENAR HEIFETZ: You know, everybody thinks about Schoenberg, his kind of composing—twelve-tone system—was far away from the music but it's not true. He could sit the whole evening and listen to a Beethoven quartet or a Mozart quartet, and we always have to know it because he really loved it. . . . So, since Schoenberg still was in Vienna, we were very close together. We came always together; he was very *gastfreundlich*. He was a wonderful host, and I remember the way he used to say—we were all very arrogant because, under Schoenberg and Alban Berg, nobody could compose so—but he always said, "There is no bad composition. If the composer doesn't have talent, he knows how to write. He has a gift to write. Sometimes he does it, he has a talent but he doesn't know how to write. So every composition has something good."[28] You wouldn't believe that Schoenberg would say this. And, for instance, he always used to ask us, "Why don't you play [an] Edvard Grieg quartet?" "Schoenberg, how could we play such music today?" And he said, "You know, I always hear the way he composed it, and when he composed it, the harmonies were absolutely new to us." So he was very gracious and very—he hated the world because they hated him. He was suspicious and very stubborn.

HUMPHREY SEARLE: I think the interesting thing was that he [Webern] didn't feel that atonal music and twelve-tone music were a break from the past; they were sort of a continuation of it. That was sort of his point of view.

SMITH: At the time that it all happened, did you feel that this was a development—a natural development—out of what he had been doing before, or that this was something new—that it was more like an invention?

KOLISCH: Ja, it appeared as something new. We could not see this from this perspective yet. That appeared really as something very fundamentally drastic.

OSKAR KOKOSCHKA: [About twelve-tone music] And that we knew, so there was no discussion. The past was active at that time still. For us, it was the past. It was out of discussion. We talked about when he wrote something—this passage, whether it expresses what he meant to do— about such things we were talking—would it be better in that way or in that way and so on. But mostly, they played. Bach he played. He liked Bach very much. . . . These tendencies like Poulenc or like the Russian [Prokofiev], that wasn't clean for us. Purist he was in that way, and me too, of course, and that's why we liked each other, because we were both in different ways common. . . .

SMITH: When you came back in 1924, Schoenberg had already developed the twelve-tone method. Did he talk to you about this or did you have any feelings about it at the time?

KOKOSCHKA: We all thought it's *the* music, so there was no dispute about it. It was just *the* fact. All the others were behind and didn't understand it, so we thought. . . . But we all agreed that the late Beethoven was the tower. We even thought Schoenberg was building on the late Beethoven, and not only building on it but now trying to open our ears for Beethoven. That's what we thought, at least I understood it in that way. As a nonmusician, I didn't care for these fights between the musicians— didn't know even about it. I only knew that Alban Berg, for example—and I think Schoenberg thought the same way—that he wanted to be on the safe side, so he was inclined to be the bridge between the past and this new music. Just as I thought new painting is when you paint what you really see and not what you have learned or routine or convention—what you really not only see but in a way feel as the expression of the period in which you live—the *Geist*, the spirit, of the period—so he thought he reflects in his music the spirit of his time and all the others didn't. . . . We were like *Auswanderer* . . . like immigrants, but in your own town. Of course afterwards, they discovered that we had been the real ones, but it's always the same.

Notes

1. Arnold Schoenberg, "Composition with Twelve Tones (1)," in *Style and Idea*, ed. Leonard Stein, trans. Leo Black (London: Faber and Faber, 1975), p. 216.

2. Anton Webern, "The Path to Twelve-Note Composition," in *The Path to the New Music*, ed. Willi Reich, trans. Leo Black (Bryn Mawr, Pa.: Theodore Presser; London: Universal Edition, 1963), pp. 42–56.

3. Ibid., p. 48.

4. H. H. Stuckenschmidt, *Arnold Schoenberg: His Life, World and Work*, trans. Humphrey Searle (New York: Schirmer Books, 1978), p. 442.

5. Webern, "The Path to Twelve-Note Composition," p. 51.

6. Schoenberg, *Style and Idea*, p. 217.

7. Arnold Schoenberg, "Composition with Twelve Tones (2)," in *Style and Idea*, p. 247.

8. Stuckenschmidt, *Schoenberg*, p. 442–443.

9. Webern, "The Path to Twelve-Note Composition," pp. 51–52.

10. Theodor W. Adorno, *Musikalische Schriften*, vol. 1: *Klangfiguren* (Frankfurt am Main: Suhrkamp Verlag, 1959), p. 171, quoted in Walter Kolneder, *Anton Webern: An Introduction to His Works*, trans. Humphrey Searle (Berkeley: University of California Press, 1968), pp. 83, 85.

11. Quoted in Ludwig Münz and Gustav Künstler, *Adolf Loos: Pioneer of Modern Architecture*, trans. Harold Meek (New York: Frederick A. Praeger, 1966), p. 51.

12. Stuckenschmidt, *Schoenberg,* p. 442.

13. George Perle, review of *Studien zur Entwicklung des dodekaphonen Satzes bei Arnold Schönberg. I. Chronologischer Teil. II. Analytischer Teil. III. Notenbeilage,* by Jan Maegaard, *Musical Quarterly* 63 (April 1977):274–275.

14. Ibid., pp. 275–276.

15. Schoenberg, *Style and Idea,* pp. 246–247.

16. See especially Josef Matthias Hauer, *Vom Wesen des Musikalischen: ein Lehrbuch der Zwölftonmusik* (Leipzig: Waldheim-Eberle, 1920). Reprinted as *Ein Lehrbuch der atonalen Musik* (Berlin: Schlesinger, 1923); and *Zwölftontechnik: die Lehre von den Tropen* (Vienna: Universal Edition, 1926).

17. See, for instance, Schoenberg's letters to Hauer in Arnold Schoenberg, *Letters,* ed. Erwin Stein, trans. Eithne Wilkins and Ernst Kaiser (New York: St. Martin's Press, 1965), pp. 103–107.

18. Bryan R. Simms, "The Society for Private Musical Performances: Resources and Documents in Schoenberg's Legacy," *Journal of the Arnold Schoenberg Institute* 3 (October 1979):134.

19. See Fritz Heinrich Klein, "Die Grenze der Halbtonwelt," *Musik* 17 (January 1925):281–286.

20. Simms, "The Society for Private Musical Performances," p. 135.

21. Schoenberg, *Style and Idea,* p. 247.

22. For a more detailed discussion of the mathematical significance of the twelve-tone method, see Milton Babbitt, "Some Aspects of Twelve-tone Composition," *Score* 12 (June 1955):53–61; and "Twelve-tone Invariants as Compositional Determinants," *Musical Quarterly* 46 (April 1960):246–259.

23. Interview of Felix Greissle by Hans Keller, BBC, 4 November 1965.

24. Stuckenschmidt, *Schoenberg,* pp. 443–444.

25. Schoenberg, *Style and Idea,* p. 216.

26. Alban Berg, *Letters to His Wife,* ed. and trans. Bernard Grun (London: Faber and Faber, 1971), p. 310.

27. Schoenberg, *Style and Idea,* p. 244–245.

28. See Schoenberg, *Style and Idea,* p. 366; quoted in Chapter 7, p. 134 of this work.

PART V

The Berlin Years

Even in those days, whatever was new was derided after several performances in Berlin, whereas in Vienna it needed only one performance. In extreme cases—in both places—no performance at all.

Arnold Schoenberg

≈ 10 ≈

The Prussian Academy of Fine Arts

The years following the development of the twelve-tone method were ones of great change for Schoenberg. On 27 June 1924, Ferruccio Busoni died. Busoni had taught a masterclass in composition at the Prussian Academy of Fine Arts in Berlin, and Schoenberg was invited to replace him. The appointment was a prestigious one, and the terms were highly satisfactory.[1] Schoenberg was expected to be in Berlin for six months out of every year and to teach classes of his own design to those students who seemed to him qualified. The appointment was a lifetime one and carried with it a generous stipend which promised Schoenberg financial security for the first time.

The Viennese were impressed by this new success and suddenly seemed eager to keep Schoenberg in Vienna. Schoenberg finally responded to this belated show of affection in a letter to the editor of the *Neues Wiener Journal:*

> It is my most intense desire to depart from Vienna as
> unnoticed as I have always been while I was here. I desire
> no accusations, no attacks, no defence, no publicity, no
> triumph!
> only: *peace!*[2]

After a delay caused by appendicitis, Schoenberg took up
his position in Berlin in January of 1926.

Berlin had changed considerably since Schoenberg's pre-
war days there. After the chaos of the postwar years, it had
risen to be one of the cultural capitals of Europe. Roberto
Gerhard[B], a Schoenberg pupil in both Vienna and Berlin,
described the situation as follows:

> The Berlin of the middle Twenties hardly bore any
> resemblance to the topsy-turvy Berlin of the post-war
> years and the crazy inflation, when the underworld sat at
> the West End Cafés and the population of the Reich's capi-
> tal seemed to consist mainly of spivs. From the squalid,
> catastrophic city of those chaotic years, Berlin had become
> a brilliant metropolis, almost overnight, with characteristi-
> cally German powers of recovery. For a brief period
> stretching from the middle Twenties to the seizure of
> power by the Nazis, Berlin was the cultural center of the
> world. Even Paris looked a little dim by comparison then.
> Musically, at any rate, Berlin was undoubtedly on top.[3]

Schoenberg's teaching situation was different from what
he had been accustomed to in Vienna. Now, instead of private pupils, he had small classes that met in his home. He
had an assistant, Josef Rufer[B], who taught the more elementary subjects, while Schoenberg confined himself exclusively to the teaching of composition. Although the substance of his teaching changed little from the Vienna period,
his approach was now quite different. Instead of instructing
his students individually, he now lectured. He encouraged
his students to discuss their works together, a practice that
often resulted in vigorous argument. In addition, he now
had students who were already interested in the twelve-tone

method and who wanted to compose twelve-tone music. Although he carefully scrutinized student twelve-tone works and made helpful suggestions, he did not lecture on the subject. He still stressed knowledge of the classic and romantic literature, but contemporary pieces were also discussed. Roberto Gerhard recalled the differences between the Vienna teaching and the Berlin classes:

> During lessons [in Vienna], Schoenberg talked a good deal, rationalising everything that could possibly be rationalised, trying all the time to go to the heart of the matter and show you what to expect there, what to look for. Sometimes he would say, "I'll just show you." He would take pencil and paper and start sketching whatever it was he wanted to show. No word was spoken then, one just looked on. It was in this way that I had some of the greatest and most vividly illuminating experiences with Schoenberg as a teacher. It was fascinating to watch how his mind worked, the amazing speed and even flow of thought; to observe the occasional hesitations or corrections, suddenly to realise the reason for the correction and how many draws ahead he had been thinking; to be able to follow with one's own eyes the actual morphogenetical process and sequence of events; to see how the thing grew; the order in which the various elements appeared, their interplay, their repercussions and metamorphosis; in short, the teamwork of chance, choice, and deliberation. It was a breathtaking adventure. . . .
>
> The *Meisterklasse* in Berlin was very different from that. It was in a more academic style. Schoenberg lectured to us. He would pace up and down the room and expound the subject which would be developed in a whole series of lectures, and also give indications as to the work he expected us to do. Every point would be abundantly illustrated and exemplified with passages or entire works taken from the repertoire ranging roughly from Bach to Brahms. Only very occasionally would a modern work be chosen for analysis. Exactly as in his *Harmonielehre*, Schoenberg taught composition strictly on the lines of the classic models. . . . Some of the members of the *Meisterklasse* who had joined more recently decided one day to ask

Schoenberg to give the class an exposé of the twelve-tone technique. He refused. And these were the reasons he gave: not that he doubted that the twelve-tone technique was the right and only possible way for himself; but he was emphatically not prepared to say that it was so for anyone else. Above all he taught one to be true to oneself.[4]

Despite severe problems with asthma, exacerbated by the harsh winters, Schoenberg's Berlin years were fruitful ones compositionally, producing many of the major twelve-tone works, including the Suite, Op. 29; the Variations for Orchestra, Op. 31; the Third String Quartet, Op. 30; the Piano Pieces, Op. 33a and b; *Von Heute auf Morgen;* and the opera *Moses und Aron.*

Schoenberg's life in Berlin differed in other respects from his early Vienna years. Not only was he now a permanent member of the musical establishment and as such at last awarded at least temporarily the respect that he felt his due, but his days of youthful experimentation being at an end, he associated less with achievers in disciplines outside his own. Always somewhat reclusive, he now confined himself more and more to the narrow circle of his students and immediate friends.

By the time Alfred Keller and Erich Schmid studied with Schoenberg in Berlin, knowledge of the twelve-tone idea had spread. Students came to Schoenberg in order to study the method, and although he rarely mentioned it in his classes, he felt obliged to assist those students who used it in their compositions. The Swiss student Alfred Keller returned to a small town in Switzerland following his studies and has remained there. He remembers his years of study with Schoenberg as among the most exciting of his life. He is a charming, generous man, provincial yet interested in new developments. Erich Schmid, also from Switzerland, has a very different sort of life. As a conductor, he travels widely and is acquainted with recent developments in music theory. Hans Curjel came from a theatre background and knew Schoenberg in that context. His knowledge of the twelve-tone method was not technical, but he had more personal contact with Schoenberg in Berlin than did anyone else interviewed.

JOAN ALLEN SMITH: When did you study with Schoenberg?

ALFRED KELLER: From 1927 to 1930 in Berlin.

SMITH: And were you in a class?

KELLER: Yes, the composition master class at the Prussian Academy of Fine Arts in Berlin.

SMITH: And who studied with you there?

KELLER: My fellow students? Walter Goehr[B], Winfried Zil-lig[B], Peter Schacht[B], Nikos Skalkottas[B], Norbert Han-nenheim[B], Josef Zmigrod, Walter Gronostay[B]. Those are the most important as far as I recall.[5]

(Alfred Keller) Instruction in the Berlin master class was free of all formality. We met as the occasion arose in Schoenberg's apartment; we smoked heavily, and for a while Schoenberg contributed to the general haze with his large, fat cigars. Classes were entirely informal, due additionally to Schoenberg's custom of first having his students discuss and evaluate each other's compositions. This often led to loud and fierce disagreements. When things threatened to get out of hand, however, Schoenberg would calm us down and ask us to get on with our business. At times, however, he felt forced to be authoritative and then offered his own opinion. It was not uncommon for him then to find useful ideas where the students had only found a work's insufficiencies and lacks—attempts which under his painstaking tutelage were transformed into musical thoughts and forms worth developing. Now and then, the conversation turned to other art forms: painting, sculpture, architecture, literature. We also discussed ideological things, especially concerning politics, and Schoenberg played an active role in the discussions. He presented his often singular opinions very decisively with the sparkling eloquence peculiar to him.[6]

SMITH: When you studied with Schoenberg, did he talk much about twelve-tone music?

KELLER:[7] Twelve-tone music, and particularly dodeca-
phonic compositional technique, was very rarely discussed and then only on special occasions. Schoenberg
was aware of the effect of his commanding personality
and of the danger this could pose to the individual
development of his students. For this reason, he was
always very mindful of never influencing the still unfo-
cused personality of the young composer. Rather, he
tried to lead him as inconspicuously as possible. This
effort probably explains his hesitancy to use his own
compositions in teaching, to discuss them, or to allow
his students to analyze them. He would allude to this in
a humorous vein, with slightly ironic undertones, saying, "I consider twelve-tone composition strictly a family
matter."

During the three years of my studies, from 1927 to
1930, I can remember only two occasions on which
Schoenberg's works were discussed. Once, a student had
attempted rather complicated compositional techniques—
not totally successfully, as Schoenberg felt. At this point,
he gave a rather lengthy explanation. To make it quite
clear and to our great surprise, he took out the score of
the Variations for Orchestra, Op. 31, and showed us in
musical examples how such difficulties might be over-
come. He concluded his performance by saying, "This is
how I handled it. But it can also be handled differently.
You should, and even must, do it differently—each in
his own way."

Later, in a similar situation, Schoenberg was not
totally convinced of the composer's techniques and ob-
jected. The student defended himself, the teacher like-
wise. I thought I could help my fellow student by referring
to the second movement of Schoenberg's Third String
Quartet. The master seemed taken aback, even somewhat indignant, and hurried with a quick step, as was
his way, to the music cabinet, produced the score, and
placed it on the piano, directing the following curt challenge
toward his imprudent student: "So now, prove it." An
hour later, as I finished my presentation, Schoen-

berg replied to the discussion of his work, which at first had been obviously unwelcome, in a manner which, coming from him, was intended as praise: "Well, you studied that quite thoroughly." With new students, Schoenberg first wanted to ascertain their degree of accomplishment in tonal composition. He was in the habit of assigning such work for this purpose. Thus, for example, I had to write string quartet variations on the nineteen bar first theme of the second movement of Mozart's String Quartet in D, K. 575.

SMITH: Did Schoenberg sometimes talk about twelve-tone music in the same way in which he would talk about other music, about Mozart or Bach?

KELLER: Aside from the above example of the Variations, Op. 31, Schoenberg only spoke of twelve-tone composition when students presented such works to him. This was seldom the case, for we wisely refrained from doing this—with good reason. The only exception was Norbert v. Hannenheim who composed exclusively in the twelve-tone system. Schoenberg discussed the tonal masterpieces and free tonal student work. He always tested the clarity of presentation, thematic work, continuity of form, variation of repetitions, et cetera, and then he covered his explanations with reference to the works of Beethoven, Mozart, Brahms, et cetera. I can't remember the exact occasion, but it was probably during a discussion of one of Hannenheim's pieces that Schoenberg said: "The ignorant claim that it is only necessary to set up certain successions in twelve-tone composition, whereupon everything else will fall into place by itself, and that, therefore, composing has become easier. I can't warn my students enough against this mistake; the opposite is true. Composing has now become much more difficult."

Analysis of masterpieces from the preclassical, classical, and romantic periods and even tonal composition from the turn of the century (Mahler, Strauss, Reger, Wolf) was given considerable attention in class; it sometimes happened that Schoenberg dedicated several hours to the exclusive analysis of a work by Bach, Mozart, Beethoven, Schubert, or Brahms.

ERICH SCHMID: I was with Schoenberg one year, '30 until '31. It was the last class in Berlin. . . . I was with Schoenberg at the Akademie der Künste. I was in his master class, into which one was admitted only after having completed studies at the conservatory. I had to show Schoenberg my earlier theoretical work, counterpoint, studies of form, and my own compositions. It was on the basis of such work that one was admitted. Thus, we studied neither harmony nor counterpoint with him. Earlier, in Vienna, that was probably different. In the course of my studies with him, he continually asked for work in strict style—this was the so-called Palestrina style—based on Bellermann, which was the strictest textbook of the time, going back to Fux. This book is hardly known today. Schoenberg considered such work important, in a way like "brain hygiene" [Gehirnwäsche] as he once called it. The classes were not lectures. They were discussion groups led by Schoenberg. (Classmates were Norbert v. Hannenheim, Peter Schacht, Nikos Skalkottas, Rudolf Goehr.) We had to play everything we discussed on the piano, sometimes four hands. We also played our own compositions and works like Beethoven's string quartets. It was important to Schoenberg to see how we made music. He had us play a theme. Schoenberg demanded clear articulation. Thus, we not only studied composition with him, but we also learned a considerable amount of interpretation.

SMITH: When you went to Schoenberg, he was already quite established, and it was some time after he had first begun working with the twelve-tone method. Did he ever talk to you about how this came about?

SCHMID: In this time, he was never teaching twelve tone. We worked only with examples from Mozart, the classic, romantic, Brahms, etc. I wrote a quartet in twelve

tone and he made corrections; and, for example, I said,
"You know, I cannot make a change here. This is twelve-
tone." "Ah, good, twelve-tone. Then do this—this is what
you should try." But he was not interested in technical
twelve tone. . . . He did show us twelve-tone pieces of
his, for example, the Quintet for Winds. But he [showed]
us little of the twelve-tone construction in this work.
That is one very important work in the development of
twelve-tone composition, the Quintet. . . . But for him, it
was much more important than he had written a classical piece, with classical forms, and he showed us these
classical forms—theme, development—first theme,
second theme—he showed all of this in the twelve-tone
piece. . . . What I want to say is that he did speak about
twelve tone, but he didn't teach it. . . . For example, he
did illustrate the development of twelve-tone music in
his early works. This is, the development from atonality
to twelve tone. He showed us the variations from the
Serenade, for instance. . . . But he showed more which
related to classical formulation and not to a technical
renunciation of classic composition. He may have used
as illustrations something like that in the variations of
Mozart, variations of Brahms, and showed how that is.
Reger too. But not really twelve tone—never during
that time.

SMITH: Whom did he mention when he talked about philosophy and art?

KELLER: Literature comparatively little. He often spoke
about painting—Kandinsky[B]. And then above all also
about architecture—Loos, then sculptor—painter he
was—Klimt[B], about whom he really spoke often, he
spoke pretty often. Literature, comparatively little.

SMITH: Did he ever discuss things with you other than
music—art, or philosophy, or literature?

SCHMID: Yes. On the first day on which I was with him,
therefore we were in the class, he really didn't talk

about music. He talked about other arts—about architecture, about painting, about everything that there was and not at all about music, and one was always conscious of it anyway. There is—it is all one thing, and not music here and something else there, but all one thing, one idea. . . . That is also art. Form, no? That was for him also art. Everything that he did. . . . He was very interested in many things—very interested.

SMITH: Did Schoenberg ever talk to you about other things which were not music, such as theatre or literature or art?

KELLER: Yes. Especially politics.

SMITH: Was he conservative politically?

KELLER: . . . He was strictly conservative. And as for us students, he always [said] that we were communists. He said to me, "You are a red." A red one.

SMITH: Was Hanns Eisler[B] in Berlin when you were there?

HANS CURJEL: I knew him, yes, but not too much.

SMITH: Was he close to Schoenberg?

CURJEL: At the time, not too much. It was already at the time when he started politics.

SMITH: Was Schoenberg more conservative politically?

CURJEL: Schoenberg was as Karl Kraus. More conservative, yes.

SMITH: Was he a pacifist?

CURJEL: I don't know, but I think he was not a pacifist, no. He should have been, but the mentality was bellicose.

SMITH: Did you see Schoenberg also socially?

SCHMID: Yes, this is a problem. . . . He was a respected person, yes. He was however very nice. And he was very concerned about what happened to his students. Until the war, I often received postcards from him. That was our contact. He had contact, but not so that one went ever to his house to eat, or for walks together with him, or to a restaurant together, or whatever. . . . However, one should perhaps—one must say that in this year when I was with him, he was not very well. He had always his asthma—he had a history of it—and the winter in Berlin, when I was in Berlin, was very hard and very cold. . . . He was from time to time very ill. I know only that when spring came—there is a letter from me to my parents where I write, "It is wonderful weather. It is now finally beautiful, this beautiful weather, and one can see also in Schoenberg that it is beautiful weather. He is much more cheerful."

Notes

1. The documents concerning Schoenberg's appointment are published in Josef Rufer, *The Works of Arnold Schoenberg: A Catalogue of His Compositions, Writings and Paintings.* trans. Dika Newlin (London: Faber and Faber, 1962), pp. 207–210.

2. Arnold Schoenberg, *Letters*, ed. Erwin Stein, trans. Eithne Wilkins and Ernst Kaiser (New York: St. Martin's Press, 1965), p. 112.

3. Roberto Gerhard, "Schoenberg Reminiscences," *Perspectives of New Music* 13 (Spring–Summer 1975):59.

4. Ibid., pp. 63–64.

5. For a more complete list of Schoenberg's students during this period, see H. H. Stuckenschmidt, *Schoenberg: His Life, World and Work*, trans. Humphrey Searle (New York: Schirmer Books, 1978), pp. 540–541.

6. Alfred Keller, "Arnold Schönberg, Erinnerungen eines Schülers an seinen grossen Lehrer." Radio broadcast by Radio Basel, pp. 1–2.

7. Interview material rewritten by Alfred Keller.

~ 11 ~

Epilogue

On the surface, it seemed that Schoenberg was settled at last in Berlin. Berlin had become a great cultural center and had much to offer the composer in addition to the obvious amenities of financial security and considerable free time to travel and compose. However, this situation proved not to be ideal, and in any case it was short-lived.

Although Schoenberg had achieved recognition as a teacher by his appointment to the Prussian Academy of Fine Arts, his works were still not universally accepted. The days of demonstrations were over, replaced by a situation of limited approval by a few people. In a letter of 18 June 1930 to the *Deutsche Allgemeine Zeitung*, Schoenberg related his dissatisfaction:

> Even before the war people in Vienna were rightly and wrongly proud and ashamed of being less active than Berlin.
>
> Even at that time Berlin showed a lively and intense interest in recognising and explaining the symptoms of a work of art, something that was missing in Vienna, thanks to centuries of experience in composing.
>
> Even in those days whatever was new was derided after several performances in Berlin, whereas in Vienna it

235

needed only one performance. In extreme cases—in both places—no performance at all.

Even in those days, in both cities, the public had discovered that there is always plenty of time to honour a great man after he is dead.[1]

During Schoenberg's stay in Berlin, only two of his works received their premieres there: the Variations for Orchestra, Op. 31, by the Berlin Philharmonic conducted by Wilhelm Furtwängler; and the *Begleitungsmusik zu einer Lichtspielszene*, Op. 34, by the orchestra of the Kroll Opera conducted by Otto Klemperer.

Other factors also combined to make Schoenberg's last stay in Berlin an unpleasant one. Suffering from emphysema, he found the winters in Berlin impossible to tolerate, and his health steadily deteriorated. As his contract allowed him to be absent from Berlin for six months of the year, he tried to spend the coldest months in Barcelona. By 13 May 1932, his condition had declined to such an extent that he wrote to Dr. Joseph Asch (unsuccessfully) for help in obtaining a stipend so that he could move permanently to Barcelona:

> For some time I have been living in the South for reasons of health, and on these grounds, but also because of political conditions, am very reluctant to go back to Germany at this juncture. . . .
>
> I am told you have enough influence to achieve something. . . . I was told that quite some time ago. But it is only today that I can bring myself to approach you about it. Will you try it, will you see if you can get some rich Jews to provide for me so that I don't have to go back to Berlin among the swastika-swaggerers and pogromists?[2]

This letter, written two months before the elections of July 1932, shows that the political situation was already causing Schoenberg much concern. In the July elections, the Nazi party became the largest party in the Reichstag. Writing to Kolisch that same month, Schoenberg remarked, "When do you all expect to be in Berlin? The elections are over and done with, anyway. I'm curious to see what's going to come of it all. I simply can't imagine."[3] By September, he was able to imagine; in a letter to Berg of 23 September, Schoenberg had already realized that relocation might be necessary but seemed to have had difficulty in accepting the decision:

> But it isn't only that; there's also a sort of depression, which is undoubtedly connected with having to be in Berlin, that takes away all my pleasure in work. For here I'm constantly obliged to consider the question whether and, if so, to what extent I am doing the right thing in regarding myself as belonging here or there, and whether it is forced upon me. Even without the nationalistic hints one has been getting in recent years, naturally I know where I belong. Only such a change of milieu isn't as easy as one might think.[4]

On 27 February 1933, a fire that burned the Reichstag building was blamed on the communists. In the resulting political upheaval, the Nazis, together with their allies the Nationalists, achieved a majority in the Reichstag on 5 March. On the first of March, Schoenberg attended a meeting of the Senate of the Academy. There, the composer and President of the Academy, Max von Schillings, stated that the government wished Jewish influence in the Academy to be eliminated. Saying that he never stayed where he wasn't wanted, Schoenberg left the meeting. On March 20, three days before the Reichstag handed over its power to Hitler's cabinet by passing the so-called Enabling Act,[5] Schoenberg resigned from the Academy and requested payment of his salary until 30 September 1935 as stipulated in his contract.[6] This request was refused, and Schoenberg was paid only through October 1933. In May 1933, Schoenberg left Germany and went first to France, there formally re-embracing the Jewish faith, and then, in October, to the United States, where a position at the small Malkin Conservatory in Boston awaited him. Unable to tolerate the Boston winters, Schoenberg soon moved to Los Angeles where he taught first at the

University of Southern California and then from 1936 until his retirement in 1944 at the University of California at Los Angeles.

The other members of Schoenberg's immediate circle stayed in Vienna where they continued to work and teach. There was for a while the possibility that Berg might also move to Berlin to teach at the Musikhochschule.[7] Berg seriously considered this offer, even after Schoenberg had been forced to leave Berlin,* but in the end remained in Vienna where he died on December 24, 1935 of blood poisoning resulting from the lancing of a boil.

Webern stayed in Mödling and continued to teach throughout the war, sometimes secretly, and seemed, at times at least, to feel some affinity for National Socialism.† However, the Nazi government prohibited him from conducting. At the war's end, he was accidentally killed by an American soldier as he stepped outside of his son-in-law's house to smoke a cigarette.[8]

Loos and Kraus were both spared the worst of Nazism; Kokoschka alone survived to flee to England. Loos, after suffering for some time from nervous disorders, died 23 August 1933 in a sanatorium in Vienna. Karl Kraus, who had long anticipated the German crisis, ceased publication of *Die Fackel* in 1936, saying he had nothing more to say since what he had warned against was already coming true. Kraus died of natural causes on 12 June 1936 and missed both the *Anschluss* and the subsequent destruction of his library and the offices of *Die Fackel*. Berthold Viertel[B], in an

---

*That Berg was still considering the possible offer is indicated by his letter to Helene Berg of 15 May 1933 in which he described being approached on the subject by Hindemith[B]. He was not completely inclined to take up the position but remarked significantly that "it would be more feasible now than before, as S. is no longer in Berlin." Alban Berg, *Letters to His Wife*, ed. and trans. Bernard Grun (London: Faber and Faber, 1971), pp. 412–413.

†Rumors of Webern's connection with the Nazi party abound. It seems possible that he had advance knowledge of the *Anschluss*, and there is indication that he was in sympathy with at least some of the programs advocated by the Nazis. This sympathy may have been accompanied by naïveté. Whatever his feelings about socialism, or National Socialism, there is no evidence that Webern was anti-Semitic.

article for Kraus's sixtieth birthday volume, summed up Kraus's contribution:

> Karl Kraus had turned sixty. When we were boys of four-teen . . . we read his *Fackel* while hiding it under our school benches. We never stopped reading it—but now he has stopped writing it. After a lifetime of powerful speech this warner is now silent. For there no longer is anything to warn about. Everything happened the way he knew it beforehand, foresaw and foretold it. All horrors have come to pass—that war and this peace. He has had the harshest fate: to be proved right in such a frightful way. So he finally fell silent, like the prophet Samuel who went up on the mountain and did not look down upon the lost city. The harshest fate, the fate of the prophet who is con-firmed by misfortune.[9]

For the students and associates of Schoenberg, many of whom were younger than himself, the Nazi invasion of Aus-tria meant the end of a way of life. Most left their homeland and emigrated either to England (Erna Gál, Roberto Ger-hard[B], Erwin Stein[B], Lona Truding) or to the United States (Felix Galimir, Felix Greissle, the Kolisch Quartet, Alma Mahler[B], Paul Pisk, Edward Steuermann[B]). What followed were hard times of adjustment and unemployment. Al-though most eventually found rewarding occupation, this was all too often achieved at the expense of sacrificed ideals and forgotten goals.

JOAN ALLEN SMITH: What sort of reception did you get from Schoenberg's works at the time?

FELIX GALIMIR: Different. Different. . . . As long as we played it within the group, the ISCM [International Society for Contemporary Music], then of course there was always excitement and great enthusiasm, but the moment you went outside, Schoenberg's music was unfortunately not too easily acceptable. . . . It's this enormously complicated counterpoint and the constant interwoven voice-leading that keeps people from understanding it. I love it, but the outside impression is not quite acceptable.

SMITH: When you played the Third Quartet, you said that there was no longer this reaction against Schoenberg's works. That was 1927 already. Were there positive feelings towards his work at that time?

RUDOLF KOLISCH: Yes. Of course it really reached only a minority. But the attitude had changed around this time. The noisy, boisterous refusal was gone—was not any more.

HANS CURJEL: [About his work at the Kroll Opera] The elite was very enthusiastic—an elite of 500 people, not the big public. But we did a lot of modern operas. . . .

SMITH: How much did Schoenberg himself have to do with the performances? Did he come to the rehearsals?

CURJEL: Yes, the last rehearsals only, but he rehearsed with the singers but not with orchestra. But he came to three or four rehearsals.

EUGEN LEHNER: Well, to make a long story short, then came the summer . . . when we had to learn the Third Quartet from Schoenberg for the premiere in Europe. . . . And I remember once, when Schoenberg came to Vienna with the manuscript, we were sitting in a circle and Schoenberg was trying to conduct so that we could play through. And I was just playing and thought, "Jesus, if that is music, I will eat my head. That might be anything, but music it is not." So, with that, finally came the summer, and we went off to a little forlorn Austrian [village] and settled down and started to learn—study. And, you know, every day something happened. All of a sudden, "Gee, that must have been a mistake, it sounded like music." And it probably was in a week or two, I don't know any more, but all I know is that I never could take anything else seriously. . . . And no other composer country by country I could take even halfway seriously, and I still believe that the Third and the Fourth Quartets and the String Trio are probably the most beautiful music written in the twentieth century. . . .

I remember, for example, . . . [a] performance of the Orchestra Variations. It was in Frankfurt in the radio station. Schoenberg was himself conducting. It must have been the very late twenties or the very early thirties, and during the performance, I loved it—I was absolutely crazy for it, and I told afterwards to Trudy Schoenberg—that's his wife, Kolisch's sister—and I said, "Gee, I never heard anything so beautiful as this music." And she said to me, "Don't tell it to me, tell it to Arnold." "What do you mean? I can't go to Mr. Schoenberg and tell him that I think his music is beautiful." "Are you a fool? He would love to hear it if you really mean it." So, I went to Schoenberg and I told him, "Mr. Schoenberg, I must tell you, I think that your music—the variations are simply beautiful." And he was so happy. . . . He was a human being, the warmest and [most] inspiring and why must only the whole world [see] this forbidding, mathematical, crude, arrogant, disagreeable, aggressive person? . . .

But everything—he had to write it up, there was a system to it. He was incredibly addicted to tennis playing, both to tennis and to table tennis. Once, one evening in Berlin—there was this chess master, [Emanuel] Lasker. I remember Lasker—he's a mathematical philosopher— and after dinner, fortunately, Lasker was kind enough to ask Schoenberg about his ping-pong playing about which he was very proud. So right away we repaired ourselves to the ping-pong table, and I was selected to play an exhibition game with Schoenberg. Of course, as every child knew, you must let Schoenberg win in such a case, when it is an exhibition game. And so I started to smash everything, but . . . the most improbable thing— impossible you would have thought—it came through. So I noticed that Kolisch was making all kinds of alarm signals and things. . . . At long last, in the last minute, I was able to lose this game. And so was everything happy. After

Lasker was gone, Schoenberg explained to me why he thinks he won this game, and made a perfect theory about it.

SMITH: Did you find Schoenberg himself to be intimidating or overbearing?

CURJEL: No, because I knew him very well. I played every morning tennis with him in the summer time at seven o'clock. He was an extremely strong personality. . . . He was one for whom one had at the first moment respect, but he was a little turned. He was a little complicated. For instance, if we played tennis and—I was younger, I was much younger than Schoenberg—I played better, and when he failed a ball, he came and explained why he failed. Typical for Schoenberg.

ERWIN RATZ: I was friendly with Webern until 1945, shortly before his death. But I would like to make one thing clear; namely, as we see it, the major importance of Schoenberg came before twelve-tone music. The orchestral variations are a wonderful and perfect work; that is certain. But then came these big external crises— emigration and all that—and I have the impression that Schoenberg could never get used to America. You can see that even his theoretical works are written for a *niveau* [level] which is rather primitive, and that, there- fore, one could hardly draw any conclusions about Schoenberg as a theoretician. What Schoenberg was, what he represented, came before twelve-tone music. Twelve-tone music began slowly at first, 1923, and this was quite bristly, that is, rather hard to enjoy. It reminds me of the first time we heard the Wind Quintet, which was somewhat difficult for us, and we only slowly began to understand it. Today, I value the Wind Quintet; it is not as unfathomable to me as it was then, but since you place so much stress on twelve-tone composition— that is, I can't say that Schoenberg was fundamentally a twelve-tone composer, for his great works—that is, both operas, the *Glückliche Hand* and *Erwartung*—are the real Schoenberg for us—the atonal but not twelve-tone Schoenberg. This may sound like heresy to many, but after all, we grew up with that music. Imagine something like the operas; the twelve-tone works no longer have such strong radiance. I felt endless sorrow for Schoenberg because he had been dealt such a fate. It is like two separate worlds: what Schoenberg was, how he was in Vienna—we heard countless rehearsals of *Pierrot lunaire*, for instance, under Schoenberg's direction. It is also true that no one can imagine how this work should be played. If you listen to the recording of *Gurrelieder*, your hair will stand on end. There is none of the warmth in the music that there used to be under Schoenberg's direction. All right, he needed ten rehearsals or even more, but what rehearsals! One's heart opened, he made music so wonderfully; he was a magnificent performer! He didn't have manual dexterity, but when he had sufficient time at his disposal, things turned out splendidly—and also, when he demonstrated the *Sprecher*'s part in the third section of *Gurrelieder*, "O schwing dich aus dem Blumenkelch, Marienkäferlein," and when you hear that on records, you would like more than anything to break them. How one can have no feelings for such warmth! After all, Schoenberg was an immensely uncomplicated and deeply emotional person, who was constantly thrust into paradoxical positions by his opponents.

OSKAR KOKOSCHKA: He must have suffered. But he was a holy priest in this. He took it much more seriously than other people. I play with my life. I am not so convinced of the necessity of art in this world. So, what I do, I do it more or less for myself. I have no contracts; I have no dealers; I am not forced, pushed, or pressed. But he had to live also and to live, not for money's sake, but to live with a community around him who believed in him.

Notes

1. Arnold Schoenberg, *Letters*, ed. Erwin Stein, trans. Eithne Wilkins and Ernst Kaiser (New York: St. Martin's Press, 1965), p. 142.

2. Ibid., pp. 163–164.

3. Ibid., p. 165.

4. Ibid., p. 167.

5. For a further description of this act, see William L. Shirer, *The Rise and Fall of the Third Reich: A History of Nazi Germany* (New York: Simon and Schuster, 1960), p. 198.

6. Documents concerning Schoenberg's resignation from the Academy have been reprinted in Josef Rufer, *The Works of Arnold Schoenberg: A Catalogue of His Compositions, Writings and Paintings*, trans. Dika Newlin (London: Faber and Faber, 1962), pp. 208–210.

7. This was first suggested to Berg by Schoenberg in a letter of 10 April 1930, published in Schoenberg, *Letters*, pp. 137–138.

8. For an account of Webern's death, see Hans Moldenhauer, *The Death of Anton Webern: A Drama in Documents* (New York: Philosophical Library, 1961).

9. *Stimmen über Karl Kraus zum 60. Geburtstag* (Vienna: Verlag der Buchhandlung Richard Lanyi, 1934), p. 40. Quoted in Harry Zohn, *Karl Kraus* (New York: Twayne, 1971), p. 134.

APPENDIX 1

Society for Private Musical Performances in Vienna*

(A Statement of Aims, written by Alban Berg)

The Society was founded in November, 1918, for the purpose of enabling Arnold Schoenberg to carry out his plan to give artists and music lovers a real and exact knowledge of modern music.

The attitude of the public toward modern music is affected to an immense degree by the circumstance that the impression it receives from that music is inevitably one of obscurity. Aim, tendency, intention, scope and manner of expression, value, essence, and goal, all are obscure; most performances of it lack clarity; and specially lacking in lucidity is the public's consciousness of its own needs and wishes. All works are therefore valued, considered, judged, and lauded, or else misjudged, attacked, and rejected, exclusively upon the basis of one effect which all convey equally— that of obscurity.

This situation can in the long run satisfy no one whose opinion is worthy of consideration, neither the serious composer nor the thoughtful member of an audience. To bring light into this darkness and thus fulfill a justifiable need and desire was one of the motives that led Arnold Schoenberg to found this society.

To attain this goal, three things are necessary:

1. Clear, well-rehearsed performances.
2. Frequent repetitions.
3. The performances must be removed from the corrupting influence of publicity; that is, they must not be directed toward the winning of competitions and must be unaccompanied by applause, or demonstrations of disapproval.

Herein lies the essential difference revealed by a comparison of the Society's aims with those of the everyday concert world, from which it is quite distinct in principle. Although it may be possible,

*Appendix 1 material translated by Stephen Somervell, in Nicolas Slonimsky, *Music Since 1900*, 3d ed. (New York: Coleman-Ross, 1949), pp. 1307–1308.

in preparing a work for performance, to get along with the strictly limited and always insufficient number of rehearsals hitherto available, for better or worse (usually the latter), yet for the Society the number of rehearsals allotted to works to be performed will be limited only by the attainment of the greatest possible clarity and by the fulfillment of all the composer's intentions as revealed in his work. And if the attainment of these minimum requirements for good performance should necessitate a number of rehearsals that cannot be afforded (as was the case, for example, with a symphony of Mahler, which received its first performance after twelve four-hour rehearsals and was repeated after two more), then the work concerned should not, and will not, be performed by the Society.

In the rehearsal of new works, the performers will be chosen preferably from among the younger and less well-known artists, who place themselves at the Society's disposal out of interest in the cause; artists of high-priced reputation will be used only so far as the music demands and permits; and moreover that kind of virtuosity will be shunned which makes of the work to be performed not the end in itself but merely a means to an end which is not the Society's, namely, the display of irrelevant virtuosity and individuality, and the attainment of a purely personal success. Such things will be rendered automatically impossible by the exclusion (already mentioned) of all demonstrations of applause, disapproval, and thanks. The only success that an artist can have here is that (which should be most important to him) of having made the work, and therewith its composer, intelligible.

While such thoroughly rehearsed performances are a guarantee that each work will be enabled to make itself rightly understood, an even more effective means to this end is given to the Society through the innovation of weekly meetings* and by frequent repetitions of every work. Moreover, to ensure equal attendance at each meeting, the program will not be made known beforehand.

Only through the fulfillment of these two requirements— through preparation and frequent repetitions—can clarity take the place of the obscurity which used to be the only impression remaining after a solitary performance; only thus can an audience establish an attitude towards a modern work that bears any rela-

---

*At that time, every Sunday morning from ten to noon, in the Society's small concert hall.

tion to its composer's intention, completely absorb its style and idiom, and achieve that intimacy that is to be gained only through direct study—an intimacy with which the concert-going public can be credited only with respect to the most frequently performed classics.

The third condition for the attainment of the aims of the Society is that the performances shall be in all respects private; that guests (foreign visitors excepted) shall not be admitted, and that members shall be obligated to abstain from giving any public report of the performances and other activities of the Society, and especially to write or inspire no criticisms, notices, or discussions of them in periodicals.

This rule, that the sessions shall not be publicized, is made necessary by the semi-pedagogic activities of the Society and is in harmony with its tendency to benefit musical works solely through good performance and thus simply through the good effect made by the music itself. Propaganda for works and their composers is not the aim of the Society.

For this reason no school shall receive preference and only the worthless shall be excluded; for the rest, all modern music—from that of Mahler and Strauss to the newest, which practically never, or at most rarely, is to be heard—will be performed.

In general the Society strives to choose for performance such works as show their composers' most characteristic and, if possible, most pleasing sides. In addition to songs, pianoforte pieces, chamber music, and short choral pieces, even orchestral works will be considered, although the latter—since the Society has not yet the means to perform them in their original form—can be given only in good and well-rehearsed 4-hand and 8-hand arrangements. But the necessity becomes a virtue. In this manner it is possible to hear and judge a modern orchestral work divested of all the sound-effects and other sensuous aids that only an orchestra can furnish. Thus the old reproach is robbed of its force—that this music owes its power to its more or less opulent and effective instrumentation and lacks the qualities that were hitherto considered characteristic of good music—melody, richness of harmony, polyphony, perfection of form, architecture, etc.

A second advantage of this manner of music-making lies in the concert style of the performance of these arrangements. Since there is no question of a substitute for the orchestra but of so rearranging the orchestral work for the piano that it may be regarded, and should in fact be listened to, as an independent

work and as a pianoforte composition, all the characteristic qualities and individualities of the piano are used, all the pianistic possibilities exploited. And it happens that in this reproduction—with
different tone quality—of orchestral music, almost nothing is lost.
Indeed, these very works, through the sureness of their instrumentation, the aptness of their instinctively chosen tone-colors,
are best able to elicit from the piano tonal effects that far exceed
its usual expressive possibilities.

APPENDIX 2

Statutes of the Society for Private Musical Performances in Vienna*

#1. Name and Location of the Society.

The Society bears the name "Society for Private Musical Performances" and has its headquarters in Vienna.

#2. Aim and Purpose.

The Society, which is not based on profit, has the aim of enabling Arnold Schoenberg to carry out personally his objective of providing artists and music lovers with a real and exact knowledge of modern music. The Society shall strive to attain this goal through regular, and whenever possible weekly, meetings of the Society (Society evenings) during which works of modern music will be presented.

#3. The Society's Year.

The Society's year begins on December 1st of each year.

#4. Members.

The Society shall be shaped through its members; a member may be any reputable and honorable person who subscribes to the statutes of the Society. Membership follows from the undersigning of the declaration of admittance, whereby recognition and acknowledgment of the statutes are assumed, and from receipt of payment of at minimum the amount of dues for the remainder of the Society year. The Executive Committee is authorized to refuse admittance to the Society without statement of grounds. Each member shall be issued a nontransferable membership card, with photograph, that authorizes entrance to Society events.

*Appendix 2 material from the Arnold Schoenberg Institute, Los Angeles; translation by Cynthia Ovens.

#5. Rights of the Members.

The members of the Society shall have the right:

a) to take part in all events of the Society, provided they are not in arrears with their dues;

b) to select the Executive Committee of the Society and, as far as Statutes #8 and #12 have not otherwise been determined, to be selected;

c) to bring forward motions in matters of the Society to the Executive Committee or at the General Assembly.

#6. Obligations of the Members.

The members of the Society shall be obligated:

a) to promote the aims of the Society and to prevent wrongdoing;

b) to pay the membership dues for the entire current Society year, even in the case of premature resignation. The categories of dues are graduated and consist of a basic rate, that may be settled at the beginning of the Society's year or at the time of admittance to the Society, and an installment rate, which through choice is either settled:

1) from the outset, simultaneously with the basic rate, or
2) in weekly (monthly, quarterly) rates. The assessment of the payment of dues will be binding for a Society year, fixed and announced by the Executive Committee in advance. This announcement is made in such a way that each member may give notice of resignation from the Society before the beginning of the Society year for which the assessment is valid (#7a).

c) not to wrong the Society which, through principle, remains independent of public musical life, i.e., neither to write nor inspire public commentary on its performances and functions, especially reviews, notices, and discussions in periodicals.

#7. Resignation and Dismissal.

a) *Resignation.* Resignation from the Society follows from a written declaration of resignation in the form of a registered letter and is valid only for the end of the current year of the Society. If the declaration of resignation follows the 30th of June, the obligation for payment of membership dues for the next Society year is acknowledged.

b) *Dismissal.* Dismissal of a member may be ordered by the Governing Board if the member

1) grossly violates the Statutes,
2) does not meet his obligation of dues for more than three months,
3) does not accommodate himself to the performance regulations established by the Executive Committee,
4) damages the reputation of the Society or disturbs its functions (#6b).

#8. The Executive Committee.

The Executive Committee shall consist of
a) the President, Arnold Schoenberg, whose term of office is not limited,
b) from ten to twenty Governing Board members, chosen from the General Assembly in agreement with the President. The distribution of individual functions is determined by the members of the Governing Board with the consent of the President (#10).

In the case of need, the Governing Board is authorized to extend itself through co-optation. Individual members of the Governing Board who shall be obliged to devote all their energy to the duties of the Society (e.g., Director, Secretary, Archivist) shall, as soon as the resources of the Society permit, be allowed fixed stipends, the value of which to be determined by the President. The President, on the other hand, shall fill his post free of charge.

#9. The President.

The President has full authority in the direction of the Society. He determines the amount and nature of necessary expenditures for the aims of the Society, the fee for participants and the members of the Governing Board (mentioned in #10), cost of the rental of the halls, expenditures for Society evenings, administrative management, etc. He also has the right to release from obligation, either completely or in part, payment of dues by worthy and needy members. In the case that the President is not in a position to conduct the business of the Society for more than four weeks, he has the obligation to give directives for his representation to the Society's Governing Board. If he is also not in a position to do this, the powers of the President shall go to the representative named in #10.

#10. Members of the Governing Board.

1) *Directors [Vortragsmeister].*

The Directors shall apply themselves to the preparation and direction of artistic events, the direction of rehearsals for performances, and generally to the execution of all the Society's artistic duties according to the instructions of the Executive Committee.

The President shall name the first Director as his representative in artistic matters, who, for his part, may appoint two Directors for his representation. The stipend granted the Director in #8 shall be defined in the agreement.

2) *The Secretary.*

For the execution of administrative work, a Secretary shall be appointed from the members of the Governing Board to be the President's representative in administrative matters.

3) *Administrators.*

The Administrators are devoted to advising and assisting the President, the Directors, and the Secretary in the artistic and administrative duties of the Society. An Administrator shall serve as Clerk.

4) A member of the Governing Board shall serve as Archivist, another as Cashier.

#11. Announcements, Representation of the Society to the Public.

Announcements to the membership shall be in writing or through notification at Society evenings (performances).

The Society shall be represented to the public by the President or Secretary, and in their absence by their representative (the Clerk, see #9). Announcements and the issuing of instructions shall be approved by the President or by the Clerk.

#12. The General Assembly.

The regular, annual meeting of the General Assembly shall be called by the President (by his representative if he is unavailable), at the latest at the end of November.

The task of the General Assembly is to receive the statement of accounts, grant reinstatement to those dismissed, elect the new Executive Committee (in agreement with the President) and additional auditors (who may not belong to the Executive Committee); furthermore, to decide on changes in the Statutes and to decide on all resolutions of the General Assembly. Changes in the Statutes and dissolution of the Society, etc., require the consent of the President for validity.

General Assemblies shall be called at least fourteen days prior to the date held through written notification to the members with notice of agenda.

The General Assembly shall require for the passage of resolutions the presence of one-third of the regular membership. Decisions shall be made by a majority vote. Only for passage of a resolution of dissolution of the Society shall the presence or representation of three-fourths of the membership be required.

If the number present required for decisions is not attained, a second General Assembly shall then be called which, without regard to the number present, shall be enabled to pass resolutions. The calling of this second General Assembly may, if the agenda does not include dissolution of the Society, be done at the same time as the calling of the first General Assembly. The second General Assembly may be called for the same day as the first General Assembly but at a later hour and shall then, without regard to the number present, be enabled to pass resolutions. On written request of at least one-third of the membership, a special General Assembly shall be convened within one month to consider as its agenda the issues raised by those requesting the meeting.

In exceptional cases a special General Assembly may be called by the Executive Committee.

#13. Arbitration Committee.

Arbitration of Disputes within the Society.

Disputes between members in matters of the Society shall be decided through an Arbitration Committee. Each of the disputing parties may appoint two Arbiters who shall choose a fifth as Chairman. If no agreement can be reached on the selection of a Chairman, one shall be chosen from the nominees by lot.

The proposal to call the Arbitration Committee is to be prepared by the Executive Committee, which also makes known the names of the chosen Arbiters.

The five Arbiters must be members of the Society and may belong to the Executive Committee.

The convening of the Arbitration Committee by the Executive Committee shall occur, at the latest, fourteen days after the proposal. The members of the Executive Committee may attend negotiations before the Arbitration Committee.

The Arbitration Committee shall decide through independent judgment after hearing both sides and is not bound by any specific procedure.

If a decision is not reached by the Arbitration Committee after one meeting, the Executive Committee, in accordance with the acts of debate, shall prepare a written report.

#14. Management of Finances.

Should there result, from an audit by the General Assembly, a surplus in the finances, the funds will be invested in a reserve fund of the General Assembly at a fixed rate of interest.

#15. Dissolution of the Society.

Dissolution of the Society can only result from a vote of the General Assembly at which three-fourths of the membership are present or represented.

The vote of dissolution requires for enactment a three-fourths majority, and is thus an exception to the voting procedure as set out in #12.

It is the duty of the last General Assembly to decide on the disposal of the resources of the Society. If such a decision is not reached, the resources of the Society go to the Gustav Mahler-Stiftung in Vienna.

APPENDIX 3

Programs and Pieces
Performed by the Society

The following is a list of works performed from 29 December 1918 to 5 December 1921.[*] The letters in parentheses refer to the *Vortragsmeister* who prepared the piece listed: Sch = Schoenberg, W = Webern, B = Berg, St = Steuermann[B], S = Benno Sachs. (*Vortragsmeister* listed only for first year.) The numbers in parentheses refer to the concert in which a work was first performed.

1. 29 December 1918
   Alexander Skryabin, *IV. und VII. Piano Sonatas.* Edward Steuermann (Sch); Claude Debussy, *Proses lyriques, four songs.* Felicie Mihacsek[B], Ernst Bachrich[B] (W); Gustav Mahler, *VII. Symphonie e-moll.* Arrangement for piano four-hands by Alfredo Casella. Edward Steuermann, Ernst Bachrich (Sch).
2. 5 January 1919
   Max Reger, *Violoncellosonate a-moll op. 118.* Otto Stieglitz, Ernst Bachrich (W); Gustav Mahler, *Five songs from "Des Knaben Wunderhorn."* Arthur Fleischer, Edward Steuermann (W); Max Reger, *Introduktion, Passacaglia und Fuge für zwei Klaviere op. 96.* Olga Novakovic, Ernst Bachrich (W).
3. 12 January 1919
   Richard Strauss, *Don Quixote op. 35.* Arrangement for piano four-hands by Otto Singer. Edward Steuermann, Ernst Bachrich (W); Alexander Skryabin *IV. und VII. Piano Sonatas* (1); Max Reger, *Introduktion, Passacaglia und Fuge op. 96* (2).

---

[*]This list, together with an alphabetical list by composer and a list of performers, appears in Walter Szmolyan, "Die Konzerte des Wiener Schönberg-Vereins," *Oesterreichische Musikzeitschrift* 36 (February 1981):84–102. For *Vortragsmeister,* see Walter Szmolyan, "Schönbergs Wiener Verein für musikalische Privataufführungen," in *Arnold Schönberg, Gedenkausstellung 1974,* ed. Ernst Hilmar (Vienna: Universal Edition, 1974), pp. 76–80.

4. 16 January 1919

Gustav Mahler, *VII. Symphonie e-moll* (1); Claude Debussy, *Proses lyriques* (1).

5. 23 January 1919

Max Reger, *Violoncellosonate a-moll op. 118* (2); Claude Debussy, *Fêtes galantes, songs.* Emmy Heim, Edward Steuermann (W); Franz Schreker[B], *Vorspiel zu einem Drama.* Arrangement for piano four-hands. Josef Rosenstock, Felix Petyrek (B).

6. 30 January 1919

Richard Strauss, *Don Quixote op. 35* (3); Gustav Mahler, *Five songs from "Des Knaben Wunderhorn"* (2); Claude Debussy, *Trois Nocturnes pour orchestre.* Arrangement for two pianos by Maurice Ravel. Cesia Dische, Olga Novakovic (Sch).

7. 2 February 1919

Josef Hauer[B], *Nomos in sieben Teilen für Klavier op. 1.* Rudolf Réti (W); Josef Hauer, *Nomos in fünf Teilen für Klavier op. 2.* Rudolf Réti; Claude Debussy, *Trois Nocturnes* (6); Hans Pfitzner[B], *Fünf Lieder op. 26.* Felicie Mihacsek, Ernest Bachrich (W); Alban Berg, *Klaviersonate op. 1.* Edward Steuermann (B).

8. 9 February 1919

Franz Schreker, *Vorspiel zu einem Drama* (5); Béla Bartók, *Vierzehn Bagatellen für Klavier op. 6.* Cesia Dische (Sch); Claude Debussy, *Fêtes galantes* (5); Igor Stravinsky, *Trois pièces faciles for piano four-hands.* Edward Steuermann, Ernst Bachrich (Sch); Igor Stravinsky, *Cinq pièces faciles for piano four-hands.* Edward Steuermann, Ernst Bachrich (Sch).

9. 16 February 1919

Anton Webern, *Passacaglia für Orchester op. 1.* Arrangement for two pianos six-hands. Edward Steuermann, Paul Pisk, Ernst Bachrich (Sch); Béla Bartók, *Vierzehn Bagatellen op. 6* (8); Alexander Zemlinsky[B], *Vier Lieder op. 8.* Arthur Fleischer, Edward Steuermann (W); Igor Stravinsky, *Trois pièces faciles* (8); Igor Stravinsky, *Cinq pièces faciles* (8); Anton Webern, *Passacaglia op. 1.*

10. 23 February 1919

Alban Berg, *Klaviersonate op. 1* (7); Claude Debussy, *Trois Nocturnes* (6); Josef Hauer, *Nomos in fünf Teilen op. 2* (7); Josef Hauer, *Nomos in sieben Teilen op. 1* (7); Karl Weigl, *I. Streichquartett E-dur (with Viola d'amore).* Gottesmann-Quartett (Sch).

11. 2 March 1919

Julius Bittner, *Violoncellosonate.* Wilhelm Winkler, Olga Novakovic (W); Ferruccio Busoni, *Sech Elegien für Klavier.* Edward Steuermann (Sch); Karl Weigl, *Streichquartett E-dur* (10).

12. 9 March 1919

Max Reger, *Klarinettensonate B-dur op. 107*. Gustav Vogelhut, Edward Steuermann (St); Erich Wolfgang Korngold, *Violonsonate op. 6*. Rudolf Kolisch, Albert Tadlewsky (Sch).

13. 16 March 1919

Josef Suk, *Ein Sommermärchen, Tondichtung für grosses Orchester op. 29*. Arrangement for piano four-hands by Roman Vesely. Etta Werndorff, Ernst Bachrich (B and Sch); Hans Pfitzner, *Fünf Lieder op. 26* (7); Richard Strauss, *Don Quixote op. 35* (3).

14. 23 March 1919

Max Reger, *Klarinettensonate B-dur op. 107* (12); Max Reger, *Violoncellosonate a-moll op. 118* (2); Max Reger, *Introduktion, Passacaglia und Fuge op. 96* (2).

15. 30 March 1919

Joseph Gustav Mraczek, *Max und Moritz, symphonische Burleske für grosses Orchester*. Arrangement for piano four-hands. Olga Novakovic, Ernst Bachrich (W); Egon Wellesz[B], *Geistliches Lied für Mezzosopran, Geige, Bratsche und Klavier op. 23*. Emmy Heim, Hugo Gottesmann, Hugo Kauder[B], Rudolf Réti (B); Richard Strauss, *Sinfonia domestica op. 53*. Arrangement for two pianos. Cesia Dische, Ernst Bachrich [?] (B).

16. 6 April 1919

Ferruccio Busoni, *Sechs Elegien* (11); Alban Berg, *Vier Lieder op. 2*. Felicie Mihacsek, Edward Steuermann (W); Anton Webern, *Fünf Lieder op. 3*. Felicie Mihacsek, Edward Steuermann, (W); Josef Hauer, *Nomos in fünf Teilen op. 2* (7).

17. 13 April 1919

Fidelio Finke, *Fünf Klavierstücke*. Hildegard Spengler; Alban Berg, *Vier Lieder op. 2* (16); Josef Suk, *Erlebtes und Erträumtes, zehn Klavierstücke*. Rudolf Serkin (Sch); Igor Stravinsky, *Trois pièces faciles* (8); Igor Stravinsky, *Cinq pièces faciles* (8).

18. 27 April 1919

Maurice Ravel, *Gaspard de la nuit*. Edward Steuermann (St); Gustav Mahler, *VI. Symphonie a-moll*. Arrangement for piano four-hands by Alexander Zemlinsky. Edward Steuermann, Ernst Bachrich (Sch).

19. 4 May 1919

Max Reger, *Episoden op. 115, acht Klavierstücke*. Ernst Bachrich (Sch); Max Reger, *Klarinettenquintett A-dur op. 146*. Gustav Vogelhut, Bene-Jary-Quartett (W); Ferruccio Busoni, *Sechs Elegien* (11).

20. 11 May 1919

Claude Debussy, *Ile Joyeuse, piano pieces*. Edward Steuermann (St); Alexander Zemlinsky, *II. Streichquartett op. 15*. Feist-Quartett (W); Alexander Zemlinsky, *Sechs Gesänge op. 13*. Hedi Jracema-Brügelmann, Ernst Bachrich (W).

21. 17 May 1919

Gustav Mahler, *VII. Symphonie e-moll* (1); Max Reger, *Klarinettenquintett A-dur op. 146* (19);

22. 23 May 1919

Max Reger, *Klarinettensonate B-dur op. 107* (12); Gustav Mahler, *Five songs from "Des Knaben Wunderhorn"* (2); Alexander Zemlinsky, *II. Streichquartett op. 15* (20).

23. 30 May 1919

Alban Berg, *Klaviersonate op. 1* (7); Josef Hauer, *Sieben kleine Stücke für Klavier op. 3*. Edward Steuermann (St); Josef Hauer, *Tanz für Klavier op. 10*. Edward Steuermann (St); Ferruccio Busoni, *Sechs Elegien* (11); Claude Debussy, *Proses lyriques* (1); Maurice Ravel, *Gaspard de la nuit* (18); Claude Debussy, *Ile joyeuse* (20).

24. 6 June 1919

Béla Bartók, *Vierzehn Bagatellen op. 6* (8); Igor Stravinsky, *Berceuses de chat, four songs for voice and three clarinets*. Emmy Heim, Karl Gaudriot, Franz Prem, Gustav Vogelhut (Sch); Igor Stravinsky, *Pribaoutki, four songs for voice and eight instruments* (violin, viola, cello, bass, flute, oboe, clarinet, bassoon). Emmy Heim, Hugo Gottesmann, Hugo Kauder, Rudolf Mayer, Karl Fiala, Viktor Zimmermann, Simon Danzer, Gustav Vogelhut, Hugo Burghauser (Sch); Alban Berg, *Reigen, Orchesterstück op. 6, nr. 2*. Arrangement for two pianos eight-hands. Edward Steuermann, Olga Novakovic, Cesia Dische, Ernst Bachrich (W); Anton Webern, *Fünf Lieder op. 3* (16); Anton Webern, *Passacaglia op. 1* (9, Steuermann, Bachrich, Novakovic).

25. 13 June 1919

Claude Debussy, *Trois Nocturnes* (6); Alexander Zemlinsky, *Sechs Gesänge op. 13* (20); Josef Suk, *Erlebtes und Erträumtes* (17).

26. 20 June 1919

Alexander Skryabin, *IV. und VII. Klaviersonate* (1); Alexander Zemlinsky, *II. Streichquartett op. 15* (20).

27. 19 September 1919

Max Reger, *Violinsonate c-moll op. 139*. Erna Alberdingk, Ernst Bachrich (W); Richard Strauss, *Sechs Lieder op. 67*. Stefanie Bruck-Zimmer, Ernst Bachrich (W); Max Reger, *Beethoven-Variationen für Orchester op. 86*. Arrangement for two pianos. Olga Novakovic, Ernst Bachrich (B).

28. 26 September 1919
    Ferruccio Busoni, *I. Sonatine für Klavier*. Edward Steuermann (St); Maurice Ravel, *Streichquartett*. Feist-Quartett (W); Max Reger, *Fünf Gesänge aus op. 75*. Hedi Jracema-Brügelmann, Ernst Bachrich (W).

29. 5 October 1919
    Maurice Ravel, *Gaspard de la nuit* (18); Hans Pfitzner, *Klavierquintett C-dur op. 23*. Bene-Jary-Quartett, Ernst Bachrich (W). Maurice Ravel, *Trois Poèmes (Stephane Mallarmé)*. Stefanie Bruck-Zimmer, Edward Steuermann.

30. 12 October 1919
    Ferruccio Busoni, *I. Sonatine* (28); Franz Schmidt, *II. Symphonie Es-dur*. Arrangement for piano four-hands by Alexander Wunderer. Selma Stampfer, Paul Pisk (S and B); Béla Bartók, *Rumänische Volkstänze aus Ungarn für Klavier*. Olga Novakovic (Sch); Béla Bartók, *Rumänische Weihnachtslieder aus Ungarn, Neunzehn Klavierstücke*. Olga Novakovic (Sch).

31. 17 October 1919
    Alban Berg, *Vier Klarinettenstücke op. 5*. Franz Prem (B); Maurice Ravel, *Streichquartett* (28); Max Reger, *Fünf Gesänge aus op. 75* (28).

32. 24 October 1919
    Béla Bartók, *Rumänische Volkstänze* (30); Béla Bartók, *Rumänische Weihnachtslieder* (30); Alban Berg, *Vier Klarinettenstücke op. 5* (31); Claude Debussy, *Trois Chansons de Bilitis*. Emmy Heim, Olga Novakovic; Max Reger, *Violinsonate e-moll op. 122*. Oskar Adler[B], Ida Hartungen (W).

33. 31 October 1919
    Felix Weingartner, *IV. Streichquartett D-dur op. 62*. Brunner-Quartett (S); Modest Mussorgsky, *Kinderstube, sieben Lieder*. Stella Eisner, Edward Steuermann (W); Alexander Skryabin, *Le poème de l'extase op. 54*. Arrangement for two pianos. Olga Novakovic, Edward Steuermann (Sch).

34. 7 November 1919
    Paul Dukas, *Variationen für Klavier*. Claire Schwaiger (B); Richard Strauss, *Sechs Lieder op. 67* (27); Max Reger, *Beethoven-Variationen op. 86* (27);

35. 14 November 1919
    Modest Mussorgsky, *Kinderstube* (33); Max Reger, *Sechs kleine Präludien und Fugen für Klavier op. 99*. Ida Hartungen (W); Max Reger, *Violinsonate e-moll op. 122* (32).

36. 21 November 1919
    Claude Debussy, *Children's Corner, six piano pieces*. Edward

Steuermann (St); Anton Webern, *Vier Stücke für Geige und Klavier op. 7.* Oskar Adler, Edward Steuermann (W).

37. 28 November 1919

Rudolf Braun, *Streichquintett op. 38.* Bene-Jary-Quartett, Stephi Chalupny (W); Béla Bartók, *Rumänische Volkstänze* (30); Béla Bartók, *Rumänische Weihnachtslieder* (30); Claude Debussy, *La mer.* Arrangement for two pianos by André Caplet. Edward Steuermann, Ernst Bachrich (Sch).

38. 19 December 1919

Béla Bartók, *Quatre Nénies pour le piano.* Ernst Bachrich; Claude Debussy, *Children's Corner* (36); Richard Strauss, *Eine Alpensymphonie op. 64.* Arrangement for two pianos by Otto Singer. Olga Novakovic, Ernst Bachrich.

39. 2 January 1920

Gustav Mahler, *Fünf Lieder aus der Jugendzeit.* Stella Eisner, Ernst Bachrich; Gustav Mahler, *VI. Symphonie a-moll* (18).

40. 9 January 1920

Karol Szymanowski, *Des Hafis Liebeslieder, six songs.* Stefanie Bruck-Zimmer, Ernst Bachrich; Béla Bartók, *Quatre Nénies* (38); Richard Strauss, *Eine Alpensymphonie op. 64* (38).

41. 25 January 1920

Maurice Ravel, *Daphnis et Chloé, 2. Suite.* Arrangement for piano four-hands by Leon Roques. Olga Novakovic, Ernst Bachrich; Robert Fuchs, *Violinsonate g-moll.* Paula Bene-Jary, Paul Pisk; Franz Schmidt, *II. Symphonie Es-dur* (30).

42. 30 January 1920

Karol Szymanowski, *Romanze für Geige und Klavier op. 23.* Rudolf Kolisch, Selma Stampfer; Anton Webern, *Fünf Stücke für Orchester op. 10.* Arrangement for violin, viola, violoncello, piano, and harmonium. Rudolf Kolisch, Walter Seligmann, Maria Lazansky, Max Deutsch, Hans Neumann, conductor: Anton Webern. Erik Satie, *Drei Hefte Klavierstücke.* Edward Steuermann.

43. 6 February 1920

Maurice Ravel, *Daphnis et Chloé, 2. Suite* (41); Gustav Mahler, *Lieder eines fahrenden Gesellen.* Arrangement for flute, clarinet, two violins, viola, violoncello, double bass, piano, and harmonium. Stella Eisner, chamber orchestra, conductor: Arnold Schoenberg. Erik Satie, *Drei Hefte Klavierstücke* (42); Modest Mussorgsky, *Kinderstube, sieben Lieder* (33); Karol Szymanowski, *Romanze für Geige und Klavier op. 23* (42).

44. 13 February 1920

Max Reger, *Variationen und Fuge über ein Thema von J. S. Bach für Klavier op. 81.* Paul Emerich; Claude Debussy, *La mer* (37); Ferrucio Busoni, *Sechs Elegien* (11).

45. 20 February 1920
Alban Berg, *Klaviersonate op. 1* (7); Alexander Skryabin, *VII. Klaviersonate* (1); Gustav Mahler, *Fünf Lieder aus der Jugendzeit* (39); László Lajtha, *Elf Klavierstücke.* Olga Novakovic.
46. 27 February 1920
Claude Debussy, *Children's Corner* (36); Claude Debussy, *Violinsonate.* Oskar Adler, Edward Steuermann; Claude Debussy, *La mer* (37).
47. 5 March 1920
Béla Bartók, *Rumänische Volkstänze und Weihnachtslieder aus Ungarn für Klavier* (30); Igor Stravinsky, *Drei Stücke für Streichquartett.* Feist-Quartett; Maurice Ravel, *Streichquartett* (28).
48. 12 March 1920
László Lajtha, *Elf Klavierstücke* (45); Max Reger, *Variationen und Fuge über ein Thema von J. S. Bach für Klavier op. 81* (44); Claude Debussy, *Trois Nocturnes* (6).
49. 19 March 1920
Béla Bartók, *Vierzehn Bagatellen für Klavier op. 6* (8); Max Reger, *Violinsonate e-moll op. 122* (32).
50. 26 March 1920
Vitezslav Novak, *Exotikon, five piano pieces op. 45.* Rudolf Serkin; Gustav Mahler, *Fünf Lieder aus der Jugendzeit* (39); Josef Suk, *Erlebtes und Erträumtes* (17).
51. 9 April 1920
Maurice Ravel, *Daphnis et Chloé, 2. Suite* (41); Max Reger, *Violinsonate c-moll op. 139* (27); Max Reger, *Variationen und Fuge über ein Thema von W. A. Mozart für zwei Klaviere op. 132.* Selma Stampfer, Ernst Bachrich.
52. 16 April 1920
Max Reger, *Sechs kleine Präludien und Fugen für Klavier op. 99* (35); Zoltán Kodály, *Sonate für Violoncello solo.* Paul Hermann; Max Reger, *Variationen und Fuge über ein Thema von W.A. Mozart für zwei Klaviere op. 132* (51).
53. 23 April 1920
Max Reger, *Violoncellosonate F-dur, op. 78.* Wilhelm Winkler, Olga Novakovic; Béla Bartók, *I. Streichquartett op. 7.* Feist-Quartett.
54. 30 April 1920
Bernhard Sekles, *Passacaglia und Fuge für Streichquartett op. 23.* Gottesmann-Quartett; Maurice Ravel, *Valses nobles et sentimentales for piano.* Ernst Bachrich.
55. 7 May 1920
Boleslav Vomacka, *Vier Klavierstücke op. 4.* Selma Stampfer; Max Reger, *Violinsonate e-moll op. 122* (32).

56. 14 May 1920
   Josef Hauer, *Nomos für Klavier op. 19*. Josef Hauer; Karol Szymanowski, *Romanze für Geige und Klavier op. 23* (42).

57. 21 May 1920
   Max Reger, *Träume am Kamin, zwölf kurze Klavierstücke op. 143*. Ida Hartungen; Béla Bartók, *Quatre Nènies pour le piano* (38); Maurice Ravel, *Daphnis et Chloé, 2. Suite* (41).

58. 28 May 1920
   Max Reger, *Variationen und Fuge über ein Thema von W. A. Mozart für Zwei Klaviere op. 132* (51).

59. 4 June 1920
   Maurice Ravel, *Gaspard de la nuit* (18); Rudolf Réti, *Vier Lieder*. Marie Gutheil-Schoder[B], Ernst Bachrich; Claude Debussy, *En blanc et noir for two pianos*. Edward Steuermann, Rudolf Serkin.

60. 11 June 1920
   Rudolf Braun, *Phantasiestück für Viola und Klavier*. Else Stein, Ernst Bachrich; Anton Webern, *Fünf Stücke für Orchester op. 10*. Arrangement for chamber orchestra (42); Claude Debussy, *Violinsonate* (46); Alban Berg, *Vier Klarinettenstücke op. 5* (31, Karl Gaudriot); Claude Debussy, *En blanc et noir* (59).

61. 17 June 1920
   Alban Berg, *Vier Klarinettenstücke op. 5* (31, Karl Gaudriot); Egon Wellesz, *Fünf Klavierstücke op. 26*. Ernst Bachrich; Erik Satie, *Drei Hefte Klavierstücke* (42).

62. 20 September 1920
   Alexander Skryabin, *Vier Preludes für Klavier op. 33, Drei Klavierstücke op. 45, Trois Morceaux pour piano op. 49*. Ida Hartungen; Max Reger, *Sonate für Violine solo a-moll op. 91*. Rudolf Kolisch; Josef Suk, *Vom Mütterchen, Fünf Klavierstücke op. 28*. Rudolf Serkin; Igor Stravinsky, *Trois et Cinq pièces faciles for piano four-hands* (8, Selma Stampfer, Edward Steuermann).

63. 29 September 1920
   Max Reger, *Sechs Stücke für Klavier zu vier Händen op. 94*. Selma Stampfer, Ernst Bachrich; Max Reger, *Violinsonate e-moll op. 122* (32); Josef Suk, *Vom Mütterchen op. 28* (62).

64. 6 October 1920
   Claude Debussy, *Violoncellosonate*. Wilhelm Winkler, Olga Novakovic; Maurice Ravel, *Gaspard de la nuit* (18).

65. 9 October 1920
   Max Reger, *Eine romantische Suite op. 125*. Arrangement for chamber orchestra by Rudolf Kolisch. Chamber orchestra, conductor: Erwin Stein; Béla Bartók, *Rhapsodie pour le piano et*

l'orchestre op. 1. Arrangement for two pianos by Béla Bartók. Edward Steuermann, Ernst Bachrich; Arnold Schoenberg, *Zwei neue Klavierstücke (Klavierstücke op. 23/1, 2).* Edward Steuermann. Claude Debussy, *Sonata for Flute, Viola and Harp.* Wilhelm Sonnenberg, Ernst Morawetz, Steffi Goldner.

66. 13 October 1920

Arnold Schoenberg, *Drei Klavierstücke op. 11.* Edward Steuermann; Max Reger, *Violinsonate C-dur op. 72.* Oskar Adler, Ida Hartungen; Igor Stravinsky, *Petruschka, Burleske Szenen in vier Bildern.* Arrangement for piano four-hands by Igor Stravinsky. Edward Steuermann, Rudolf Serkin.

67. 18 October 1920

Max Reger, *Drei Stücke aus "Träume am Kamin" op. 143* (57); Max Reger, *Violinsonate C-dur op. 72* (66); Claude Debussy, *En blanc et noir* (59).

68. 23 October 1920

Maurice Ravel, *Gaspard de la nuit* (18); Arnold Schoenberg, *Fünf Lieder aus "Das Buch der hängenden Gärten" op. 15.* Helge Lindberg, Edward Steuermann; Arnold Schoenberg, *Zwei neue Klavierstücke* (65); Anton Webern, *Vier Stücke für Geige und Klavier op. 7* (36, Rudolf Kolisch, Edward Steuermann); Alban Berg, *Vier Klarinettenstücke op. 5* (31, Karl Gaudriot, Edward Steuermann); Maurice Ravel, *La Valse, Poème choreographique pour orchestre.* Arrangement for two pianos by Maurice Ravel. Maurice Ravel, Alfredo Casella; Maurice Ravel, *Trois Poèmes (Stephane Mallarmé)* (29, Marya Freund, Maurice Ravel); Arnold Schoenberg, *Jane Grey, Ballade aus op. 12.* Olga Bauer-Pilecka, Ernst Bachrich; Maurice Ravel, *Streichquartett* (28).

69. 27 October 1920

Max Reger, *Suite für Violine und Klavier a-moll, op. 103a.* Rudolf Kolisch, Rudolf Serkin; Boleslav Vomáčka, *Vier Klavierstücke op. 4* (55); Max Reger, *Sonate für Violine solo a-moll op. 91* (62); Josef Suk, *Vom Mütterchen op. 28* (62).

70. 1 November 1920

Max Reger, *Violinsonate c-moll op. 139* (27); Béla Bartók, *Rumänischer Tanz für Klavier aus op. 8.* Erna Lamadin; Max Reger, *Sechs Stücke für Klavier zu vier Händen op. 94* (63, three pieces only).

71. 8 November 1920

Max Reger, *Suite für Violine und Klavier a-moll op. 103a* (69); Claude Debussy, *Rhapsodie for clarinet and piano.* Viktor Polatschek, Rudolf Serkin; Joseph Marx, *Vier Lieder.* Dora

Schmeichler, Selma Stampfer; Maurice Ravel, *Le Tombeau de Couperin, six piano pieces*. Ida Hartungen.

    72. 15 November 1920

        Béla Bartók, *Quatre Nénies pour le piano* (38); Béla Bartók, *Suite für Klavier op. 14*. Ernst Bachrich; Max Reger, *Violinsonate c-moll op. 139* (27, Rudolf Kolisch, Ernst Bachrich).

    73. 22 November 1920

        Arnold Schoenberg, *Zwei neue Klavierstücke* (65); Max Reger, *Streichtrio d-moll op. 141b*. Hugo Gottesmann, Ernst Morawetz, Bohdan V. Bereznicky; Arnold Schoenberg, *Zwei neue Klavierstücke* (65); Egon Kornauth, *Violinsonate op. 9*. Rudolf Kolisch, Selma Stampfer.

    74. 29 November 1920

        Claude Debussy, *Violoncellosonate* (64, Wilhelm Winkler, Edward Steuermann); Béla Bartók, *I. Streichquartett op. 7* (53); Claude Debussy, *Violoncellosonate* (64).

    75. 6 December 1920

        Béla Bartók, *Rhapsodie pour le piano et l'orchestre* (65); Arnold Schoenberg, *Sechs kleine Klavierstücke op. 19*. Edward Steuermann; Anton Webern, *Vier Stücke für Geige und Klavier op. 7* (36, Rudolf Kolisch, Edward Steuermann); Claude Debussy, *La mer* (37).

    76. 20 December 1920

        Egon Wellesz, *Fünf Klavierstücke op. 26* (61); Anton Webern, *Vier Stücke für Geige und Klavier op. 7* (36, Rudolf Kolisch, Eduard Steuermann); Gustav Mahler, *VII. Symphonie e-moll* (1).

    77. 27 December 1920

        Arnold Schoenberg, *Drei Klavierstücke op. 11* (66); Modest Mussorgsky, *Lieder und Tänze des Todes*. Arthur Fleischer, Edward Steuermann; Claude Debussy, *Violinsonate* (46).

    78. 3 January 1921

        Arnold Schoenberg, *Kammersymphonie op. 9*. Arrangement for piano by Edward Steuermann. Edward Steuermann; Modest Mussorgsky, *Lieder und Tänze des Todes* (77); Gustav Mahler, *Three songs from "Des Knaben Wunderhorn"*. Arthur Fleischer, Edward Steuermann.

    79. 10 January 1921

        Claude Debussy, *Douze Préludes* (Ier livre, Nr. 1–7). Ernst Bachrich; Gustav Mahler, *IV. Symphonie G-dur*. Arrangement for chamber orchestra by Erwin Stein. Martha Fuchs, chamber orchestra, conductor: Erwin Stein.

    80. 20 January 1921

Arnold Schoenberg, *Zwei Lieder aus op. 8: Nr. 5 Voll jener Süsse, Nr. 6 Wenn Vöglein klagen.* Karl Fälbl, Ernst Bachrich; Arnold Schoenberg, *Zwei Lieder op. 14, Drei Lieder aus op. 6: Nr. 1 Traumleben, Nr. 4 Verlassen, Nr. 3 Mädchenlied.* Erika Wagner, Ernst Bachrich; Gustav Mahler, *IV. Symphonie G-dur* (79).

  81. 23 January 1921
  Arnold Schoenberg, *Zwei Lieder aus op. 8* (80); Arnold Schoenberg, *Zwei Lieder op. 14, Drei Lieder aus op. 6* (80, Erika Wagner, Selma Stampfer); Anton Webern, *Sechs Stücke für grosses Orchester op. 6.* Arrangement for chamber orchestra by Anton Webern. Chamber orchestra, conductor: Anton Webern; Gustav Mahler, *IV. Symphonie G-dur* (79).

  82. 24 January 1921
  Paul Dukas, *Variations, Interlude and Finale on a Theme by Rameau for piano* (34, Selma Stampfer); Max Reger, *Violinsonate c-moll op. 139* (27, Rudolf Kolisch, Ernst Bachrich).

  83. 31 January 1921
  Anton Webern, *Sechs Stücke für grosses Orchester op. 6* (81); Arnold Schoenberg, *Zwei Lieder op. 14* (80, Erika Wagner, Selma Stampfer); Claude Debussy, *Douze Préludes* (Ier livre, Nr. 1–6) (79); Anton Webern, *Sechs Stücke für grosses Orchester op. 6* (81).

  84. 7 February 1921
  Alois Hába, *Klaviersonate op. 3.* Albert Linschütz; Béla Bartók, *15 Ungarische Bauernlieder für Klavier.* Selma Stampfer; Max Reger, *Variationen und Fuge über ein Thema von W. A. Mozart für zwei Klaviere op. 132* (51).

  85. 14 February 1921
  Béla Bartók, *Suite für Klavier op. 14* (72); Claude Debussy, *Six Epigraphes antiques for piano four-hands.* Edward Steuermann, Selma Stampfer; Karol Szymanowski, *Violinsonate op. 9.* Rudolf Kolisch, Selma Stampfer.

  86. 21 February 1921
  Claude Debussy, *Violinsonate* (46); Claude Debussy, *Images for piano, II. book.* Cesia Dische; Claude Debussy, *Violoncellosonate* (64, Wilhelm Winkler, Edward Steuermann).

  87. 28 February 1921
  Paul Dukas, *Variations, Interlude and Finale on a Theme by Rameau for piano* (34, Selma Stampfer); Max Reger, *Serenade für Flöte, Violine und Viola G-dur, op. 141a.* Albert Weinschenk, Rudolf Kolisch, Jaroslav Czerny; Alois Hába, *Klaviersonate op. 3* (84).

  88. 7 March 1921

Josef Hauer, *Orientalisches Märchen für Klavier op. 9.* Ernst Bachrich; Otaker Ostrčil, *Zwei Gesänge aus op. 14.* Frl. Zeisl, Käthe Travniček; Claude Debussy, *Six Epigraphes antiques* (85); Arnold Schoenberg, *Kammersymphonie op. 9* (78).

89. 14 March 1921

Arnold Schoenberg, *Drei Klavierstücke op. 11* (66); Max Reger, *An die Hoffnung, Kantate für Alt und Orchester op. 124* (Edition for piano). Hilde Salinger, Ernst Bachrich; Claude Debussy, *Images* (86); Max Reger, *Sonate für Violine solo a-moll op. 91* (62); Arnold Schoenberg, *Sechs kleine Klavierstücke op. 19* (75).

90. 21 March 1921

Max Reger, *Sechs Intermezzi für Klavier op. 45.* Elly Lüttmann; Max Reger, *Serenade für Flöte, Violine, und Viola G-dur op. 141a* (87); Alexander Skryabin, *VII. Klaviersonate* (1); Arnold Schoenberg, *Zwei neue Klavierstücke* (65).

91. 4 April 1921

Arnold Schoenberg, *Kammersymphonie op. 9* (78); Arnold Schoenberg, *Pelleas und Melisande op. 5.* Arrangement for piano four-hands by Heinrich Jalowetz[B]. Edward Steuermann, Ernst Bachrich.

92. 11 April 1921

Claude Debussy, *Six Epigraphes antiques* (85); Rudolf Réti, *Vier Lieder* (59); Alexander Zemlinsky, *Vier Gesänge aus den Maeterlinck-Liedern op. 13* (20, Marie Gutheil-Schoder, Eduard Steuermann); Ferruccio Busoni, *Violinsonate E-dur op. 29.* Mary Dickenson-Auner, Steffi Blitz.

93. 18 April 1921

Max Reger, *Sechs Intermezzi für Klavier op. 45* (90); Anton Webern, *Vier Stücke für Geige und Klavier op. 7* (36, Rudolf Kolisch, Eduard Steuermann); Arnold Schoenberg, *Zwei neue Klavierstücke* (65); Max Reger, *Serenade für Flöte, Violine und Viola G-dur op. 141a* (87).

94. 25 April 1921

Claude Debussy, *Violoncellosonate* (64, Wilhelm Winkler, Edward Steuermann); Richard Strauss, *Eine Alpensymphonie op. 64* (38).

95. 30 April 1921

Arnold Schoenberg, *Pierrot lunaire op. 21.* Erika Wagner, Edward Steuermann, Franz Wangler, Viktor Polatschek, Rudolf Kolisch, Wilhelm Winkler, conductor: Erwin Stein.

96. 2 May 1921

Alban Berg, *Klaviersonate op. 1* (7); Max Reger, *Serenade für Flöte, Violine und Viola G-dur op. 141a* (87); Ferruccio Busoni, *Sechs Elegien für Klavier* (11); Anton Webern, *Vier Stücke für Geige und Klavier op. 7* (36, Rudolf Kolisch, Edward Steuermann).

97. 3 May 1921

Arnold Schoenberg, *Pierrot lunaire op. 21* (95).

98. 7 May 1921

Arnold Schoenberg, *Pierrot lunaire op. 21* (95).

99. 12 May 1921

Anton Webern, *Sechs Stücke für grosses Orchester op. 6* (81); Arnold Schoenberg, *Pierrot lunaire op. 21* (95, conductor: Arnold Schoenberg).

100. 23 May 1921

Willem Pijper, *Violinsonate*. Rudolf Kolisch, Elly Lütt-mann; Anton Webern, *Sechs Stücke für grosses Orchester op. 6* (81); Karol Szymanowski, *Masken, Drei Klavierstücke op. 34*. Albert Linschütz.

101. 30 May 1921

Ferruccio Busoni, *Toccata für Klavier*. Hilde Merinski; Alban Berg, *Vier Klarinettenstücke op. 5* (31, Karl Gaudriot, Edward Steuermann); Claude Debussy, *Children's Corner* (36); Willem Pijper, *Violinsonate* (100).

102. 6 June 1921

Erik Satie, *Drei Hefte Klavierstücke* (42); Igor Stravinsky, *Piano-Rag Music*. Edward Steuermann; Anton Webern, *Vier Stücke für Geige und Klavier op. 7* (36, Rudolf Kolisch, Edward Steuer-mann); Ferruccio Busoni, *Toccata für Klavier* (101); Igor Stravin-sky, *Piano-Rag Music*.

103. 26 September 1921

Claude Debussy, *Douze Etudes*. Edward Steuermann; Gustav Mahler, *Fünf Lieder aus der Jugendzeit* (39); Béla Bartók, *10 Kleine Klavierstücke "Für Kinder."* Olga Novakovic; Maurice Ravel, *Daphnis et Chloé, 2. Suite* (41).

104. 5 October 1921

Ferruccio Busoni, *Violinsonate E-dur op. 29* (92); Béla Bartók, *10 Kleine Klavierstücke* (103); Karol Szymanowski, *Masken op. 34* (100).

105. 10 October 1921

Claude Debussy, *Douze Etudes* (103); Modest Mussorgsky, *Kinderstube* (33); Willem Pijper, *Violinsonate* (100).

106. 17 October 1921
Max Reger, *Violoncellosonate F-dur op. 78* (53); Max Reger, *Violinsonate C-dur op. 72* (66).

107. 24 October 1921
Max Reger, *Sechs Intermezzi für Klavier op. 45* (90); Modest Mussorgsky, *Kinderstube* (33); Max Reger, *Violoncellosonate F-dur op. 78* (53).

108. 31 October 1921
Karol Szymanowski, *Masken op. 34* (100); Igor Stravinsky, *Piano-Rag Music* (102); Max Reger, *Violinsonate C-dur op. 72* (66).

109. 7 November 1921
Claude Debussy, *Douze Etudes* (103, only six études); Alban Berg, *Vier Lieder op. 2* (16, Ria v. Hessert, Arthur Hermelin); Willem Pijper, *Violoncellosonate*. Wilhelm Winkler, Selma Stampfer.

110. 14 November 1921
Alban Berg, *Vier Lieder op. 2* (16, Ria v. Hessert, Arthur Hermelin); Béla Bartók, *Trois Etudes for piano op. 18*. Albert Linschütz; Maurice Ravel, *Daphnis et Chloé, 2. Suite* (41).

111. 21 November 1921
Vitězslav Novák. *Winternachtsgesänge für Klavier op. 30*. Olga Novakovic; Gustav Mahler, *Fünf Lieder aus der Jugendzeit* (39); Max Reger, *Sonate für Violine solo a-moll op. 91* (62).

112. 28 November 1921
Béla Bartók, *Trois Etudes for piano op. 18* (110); Béla Bartók, *10 Kleine Klavierstücke* (103).

113. 5 December 1921
Arnold Schoenberg, *Pierrot lunaire* (95).

Biographies

Entry name set in **boldface type** indicates person inter
viewed for this book.

ADLER, Guido (1855–1941): Austrian musicologist and professor of music history at the University of Vienna from
1897 until 1927. A student of Bruckner, he succeeded Hans-
lick at the University of Vienna and became one of the
founders of modern musicology. Among his students were
Anton Webern, Paul Pisk, Egon Wellesz, Erna Gál, and
Rudolf Kolisch.

ADLER, Oskar (1875–1955): Friend of Schoenberg's youth. A
physician, Dr. Adler was also an excellent violinist. He
taught Schoenberg violin and viola and was his first
teacher of harmony.

ADORNO, Theodor Wiesengrund (1903–1969): German philosopher, sociologist, and music critic. Following university
studies in Frankfurt, he went to Vienna, where he studied
composition with Berg and Edward Steuermann. In 1931
he qualified for a university position in Frankfurt with a
dissertation on Kierkegaard. In 1933 he was expelled from
the university by the National Socialists. In 1934 he emigrated to England, settling in Oxford, where he wrote a critical study of Husserl. From 1938 to 1941, living in New York,
he directed the Princeton Radio Research Project. From
1941 until 1949 he lived in California, where he completed
his important study of anti-Semitic and authoritarian attitudes published in 1950 as *The Authoritarian Personality*.
During this time he also advised Thomas Mann on the musical aspects of *Doktor Faustus*. In 1949 he resumed his
teaching duties at the University of Frankfurt. His principal
works include: *Kierkegaard. Konstruktion des Ästhetischen*

(1933); *Dialektik der Aufklärung* (with Max Horkheimer, 1947); *Philosophie der neuen Musik* (Philosophy of Modern Music, 1949); *Jargon der Eigentlichkeit* (1965); *Negative Dialektik* (1966); and several books of musical essays.

ALTENBERG, Peter (Richard Engländer) (1859–1919): Austrian poet. He lived a bohemian life style in the Hotel Graben, spending most of his time sitting in coffee houses where Kraus, Loos, and others supported him by giving him food. He wrote poems on postcards which he sent to friends. Berg used five of these as texts for his *Five Orchestral Songs on Picture-Postcard Texts by Peter Altenberg.*

ASKENASE, Stefan (born 1896): Concert pianist, pupil of Emil von Sauer at the Vienna Musical Academy. After serving in World War I, he returned to Vienna to continue his career. He played in a Verein concert before taking up a teaching position at the conservatory in Cairo. In 1925 he moved to Belgium, presenting concerts in Holland, England, France, and Spain. He also performed in chamber music concerts with the Kolisch and Pro-Arte Quartets. In 1932 Berg saw him frequently when in Brussels for a performance of *Wozzeck.* He left Belgium for the duration of the second world war, returning at its end to continue his concert career. From 1954 until 1961 he was professor of piano at the Royal Conservatory in Brussels; he has also given master classes in Hamburg and Cologne.

BACH, David Josef (1874–1947): Austrian musicologist and critic. An early friend of Schoenberg, who credited Bach with developing his ethical and moral power. Bach founded the Arbeiter-Symphonie Concerts and assisted Webern in getting the job of conductor.

BACHRICH, Ernst (1892–1942): Pianist and conductor. A pupil of Schoenberg from 1916 to 1919, he made frequent appearances as a pianist in the concerts of the Verein für musikalische Privataufführungen.

BENJAMIN, Walter (1892–1940): German literary, cultural, and philosophical critic. Marxist in outlook, much of his work focuses on the actions of economic, social, and political forces and the degradation of humans to the status of statistical object in the industrial process. In his efforts at philosophical and philological elucidation of literature and in his humanistic concern, he recalls the activities of Karl Kraus. Some of his major works include: *Schriften* (ed. T. W. and G. Adorno, 2 vols., 1955); *Illuminations* (tr. H. Zohn, 1969); *Angelus Novus* (1966); *Reflections* (tr. E. Jephcott, 1978); and *Briefe* (ed. G. Scholen and T. W. Adorno, 2 vols., 1966).

BUSCH, Adolf (1891–1952): German violinist and composer. Soon after 1918 he founded the Busch String Quartet. He gave numerous sonata recitals with his son-in-law Rudolf Serkin. In 1933 he emigrated first to Switzerland and then to the United States where he was instrumental in establishing the Marlboro School of Music.

CURJEL, Hans (1896–1974): Administrator of the Kroll Opera in Berlin from 1927. Saw Schoenberg frequently in connection with performances of *Erwartung* and *Die glückliche Hand*.

DEHMEL, Richard (1863–1920): German lyric poet. Following studies in science, Dehmel devoted himself after 1895 to literature alone. From 1891 until 1909 he was a close friend of Detlev von Liliencron. Schoenberg and Webern both drew song texts from his works, and Schoenberg used his poems for *Verklärte Nacht*. Dehmel wrote an autobiography, *Mein Leben* (1922); several volumes of verse; stories, plays, comedies, and letters.

DEUTSCH, Max (1892–1982): French conductor and pianist of Austrian origin. Studied at the University of Vienna from 1910 to 1915 and with Schoenberg in 1913 and from 1918 to 1922. Also studied with Steuermann. In the twenties he became a theatre conductor and moved to Paris, where he conducted French premieres of works by Schoenberg, Berg, and Webern. After World War II he taught composition at the Ecole Normale de Musique. He conducted in Paris and taught composition students using the principles of Schoenberg's *Harmonielehre*.

DICK, Marcel (born 1897): Violist. Violist in the Wiener Streichquartett (later Kolisch Quartet) from 1922 to 1927. Participated in numerous first performances of Schoenberg works. After emigrating to the United States, he joined the Cleveland Orchestra and served on the faculty of the Cleveland Institute of Music.

EISLER, Hanns (1898–1962): German composer and pupil of Schoenberg and Webern 1919–1923. His Piano Sonata, Op. 1, premiered by Edward Steuermann, received the Vienna Arts Prize in 1924. He had strong Marxist convictions and in 1926 joined the German Communist Party. He was one of Schoenberg's assistants, and Schoenberg considered him to be one of his most talented students but quarreled with him in 1926 over his political views and alleged attacks on modern music. In 1930 Eisler began a friendship and collaboration with Berthold Brecht. His music was banned in 1933, and he began years of exile in several European countries and the United States. For a while he taught at the New School for Social Research in New York. Then, after three years in Mexico, he moved to Hollywood, where he taught at the University of Southern California and wrote over forty film scores before moving eventually to East Germany.

FREUND, Marya (1876–1966): French soprano of Polish origin. An eminent interpreter of German song and twentieth-century music, she sang in many performances of Schoenberg works, including the *Gurrelieder, Pierrot lunaire, Das Buch der hängenden Gärten*, and the Second String Quartet, as well works of Falla, Ravel, Stravinsky, Bloch, Milhaud, Poulenc, Prokofiev, and Kodály.

FRIEDELL, Egon (1878–1938): Viennese writer, actor, caberet director, and critic. He studied at the Universities of Berlin and Heidelberg. He wrote numerous light pieces about Viennese life, science fiction, and a massive three-volume cultural history, *Kulturgeschichte der Neuzeit: Die Krisis der europäischen Seele von der schwarzen Pest zum ersten Weltkrieg*. He committed suicide after the German occupation of Austria.

GÁL, Erna (born 1899): Pianist who performed frequently with Rudolf Kolisch. She was a pupil of Eugenie Schwarzwald. With the rise of National Socialism, she moved to London, where she continues to teach and perform.

GALIMIR, Felix (born 1910): Violinist. First violinist of the Galimir Quartet, which gave many performances of works by members of the Schoenberg circle. Since immigrating to the United States, he has had a long and active teaching and performance career in New York City.

GERHARD, Roberto (1896–1970): Spanish composer. He studied piano with Granados and composition with Pedrell before becoming a pupil of Schoenberg in 1923. He remained with Schoenberg until 1928, moving to Berlin with him in 1926. In 1929 he returned to Barcelona, where he was appointed professor of music at the Ecola Normal de la Generalitat. In 1932 he became head of the music section of the Catalan Library. Following the defeat of the Republicans in 1939, he left Spain. He spent the remainder of his life in Cambridge, England. His extensive catalogue includes ballets, symphonies, concerti, vocal and chamber music works, and several pieces for tape.

GERSTL, Richard (1883–1908): Austrian painter. He studied at the Academy in Vienna. His early works were in the style of the Vienna Secession, influenced by the decorative linearism of Klimt. By 1905 he had evolved an expressionist style, painting portraits remarkable for their psychological insight, including two groups of the Schoenberg family. His work was little known in his own time and largely ignored for many years following his suicide.

GOEHR, Walter (1903–1960): German conductor and composer. Pupil of Schoenberg in Berlin 1926–1928. From 1925 until 1931, he was conductor for the Berlin radio. In 1931 he began a successful London conducting career which included positions with the Morley College Concerts and the BBC. In 1943 he conducted the premiere of Britten's Serenade.

GREISSLE, Felix (1899–1982): Pupil of Schoenberg from about 1920, he also studied with Berg briefly. He was for a time Secretary of the Verein für musikalische Privataufführungen and did many piano reductions for their concerts. In 1921 he married Schoenberg's daughter Gertrud. In New York City, he was employed for many years by E. B. Marks, a music publisher.

GRONOSTAY, Walter (1906–1937): Composer. Pupil of Schoenberg in Berlin from 1926 through 1928. Works include film scores, chamber music, and compositions for radio.

GUTHEIL-SCHODER, Marie (1874–1935): German soprano at the Weimar Opera 1891–1900, and at the Vienna Opera from 1900 to 1927. She sang in the premiere of Schoenberg's Second Quartet with the Rosé Quartet in Vienna in

1908, and in the premiere of *Erwartung*, conducted by Alexander von Zemlinsky, in Prague in 1924. She frequently sang Strauss, and Berg admired her performances.

HANNENHEIM, Norbert von (1898–1942): Composer and pupil of Schoenberg in Berlin from 1929 to 1932. Hannenheim was a talented and prolific composer whose works unfortunately largely disappeared following his death in a mental institution in 1942.

HAUER, Josef Matthias (1883–1959): Austrian theorist and composer. Initially an elementary school teacher, Hauer was also active as an organist and choral conductor. He lived in Vienna, where he was an associate of Altenberg, Hermann Bahr, Kraus, Loos, and Itten. As early as 1913 he approached Schoenberg for an opinion of his work. Their first personal meeting, however, did not take place until 1917. Thereafter Schoenberg presented Hauer's compositions in the Verein concerts. Hauer devised an approach to composition utilizing divisions of the chromatic scale into collections, or *Tropen*, which form the material for composition. Following ten years of theoretical work, Hauer undertook serious composition utilizing *Tropen* in or around 1918. While predating Schoenberg's twelve-tone method by several years, Hauer's approach lacks its refinement. Hauer also invented a special notation for twelve-tone music. In 1938 Hauer retired completely after his music was declared decadent and degenerate art by the National Socialists. His most important theoretical works are *Deutung des Melos* (1923); *Vom Melos zur Pauke* (1925); and *Zwölftontechnik* (1926).

HEIFETZ, Benar (1899–1974): Cellist of the Kolisch Quartet. Of Russian birth, he studied at the St. Petersburg Conservatory and in Leipzig with Julius Klengl. Following extensive solo recital tours, he joined the Kolisch Quartet in 1927. Heifetz brought great technical facility to the Quartet. His warmth and the naturalness of his playing were assets to the group, whose attitude might otherwise have been too cerebral. From 1939 through 1943 he served as solo cellist first with the Philadelphia Orchestra, under Eugene Ormandy, and then with the NBC Symphony Orchestra, under Arturo Toscanini. In 1944 he founded the Albeneri Trio. After 1961, he taught at the Manhattan School of Music.

HELLER, Hugo (died 1923): Viennese bookstore and gallery owner. Heller held the first exhibition of Schoenberg's painting in his establishment in October of 1910. As an impresario, he managed Gerhart Hauptmann and Bruno Walter, along with many other important cultural figures.

HINDEMITH, Paul (1895–1963): German composer, violist, theorist, and conductor. After studies in Frankfurt in 1915 he became concertmaster of the Frankfurt Opera Orchestra and second violinist of the Rebner Quartet. Following war service in a regimental band, he became violist of the Rebner Quartet in 1919. From 1923 until 1929 he was violist of the Amar-Hindemith Quartet which toured extensively. Although not a student of Schoenberg, and not himself a composer of twelve-tone music, Hindemith was supportive of Schoenberg's endeavors. In 1927 he was appointed professor at the Musikhochschule in Berlin. From 1929 until 1934 he was in a string trio with Josef Wolfsthal and Emanuel Feuermann. In 1933 he approached Berg about accepting a position at the Musikhochschule, but this never materialized. In 1937 he moved to Switzerland and then, in 1940, to New York. From 1940 until 1953 he was a professor of theory at Yale University. In 1953 he returned to Switzerland and began a series of conducting tours.

HÜNI-MIHACZEK, Felice (1891–1976): Soprano at the Vienna State Opera from 1919 to 1926 and Bayerische Staatsoper, Munich, from 1926 to 1944. An outstanding Mozart soprano, she sang in concerts of the Verein für musikalische Privataufführungen and gave the premiere of Webern's *Fünf geistliche Lieder*, Op. 15.

ITTEN, Johannes (1888–1967): Swiss painter and illustrator. A friend of Alma Mahler and Walter Gropius, his principal artistic affiliation was with the Bauhaus where he taught from 1919 until 1923. He taught in Vienna from 1915 to 1919 and attended at least one of the open rehearsals of Schoenberg's Chamber Symphony in 1918. In 1923 he opened his own art school in Berlin. In 1938 he moved to Zurich.

JALOWETZ, Heinrich (1882–1946): Conductor and one of Schoenberg's earliest students. He held various conducting posts in Germany, including the Cologne Opera, and conducted the first Berlin performance of the *Gurrelieder* in 1923. In 1939 he emigrated to the United States where he taught at Black Mountain College until his death.

KANDINSKY, Wassily (1866–1944): Russian painter. Born in Moscow, he studied law, economics, and politics at Moscow University. In 1897 he moved to Munich, where he was influenced by the Jugendstil. In 1911 he established the *Blaue Reiter* and was co-editor of the *Blaue Reiter Almanac*. He included paintings by Schoenberg in the first exhibition of the *Blaue Reiter* in 1911 and quoted him in his book *Über das Geistige in der Kunst* (*Concerning the Spiritual in Art*, first published in 1912), one of the seminal formulations of the principles of abstraction. Kandinsky returned to Russia for World War I and then, in 1921, began to teach in the Bauhaus. When Kandinsky invited Schoenberg to join the Bauhaus in 1923, Schoenberg accused Kandinsky of anti-Semitism, but the two men later became friends again. Upon the closing of the Bauhaus by the National Socialists in 1933, Kandinsky went to Paris, where he remained until his death.

KAUDER, Hugo (1888–1972): A young composer in Vienna at the end of World War I. Kauder attended at least one of the open rehearsals of Schoenberg's Chamber Symphony and played viola several times in concerts of the Verein für musikalische Privataufführungen. He later emigrated to the United States.

KELLER, Alfred (born 1907): Swiss composer and teacher. Keller studied with Schoenberg in Berlin from 1927 to 1930. During some of this time, he assisted Schoenberg with elementary instruction. Following this period, he returned to Switzerland where he became a teacher and continued composing.

KLEIBER, Erich (1890–1956): Austrian conductor. Following an early career in Prague, Darmstadt, Düsseldorf, and Mannheim, he became the general music director of the Berlin State Opera in 1923. In 1925 he directed the premiere, after 137 rehearsals, of Berg's opera *Wozzeck*. In 1934 he conducted the first performance of the *Lulu* Suite. During the twenties and thirties, he made tours of Europe, Russia, and the United States. In 1935 he emigrated, living for a time in Buenos Aires, and was reappointed to the Berlin State Opera in 1955.

KLEIN, Fritz Heinrich (1892–1977): Pupil of Schoenberg in the Schwarzwald School Seminar during 1917 and 1918. In 1918 Klein became a pupil of Berg. The Verein für musikalische Privataufführungen awarded him a prize for his piece *Die Maschine*, which was an experiment with a kind of twelve-tone composition.

KLIMT, Gustav (1862–1918): Austrian painter and graphic artist. After studies at the Vienna School of Arts and Crafts, Klimt worked from 1883 until 1892 in a decorating business with his brother. During this time he executed commissions for the Burgtheater (1888) and the Museum of the History of the Arts (1891). He was one of the founders in 1897 of the Vienna Secession and became its first president. It was during this period that he matured as a painter. Klimt is important as a painter both for his own decorative style and for his influence on Kokoschka and Egon Schiele.

KOKOSCHKA, Olda: Kokoschka met Olda Palkovsky when he was living in Prague during the years 1934 to 1938. She was at that time a law student. They fled Prague together in 1938 and went to England where they were married in 1941.

KOKOSCHKA, Oskar (1886–1980): Austrian painter and writer. In his early years at the Vienna School of Arts and Crafts, he came under the influence of Klimt and the art nouveau. Kokoschka was discovered by Adolf Loos in the first Kunstschau, an international art exhibition of 1908. He was at this time designing postcards and fans for the Wiener Werkstätte. Loos helped to support Kokoschka and assisted him in finding commissions and in selling his works. His early works were still lifes and portraits, which were to become famous for their psychological insight and projection of the inner person. In 1910 Kokoschka moved to Berlin, where he became involved with the German Expressionists. Following a tempestuous affair with Alma Mahler which inspired some of his finest paintings, Kokoschka served in the war and received serious head injuries. Years of convalescence first in Sweden and then in Dresden followed. His paintings lost some of their luminescence and he began to favor large blocks of primary colors. That his visionary quality was not lost is evident from the landscapes that he created during extended travels from 1924 until 1931 when he returned to Vienna. In 1934 he moved to Prague, and in 1938 he emigrated to England. His last years were spent in Switzerland.

KOLISCH, Rudolf (1896–1978): Austrian violinist. He studied violin with Ševčík, composition with Franz Schreker and with Schoenberg from 1919 to 1922, and musicology with Guido Adler. After beginning his career as a stage conductor and violin soloist, he played in numerous concerts of the Verein für musikalische Privataufführungen. He then founded the Wiener Streichquartett. By 1927 the group's name had been changed to the Kolisch Quartet and consisted of Kolisch, Felix Khuner, Eugen Lehner, and Benar Heifetz. In this form, the Quartet toured successfully in Europe and in North and South America until it disbanded in 1939 following the members' emigration to the United States. The group retained close ties with the Schoenberg circle and gave first performances of Schoenberg's Third and Fourth String Quartets, Serenade, and Suite; Berg's *Lyric Suite;* and Webern's String Trio and String Quartet. Schoenberg married Kolisch's sister Gertrud in 1924. After the Quartet dispersed, Kolisch joined with surviving members of the Pro-Arte Quartet in residence at the University of Wisconsin. At his death, he was on the faculty of the New England Conservatory.

KORNGOLD, Erich (1897–1957): Austrian composer. Son of the famous critic Julius Korngold, he was a child prodigy composer, going to study with Zemlinsky on Mahler's recommendation in 1907. In 1910 his ballet *Der Schneemann* was performed by the Vienna Court Opera. His Piano Sonata in E was performed by Schnabel on European tour. Other triumphs followed and by the late twenties he was teaching opera and composition at the Vienna Staatsakademie. In 1928 a poll by the *Neue Wiener Tagblatt* named Korngold and Schoenberg as the two greatest living composers. With the rise of the National Socialists, he emigrated to the United States where he wrote film scores in Hollywood.

KRENEK, Ernst (born 1900): Austrian composer. A student of Franz Schreker from 1916 to 1923. Krenek followed Schreker to Berlin, where he became associated with Busoni, Erdmann, and Scherchen. He spent the early twenties in Switzerland and Paris before returning to Germany where he wrote his highly successful opera *Jonny spielt auf.* Although previously acquainted with members of the Schoenberg circle, he did not become closely identified with its ideas until he moved to Vienna in 1928. During the years that followed, he associated with Berg and Webern, met Karl Kraus, and adopted the twelve-tone method of composition. In 1938 he emigrated to the United States, where he taught at various universities, and retired to Palm Springs, California.

LEHNER, Eugen (born 1906): Violist with the Kolisch Quartet starting in 1927. Before joining the Quartet, he was a composition student of Zoltán Kodály in Budapest. After the disbanding of the Quartet, he joined the Boston Symphony Orchestra.

LEONARD, Lotte (1884–1976): German soprano. After training in Berlin, she held various teaching positions including Bernuth's conservatory in Hamburg. From 1924 on, she organized annual summer courses at Grundlsee in Austria. She was an internationally known soloist who appeared with many major orchestras prior to 1933 when she left Germany. From 1933 until 1940 she was a professor at the Conservatoire International in Paris. She then emigrated to the United States where she taught at the Juilliard School. After spending some time in Switzerland, she moved to Israel.

MAHLER WERFEL, Alma (1879–1964): Mahler met Alma Schindler in 1902 when she was studying composition with Alexander von Zemlinsky, and they were married soon after. Following Mahler's death in 1911, Alma Mahler associated herself with several famous men, including Oskar Kokoschka, Walter Gropius, and Franz Werfel, the latter two of whom she married. She was a close friend of Alban and Helene Berg and strong supporter of the Schoenberg circle.

MIHACZEK, Felice: see HÜNI-MIHACZEK, Felice.

MORGENSTERN, Soma (1891–1976): Austrian writer and poet. He studied law and political science at the University of Vienna but in 1925 became a columnist for the *Frankfurter Zeitung*, writing articles on Viennese theatre, literature, and music. He was a neighbor of Berg in Hietzing, a suburb of Vienna, and enjoyed discussing literary matters with him. He left Vienna with the rise of National Socialism and lived the rest of his life in New York City. His books reflect Jewish pastoral farm life in Eastern Europe. He is best known for his trilogy, *The Son of the Lost Son, In My Father's Pastures*, and *The Testament of the Lost Son*.

PFITZNER, Hans (1869–1949): German composer and conductor. After studies at the Hoch Conservatory in Frankfurt and early conducting and teaching experience with the Theater des Westens and the Stern Conservatory in Berlin, he moved to Strasbourg, where he directed the opera, conducted the symphony, and headed the conservatory. It was in Strasbourg that he composed his most famous work, the opera *Palestrina* (parodied by Schoenberg in an unpublished piece called *Palestrina's Revenge*). In 1920 he was given a master class in composition at the Prussian Academy of Fine Arts in Berlin. Well-known in his time, he was conservative in style and personality.

PISK, Paul Amadeus (born 1893): Austrian musicologist, pianist, and composer. He received a Ph.D. from the University of Vienna in 1916, following work with Guido Adler. He studied composition with Franz Schreker and with Schoenberg from 1917 to 1919. Secretary of the Verein für musikalische Privataufführungen, he also performed as a pianist in many of its concerts. From 1921 until 1934 he was music editor for the *Wiener Arbeiter-Zeitung*. From 1920 until 1928 he served as co-editor of the *Musikblätter des Anbruch*. He also, from 1922 until 1934, directed the music department of the Volkshochschule in Vienna and taught at the New Vienna Conservatory. In 1936 he emigrated to the United States where he taught at the University of Redlands, the University of Texas at Austin, and Washington University in St. Louis.

PLODERER, Wolfgang (born 1915): Ploderer's father, Rudolf Ploderer, was a lawyer and a friend of Berg. As a child Ploderer went with his father to concerts where Webern conducted, as well as to concerts of the Verein für musikalische Privataufführungen.

POLNAUER, Josef (1888–1969): Railroad official and student of Schoenberg from 1909 to 1911; and of Berg from 1911 to 1913. From 1917 to 1920 he was Schoenberg's assistant in the Schwarzwald School Seminar. Polnauer was intimately concerned with the Verein für musikalische Privataufführungen and served as Archivist.

POPPER, Karl Raimund (born 1902): Austrian philosopher of natural and social science. Following studies in mathematics, physics, and philosophy at the University of Vienna, he became closely associated with several of the Vienna Circle of logical positivists including Rudolf Carnap, although he was never himself a member of the circle. His first book, *Logik der Forschung*, was published in 1935 in the circle's series. From 1937 until 1945 Popper served as senior lecturer at Canterbury University College in Christchurch, New Zealand. After 1949 he was associated with the London School of Economics. His most important works include *The Open Society and Its Enemies* (1945); *The Poverty of Historicism* (1957); and *Conjectures and Refutations; The Growth of Scientific Knowledge* (1963).

RANKL, Karl (1898–1968): Austrian conductor and composer. He studied with Schoenberg from 1918 to 1921, and later with Webern. He had an active conducting career culminating in his appointment as conductor of the Kroll Opera in Berlin in 1928. In 1937 he became director of the German Theatre in Prague, where he conducted the premiere of Krenek's *Karl V* in 1938. In 1946 he moved to England, where he became director of the opera at Covent Garden.

RANKL, Kristina: Friend of the Kolisch family and wife of Karl Rankl.

RATZ, Erwin (1898–1973): Austrian musicologist and theorist. From 1918 until 1922 he studied musicology with Guido

Adler while also studying with Schoenberg. In 1918 he organized ten public rehearsals of Schoenberg's Chamber Symphony, Op. 9, and from 1918 until 1921, he was actively involved in the Verein für musikalische Privataufführungen. In 1925 he studied with Webern and thereafter remained a close friend. He remained active in Viennese musical life, teaching theory at the Musikakademie. In his later years, he was president of the International Mahler Society and editor of the Mahler Complete Edition. From 1953 until 1968 he served as president of the Austrian chapter of the International Society for Contemporary Music.

REINHARDT, Max (1873–1943). Austrian theatre producer. Famous for his Vienna production of *Oedipus Rex*, staged in 1910 in a circus, he mounted many extravagant productions with huge casts. He influenced Strauss and Hoffmannsthal, and both *Salome* and *Elektra* were inspired by his earlier dramatic versions. He produced the premiere of *Der Rosenkavalier* as well as that of the original version of *Ariadne auf Naxos*.

ROSÉ, Arnold (1863–1946): Austrian violinist. Following studies at the Vienna Conservatory, he became concertmaster of the Vienna Court Opera Orchestra and also of the Vienna Philharmonic. He taught at the Vienna Academy of Music from 1893 to 1924 and, starting in 1888, frequently performed at the Bayreuth Festival. In 1882 he founded the Rosé Quartet which played premieres of late Brahms, Pfitzner, and Reger quartets. The Quartet also gave first performances of Schoenberg's First and Second Quartets and, augmented by Vienna Philharmonic players, of the first Chamber Symphony. The Quartet played the two Schoenberg quartets at the opening of Schoenberg's art exhibition in Hugo Heller's bookshop and gallery in 1910. In 1938 Rosé, by then one of Austria's most revered musicians, emigrated to England.

RUFER, Josef (1893–1985): Austrian composer and author. A student of Zemlinsky and Schoenberg from 1919 to 1922 and Schoenberg's assistant in Berlin from 1925 to 1933. From 1928 until 1940 he was music critic of the Berlin *Morgenpost* and also for *Die Welt*. His book, *Die Komposition mit zwölf Tönen* (*Composition with Twelve Tones*, 1955) was the first major work to appear on the subject. During the years 1957 to 1959 he catalogued Schoenberg's estate. *Das Werk Arnold Schönbergs* (*The Works of Arnold Schoenberg*) was published in 1959. In 1961 Rufer became editor of the Schoenberg Complete Edition.

SCHACHT, Peter (1901–1945): Composition pupil of Schoenberg in Berlin from 1927 to 1930. He died in action in World War II. Works include chamber music and piano variations.

SCHENKER, Heinrich (1867–1935): Austro-Polish musicologist and theorist. Studied under Bruckner at the Vienna Conservatory. After taking a degree in law, he taught piano and theory privately. His pupils included Wilhelm Furtwängler, Anthony von Hoboken, Oswald Jonas, Felix Salzer, Otto Vrieslander, and Hans Weisse. During the years 1921 to 1924, he edited a periodical, *Der Tonwille*, devoted to his theoretical work. His major works included his *Harmonielehre* (1906); *Das Meisterwerk in der Musik* (1925–1930); *Der freie Satz* (*Free Composition*, 1935); and his edition of the Beethoven piano sonatas.

SCHERCHEN, Hermann (1891–1966): German conductor. A violist in the Berlin Philharmonic from 1907 to 1910. He turned down the opportunity to play violin in the premiere of *Pierrot lunaire* but attended the rehearsals, and when *Pierrot lunaire* went on tour during 1912 and 1913, shared conducting duties with Schoenberg. From then on Scherchen was a frequent conductor of works by members of the Schoenberg circle, conducting premieres of Berg's Chamber Concerto (1927), and *Der Wein* (1930); and Webern's *Das Augenlicht* (1938), and Variations, Op. 30 (1943). In addition in 1919 he founded the music journal *Melos* and from 1933 to 1936 edited the periodical *Musica Viva* in Brussels. In 1922 he succeeded Furtwängler as director of the Frankfurt Museumskonzerte, and he was frequently the principal conductor at festivals of the International Society for Contemporary Music. In 1954, with the support of UNESCO, he opened a studio for electroacoustic research in Switzerland.

SCHMID, Erich (born 1907): Swiss conductor and composer. After completing theory and composition studies at the Frankfurt Conservatory, he studied with Schoenberg in

Berlin from 1930 to 1933. He has conducted many works of the Schoenberg circle and published studies of Schoenberg's quartets.

SCHREKER, Franz (1878–1934): Austrian composer and teacher. He conducted the premiere of the *Gurrelieder* in Vienna in 1913 and remained a friend of Schoenberg off and on from that time. He met Berg in 1917. In 1920 he became director of the Musikhochschule in Berlin. In this position he was able to recommend that Schoenberg be appointed to replace Busoni at the Prussian Academy of Fine Arts in 1924, and he tried to get a position for Berg at the Musikhochschule. In 1932 he held a master class in composition at the Prussian Academy. He had many students, including Ernst Krenek, Paul Pisk, Alois Haba, and Jascha Horenstein. He was removed from his position by the Nazis and died in obscurity.

SCHWARZWALD, Eugenie (1873–1940): Head of a progressive girls' school in Vienna. Schoenberg and Kokoschka both taught at this school. During World War I, she helped Schoenberg both with his army problems and with his finances. She also founded inexpensive restaurants, called WÖK, for intellectuals. She was friendly with many important figures of the time, including Loos, and invited many of them, along with her students, to her summer home in Grundlsee.

SEARLE, Humphrey (1915–1982): English composer and writer. He studied first as a classical scholar at Oxford from 1933 to 1937, then at the Royal College of Music in 1937 and the New Vienna Conservatory from 1937 to 1938, during which time he studied with Webern. In 1938 he joined the music staff of the BBC in London. After 1946 nearly all of his compositions utilized the twelve-tone method of composition.

SEIDLHOFER, Bruno (born 1905): Pianist. He studied piano and composition in Vienna at the Akademie für Musik und darstellende Kunst from 1921 to 1929 and with Berg around 1923. In 1943 he was appointed lecturer and in 1956 professor of piano at the Akademie für Musik und darstellende Kunst.

SKALKOTTAS, Nikos (1904–1949): Greek composer and violinist. Graduated in 1920 from the Athens Conservatory. In

1921 he went to Berlin where he studied at the Hochschule für Musik. A pupil of Schoenberg from 1927 to 1931, he was one of his most successful students. In 1933 he returned to Athens where, in ill health and with financial problems, he worked as an orchestral violinist. His works are faithful to neoclassical ideals; they are mostly twelve-tone and utilize traditional forms.

STEFAN, Paul (1879–1943): Austrian music critic and author. He studied at the University of Vienna and possibly briefly with Schoenberg. He was chiefly a critic for *Die Stunde* and various foreign periodicals, including *Musical America*. In 1921 he was appointed editor of the periodical *Musikblätter des Anbruch* after Berg. He attended and wrote about many concerts of the Schoenberg circle. In addition he wrote numerous books, including *Neue Musik und Wien* (1921) and *Arnold Schönberg* (1924).

STEIN, Erwin (1885–1958): Austrian critic and writer. He studied at the University of Vienna from 1905 to 1908, and with Schoenberg from 1906 to 1910. He was a close friend of Berg and Webern. During the period 1910 to 1919 he held various conducting posts. From 1919 to 1923 he was deeply involved in the Verein für musikalische Privataufführungen, serving first as *Vortragsmeister* and later, when Schoenberg went to Holland, as President. He conducted *Pierrot lunaire* on tour with Erika Stiedry-Wagner in 1923. From 1924 until 1930 he edited the music periodical *Pult und Taktstock*. Until 1938 he was artistic advisor to Universal Edition. In 1938 he moved to England, where he was employed by Boosey and Hawkes, music publishers. He was the author of numerous essays, and in 1958, he published an edition of Schoenberg's letters.

STEUERMANN, Clara (1923–1982): Pianist and student of Schoenberg in Los Angeles. While a student of Schoenberg, she studied piano with Edward Steuermann and they later married. Until her death, she was Archivist of the Arnold Schoenberg Institute.

STEUERMANN, Edward (1892–1964): Polish pianist and composer. He studied piano with Busoni in Berlin from 1911 to 1912, and Busoni encouraged him to study composition with Schoenberg, which he did during the years 1912 to

1914. Thereafter he became extremely involved with the performance of music of the Schoenberg circle and performed extensively both in the Verein für musikalische Privataufführungen, where he served also as *Vortragsmeister*, and on tour. He gave first performances of nearly all of Schoenberg's piano music and chamber music with piano, including *Pierrot lunaire* and the Piano Concerto, Op. 42, and of Berg's Sonata, his Chamber Concerto, and most of Webern's chamber music for piano. He occasionally served as pianist for Karl Kraus. He also made numerous piano reductions of Schoenberg scores for publication and for use in the Verein. He taught at the Juilliard School in New York from 1952 to 1964. He had many pupils, including Adorno, Brendel, Gimpel, Hollander, and Lili Kraus.

STIEDRY-WAGNER, Erika (1892–1974): Actress. When she came to Vienna in 1907 for her debut at the Vienna Burgtheater, she was given the address of the Bergs, with whom she subsequently became friends. As she was also a singer, she was asked to perform *Pierrot lunaire* in a concert of the Verein für musikalische Privataufführungen in 1922. In 1923 she performed *Pierrot* on tour with Erwin Stein conducting, and in 1942 she recorded the work under Schoenberg's direction.

STUTSCHEWSKY, Joachim (1891–1982): Israeli cellist and composer. Studied at the Leipzig Conservatory, and in 1912 became a member of the Jena String Quartet. After an early career in Germany and Switzerland, he moved to Vienna in 1924 and became cellist of the Wiener Streichquartett. He left the Quartet in 1927, but he remained in Vienna until 1938, making a reputation as a teacher, soloist, and editor. In 1928 Stutschewsky founded the Society for the Development of Jewish Music in Vienna; he moved to Palestine in 1938.

TRAUNECK, Josef (1898–1975): Conductor. He studied with Schoenberg from 1918 to 1922. After a varied conducting career in Prague and several cities in Germany, he went to South Africa in 1933. Later he returned to Austria.

TRUDING, Lona: Pianist and student of Schoenberg at the Schwarzwald School Seminar. She attended the University of Vienna. She played in some concerts of the Verein für musikalische Privataufführungen. She emigrated to England to avoid the Nazis.

ULLMANN, Viktor (1898–1944): Austro-Hungarian composer and conductor. He studied in Vienna with Schoenberg from 1918 to 1921. In Prague he was active as an accompanist and conductor for the New German Theatre. He was also a member of the Prague Society for Private Musical Performances. From 1935 until 1937 he studied in Haba's quarter-tone music department at the Prague Conservatory. He was arrested by the National Socialists in 1942, and in 1944 was deported to Auschwitz.

VIERTEL, Berthold (1885–1953): Austrian poet, author, and theatre director. In the mid-twenties, he moved from Vienna to Berlin, where he managed the Reinhardt Theatre. He was active as a director throughout the twenties and thirties. In the mid-thirties, he emigrated to the United States, where he continued to work in New York until his death. He was the husband of Salka Viertel.

VIERTEL, Salka (1889–1978): Actress and screen writer. As a sister of Edward Steuermann, Salka Viertel first met Schoenberg in 1912, before she became a successful actress. When she moved to the United States, she became a prominent screen writer in Hollywood, writing scripts for Greta Garbo. Her friendship with Berthold Brecht resulted in her being blacklisted in the 1950s.

WAGNER, Erika: See Stiedry-Wagner, Erika.

WELLESZ, Egon (1885–1974): Austrian composer and musicologist. He graduated from the University of Vienna, after work in musicology with Guido Adler. He studied with Schoenberg from 1904 to 1905, and he became a close friend of Webern. He then decided to compose on his own but maintained contact with Schoenberg and had several works performed in concerts of the Verein für musikalische Privataufführungen. He was a pioneering figure in the International Society for Contemporary Music. His book, *Arnold Schönberg*, was published in Vienna in 1921. After serving as a professor at the University of Vienna, he emigrated to England in 1938, where he taught at Oxford University.

ZEHME, Albertine (1857–1946): Actress. After a first engagement in Oldenburg, she became associated with the Leipzig Stadt Theater, where she played Thekla in *Wallenstein* and Desdemona in *Othello*. In 1904 Zehme performed some of Otto Vrieslander's settings of *Pierrot*. She commissioned Schoenberg to write *Pierrot lunaire* in 1912 and presented the premiere of it.

ZEMLINSKY, Alexander von (1872–1942): Austrian conductor and composer. After training at the Vienna Conservatory, he embarked upon what was to become a successful conducting career, first in Vienna and later in Prague. He was highly regarded in Vienna as a conductor, a composer, and especially as a teacher. He was essentially Schoenberg's only composition teacher, and the two men became close friends. In 1899 he became Kapellmeister at the Carltheater in Vienna. Schoenberg married Zemlinsky's sister, Mathilde, in 1901. From 1911 until 1927 he was opera conductor of the Deutsches Landestheater in Prague. Zemlinsky conducted many performances of works by members of the Schoenberg circle, including the premiere of *Erwartung* in 1924. In 1921 he founded the Prague Verein für musikalische Privataufführungen. From 1927 through 1930, he was Kapellmeister under Klemperer at the Kroll Opera in Berlin. He emigrated to the United States in 1938.

ZILLIG, Winfried (1905–1963): German conductor, composer, and writer. After studies of law and music at Würzburg, he went to Vienna to study with Schoenberg in 1925. In 1926 he followed Schoenberg to Berlin and continued to work with him until 1928. During 1927 and 1928 he was music assistant to Erich Kleiber at the Berlin Staatsoper. He conducted numerous performances of Schoenberg's works, including the European premiere of the Violin Concerto. From 1940 through 1943 he was music director of the Poznań Opera and, during the years 1947 through 1951, was chief conductor of the Hesse Radio in Frankfurt. From 1959 until his death Zillig was director of the music division of the North German Radio in Hamburg. In addition he prepared the vocal scores for *Moses und Aron* and *Die Jakobsleiter*.

ZUCKMEYER, Carl (1896–1977): German dramatist and poet. After studies in Mainz and military service in World War I,

Bibliography

This bibliography is a selection of readings that the author found interesting and useful. It includes neither all sources mentioned in the text nor all sources consulted by the author. In an effort to avoid meaningless categorization, it has been organized by subject rather than by type of source. A much more extensive bibliography, containing a particularly valuable section of memoirs, is found in William Johnston, *The Austrian Mind.*

General Sources

ARENDT, HANNAH. *Between Past and Future: Eight Exercises in Political Thought.* Rev. ed. New York: Viking Press, 1968; Penguin Books, 1978.

———. *Men in Dark Times.* New York: Harcourt Brace Jovanovich, 1968.

BAREA, ILSA. *Vienna: Legend and Reality.* London: Secker and Warburg, 1966.

BREICHA, OTTO, and GERHARD FRITSCH, eds. *Finale und Auftakt: Wien 1898–1914.* Salzburg: Otto Müller Verlag, 1964.

COLLINGWOOD, R. G. *The Idea of History.* London: Clarendon Press, 1946; Oxford University Press, 1974.

FISCHER, DAVID HACKETT. *Historians' Fallacies: Toward a Logic of Historical Thought.* New York: Harper and Row, 1970.

GARDINER, PATRICK. *The Nature of Historical Explanation.* London: Oxford University Press, 1961.

———, ed. *Theories of History.* New York: Free Press, 1959.

GAY, PETER. *Weimar Culture: The Outsider as Insider.* New York: Harper and Row, 1968.

HAAS, WILLY. *Die Belle Epoque.* Munich: Verlag Kurt Desch, 1967.

JANIK, ALLAN, and STEPHEN TOULMIN. *Wittgenstein's Vienna.* New York: Simon and Schuster, 1973.

JOHNSTON, WILLIAM M. *The Austrian Mind: An Intellectual and Social History, 1848–1938.* Berkeley: University of California Press, 1972.

MIESEL, VICTOR H., ed. *Voices of German Expressionism*. Englewood Cliffs, N.J.: Prentice-Hall, 1970.

SCHORSKE, CARL. *Fin-de-Siècle Vienna: Politics and Culture*. New York: Knopf, 1979.

SHIRER, WILLIAM L. *The Rise and Fall of the Third Reich: A History of Nazi Germany*. New York: Simon and Schuster, 1960.

SORELL, WALTER. *The Duality of Vision: Genius and Versatility in the Arts*. London: Thames and Hudson, 1970.

STEINER, GEORGE. *In Bluebeard's Castle: Some Notes Towards the Redefinition of Culture*. New Haven: Yale University Press, 1971.

TAYLOR, A. J. P. *The Habsburg Monarchy 1809–1918: A History of the Austrian Empire and Austria-Hungary*. London: Hamish Hamilton, 1948; New York: Harper Torchbooks, 1965.

——. *The Origins of the Second World War*. 2nd ed. Greenwich, Conn.: Fawcett, 1961.

TUCHMAN, BARBARA W. *The Guns of August*. New York: Macmillan, 1962.

——. *The Proud Tower*. New York: Macmillan, 1966.

VIERTEL, SALKA. *The Kindness of Strangers*. New York: Holt, Rinehart and Winston, 1969.

ZWEIG, STEFAN. *The World of Yesterday*. London: Cassell, 1953.

Art and Architecture

"Arnold Schoenberg: Paintings—Drawings—Sketches." *Journal of the Arnold Schoenberg Institute* 2 (June 1978): 185–231.

COMINI, ALESSANDRA. *Gustav Klimt*. New York: George Braziller, 1975.

CZECH, HERMANN, and WOLFGANG MISTELBAUER. *Das Looshaus*. Vienna: Verlag Löcker und Wögenstein, 1976.

GOLDSCHEIDER, LUDWIG. *Kokoschka*. 3rd ed. London: Phaidon Press, 1963.

GUBLER, JACQUES, and GILLES BARBEY. "Loos's Villa Karma." *Architectural Review* 145 (March 1969): 215–216.

HODIN, J. P. *Oskar Kokoschka: The Artist and His Time*. London: Cory, Adams and Mackay, 1966.

——, ed. *Bekenntnis zu Kokoschka: Erinnerungen und Deutungen*. Berlin: Florian Kupferberg, 1963.

HOFFMANN, EDITH. *Kokoschka: Life and Work*. London: Faber and Faber, 1947.

KANDINSKY, WASSILY. *Concerning the Spiritual in Art.* Translated by Francis Golffing, Michael Harrison, and Ferdinand Ostertag. New York: George Wittenborn, 1970.

———. "The Paintings of Schoenberg." Translated by Barbara Zeisl. *Journal of the Arnold Schoenberg Institute* 2 (June 1978): 181–184.

KANDINSKY, WASSILY, and FRANZ MARC, eds. *The Blaue Reiter Almanac.* New documentary edition by Klaus Lankheit. Translated by Henning Falkenstein, Manug Terzian, and Gertrude Hinderlie. New York: Viking Press, 1974.

KOKOSCHKA, OSKAR. *My Life.* Translated by David Britt. London: Thames and Hudson, 1974.

———. *Das schriftliche Werk,* 2 vols. Edited by Heinz Spielmann. Hamburg: Hans Cristians Verlag, 1974.

———. *A Sea Ringed with Visions.* Translated by Eithne Wilkins and Ernst Kaiser. London: Thames and Hudson, 1962.

KOSSATZ, HORST-HERBERT. "The Vienna Secession and Its Early Relations with Great Britain." *Studio International* 181 (January 1971): 9–20.

KUBINSZKY, MIHALY. *Adolf Loos.* Berlin: Henschelverlag Kunst und Gesellschaft, 1970.

KULKA, HENRY. "Adolf Loos, 1870–1933." In *Architects' Yearbook* 9, pp. 7–29. Edited by Trevor Dannatt. New York: Chemical Publishing, 1960.

LOOS, ADOLF. *Ins Leere Gesprochen: 1897–1900.* Edited by Adolf Opel. Vienna: Georg Prachner Verlag, 1981.

———. *Die Potemkin'sche Stadt: Verschollene Schriften, 1897–1933.* Vienna: Georg Prachner Verlag, 1983.

———. *Spoken Into the Void: Collected Essays 1897–1900.* Translated by Jane O. Newman and John H. Smith. Cambridge, Mass.: MIT Press, 1982.

———. *Trotzdem: 1900–1930.* Edited by Adolf Opel. Vienna: Georg Prachner Verlag, 1982.

LOOS, ELSIE ALTMANN. *Adolf Loos der Mensch.* Vienna: Verlag Herold, 1968.

MÜNZ, LUDWIG, and GUSTAV KÜNSTLER. *Adolf Loos: Pioneer of Modern Architecture.* Translated by Harold Meek. New York: Frederick A. Praeger, 1966.

NEUTRA, RICHARD. Review of *Adolf Loos: Pioneer of Modern Architecture,* by Ludwig Münz and Gustav Künstler. *Architectural Forum* 125 (July–August 1966): 88–89, 116.

OPEL, ADOLF, ed. *Kontroversen Adolf Loos: Im Spiegel der Zeitge-nossen.* Vienna: Georg Prachner Verlag, 1985.

SCHLEIFFER, HEDWIG. "Kokoschka, Pioneer in Art Education." *School Arts* 59 (June 1960): 29–32.

SCHMALENBACH, FRITZ. *Oskar Kokoschka.* Translated by Violet M. Macdonald. Greenwich, Conn.: New York Graphic Society, 1967.

SCHOENBERG, ARNOLD. "Painting Influences." Translated by Gertrud Zeisl. *Journal of the Arnold Schoenberg Institute* 2 (June 1978): 237–238.

"Schoenberg Talks about His Paintings." In *Arnold Schönberg, Gedenkausstellung 1974,* pp. 109–111. Edited by Ernst Hilmar. Vienna: Universal Edition, 1974. Reprinted as "A Conversation with Schoenberg about Painting." *Journal of the Arnold Schoenberg Institute* 2 (June 1978): 178–180.

VERGO, PETER. *Art in Vienna 1898–1918.* London: Phaidon Press, 1975.

WAGNER, OTTO. *Moderne Architektur.* Vienna, 1895. Reprinted as *Die Baukunst unserer Zeit: dem Baukunst jünger ein Führer auf diesem Kunstgebiete.* Vienna: A. Schroll, 1914.

WHITFORD, FRANK. *Expressionism.* London: Hamlyn, 1970.

WILLETT, JOHN. *Expressionism.* New York: McGraw-Hill, 1970.

Literature, Philosophy, and Psychology

BENJAMIN, WALTER. *Illuminations.* Edited by Hannah Arendt. Translated by Harry Zohn. New York: Schocken Books, 1969.

———. *Reflections: Essays, Aphorisms, Autobiographical Writings.* Edited by Peter Demetz. Translated by Edmund Jephcott. New York: Harcourt Brace Jovanovich, 1978.

BLOCH, ALBERT. "Karl Kraus' Shakespeare." *Books Abroad* 11 (1937): 21–24.

CANETTI, ELIAS. *Auto-Da-Fe.* Translated by C. V. Wedgewood. New York: Farrar, Straus, and Giroux, 1984.

———. *The Conscience of Words.* Translated by Joachim Neugroschel. New York: Seabury Press, 1979.

CLARK, RONALD W. *Freud: The Man and the Cause.* New York: Random House, 1980.

ENGLEMANN, PAUL. "Kraus, Loos, and Wittgenstein." In *Letters from Ludwig Wittgenstein, with a Memoir.* Edited by B. F. McGuinness. Translated by L. Furtmüller. New York: Horizon Press, 1968.

FIELD, FRANK. *The Last Days of Mankind: Karl Kraus and His Vienna.* London: Macmillan, 1967.

FISCHER, HEINRICH. "The Other Austria and Karl Kraus." In *In Tyrannos: Four Centuries of Struggle against Tyranny in Germany,* pp. 309–328. Edited by Hans J. Rehfisch. London: Lindsay Drummond, 1944.

HAMBURGER, MICHAEL. *Contraries: Studies in German Literature.* New York: E. P. Dutton, 1970.

HELLER, ERICH. "Dark Laughter." *New York Review of Books* 20 (3 May 1973): 21–25.

———. *The Disinherited Mind: Essays in Modern German Literature and Thought.* Expanded ed. New York: Harcourt Brace Jovanovich, 1975.

IGGERS, WILMA ABELES. *Karl Kraus: A Viennese Critic of the Twentieth Century.* The Hague: Martinus Nijhoff, 1967.

JONES, ERNEST. *The Life and Work of Sigmund Freud.* London: Hogarth Press, 1953. Edited and abridged by Lionel Trilling and Steven Marcus. Garden City, N.Y.: Anchor Books, 1963.

KRAUS, KARL. *Briefe an Sidonie Nádherný von Borutin: 1913–1936,* 2 vols. Edited by Heinrich Fischer and Michael Lazarus. Munich: Kösel Verlag, 1974.

———. "In dieser grossen Zeit." *Die Fackel,* no. 404 (December 1914), pp. 1–19.

———. *In These Great Times: A Karl Kraus Reader.* Edited by Harry Zohn. Translated by Joseph Fabry, Max Knight, Karl Ross, and Harry Zohn. Montreal: Engendra Press, 1976.

———. *Half-Truths and One-and-a-Half Truths: Selected Aphorisms.* Edited and translated by Harry Zohn. Montreal: Engendra Press, 1976.

———. *The Last Days of Mankind.* Edited and abridged by Frederick Ungar. Translated by Alexander Gode and Sue Ellen Wright. New York: Frederick Ungar, 1974.

———. *No Compromise: Selected Writings of Karl Kraus.* Edited by Frederick Ungar. Translated by Sheema Z. Buehne, Edward Mornin, Helene Scher, Marcus Bullock, Michael Bullock, Frederick Ungar, and D. G. Wright. New York: Frederick Ungar, 1977.

———. "Warum die Fackel nicht erscheint." *Die Fackel,* nos. 890–905 (July 1934), pp. 1–313.

———. *Werke.* 14 vols. Edited by Heinrich Fischer. Munich: Kösel Verlag, 1955–1964.

KUNCZ, ALADAR. *Black Monastery.* Translated by Ralph Murray. New York: Harcourt Brace, 1934.

MUSIL, ROBERT. *The Man Without Qualities.* 3 vols. Translated by Eithne Wilkins and Ernst Kaiser. London: Secker and Warburg, 1954; Pan Books, 1979.

OPHULS, MARCEL. *The Sorrow and the Pity.* Introduction by Stanley Hoffmann. Translated by Mireille Johnston. New York: Berkley, 1975.

POPPER, KARL. *Unended Quest: An Intellectual Autobiography.* La Salle, Ill.: Open Court, 1976.

ROAZEN, PAUL. *Freud and His Followers.* New York: New American Library, 1976.

SCHILPP, PAUL ARTHUR, ed. *The Philosophy of Rudolf Carnap.* La Salle, Ill.: Open Court, 1963.

SCHOENBERNER, FRANZ. *Confessions of a European Intellectual.* New York: Macmillan, 1946; Collier, 1965.

———. *The Inside Story of an Outsider.* New York: Macmillan, 1949.

SOKEL, WALTER H. *The Writer in Extremis: Expressionism in Twentieth-Century German Literature.* Stanford, Calif.: Stanford University Press, 1959.

———, ed. *Anthology of German Expressionist Drama: A Prelude to the Absurd.* Garden City, N.Y.: Doubleday, 1963.

Stimmen über Karl Kraus zum 60. Geburtstag. Vienna: Verlag der Buchhandlung Richard Lanyi, 1934.

ZOHN, HARRY. *Karl Kraus.* New York: Twayne, 1971.

Music

ADORNO, THEODOR. *Alban Berg: Der Meister des kleinsten übergangs.* Vienna: Verlag Elisabeth Lafite and Oesterreichischer Bundesverlag, 1968.

———. *Musikalische Schriften.* Vol. 1: *Klangfiguren.* Frankfurt am Main: Suhrkamp Verlag, 1959. Vol. 2: *Quasi una Fantasia.* Frankfurt am Main: Suhrkamp Verlag, 1963.

———. "Kolisch und die neue Interpretation." *Frankfurter Allgemeine Zeitung,* 20 June 1956.

———. *Philosophy of Modern Music.* Translated by Anne G. Mitchell and Wesley V. Blomster. New York: Seabury Press, 1973.

ARMITAGE, MERLE, ed. *Schoenberg.* Freeport, N.Y.: Books for Libraries Press, 1937; reprint, 1971.

Arnold Schönberg in höchster Verehrung von Schülern und Freunden. Munich: R. Piper Verlag, 1912.

Arnold Schönberg zum fünfzigsten Geburtstage, 13. September 1924. Vienna: Sonderheft der Musikblätter des Anbruch, 1924.

BERG, ALBAN. *Briefe an seine Frau.* Munich: Albert Langen and Georg Müller Verlag, 1965; *Letters to His Wife.* Edited, translated [and abridged] by Bernard Grun. London: Faber and Faber, 1971.

————. "Die musikalische Impotenz der 'neuen Aesthetik' Hans Pfitzners." *Musikblätter des Anbruch* 2 (June 1920). Reprinted in Willi Reich, *Alban Berg,* pp. 205–218. Translated by Cornelius Cardew. New York: Harcourt, Brace and World, 1965.

CARNER, MOSCO. *Alban Berg: The Man and the Work.* London: Gerald Duckworth, 1975.

DEVOTO, MARK. "Berg and Pacifism." *International Alban Berg Society Newsletter,* no. 2 (January 1971), pp. 8–11.

DORIAN, FREDERICK DEUTSCH. "Webern als Lehrer." *Melos* 27 (April 1960): 101–106.

FREITAG, EBERHARD. *Arnold Schönberg, in Selbstzeugnissen und Bilddokumenten.* Reinbeck bei Hamburg: Rowohlt Taschenbuch Verlag, 1973.

GERHARD, ROBERTO. "Schoenberg Reminiscences." *Perspectives of New Music* 13 (Spring–Summer 1975): 57–65.

HAUER, JOSEF MATTHIAS. *Vom Wesen des Musikalischen: ein Lehrbuch der Zwölftonmusik.* Leipzig: Verlag Waldheim-Eberle, 1920. Reprinted as *Ein Lehrbuch der atonalen Musik.* Berlin: Schlesinger, 1923.

————. *Zwölftontechnik: die Lehre von den Tropen.* Vienna: Universal Edition, 1926.

HILMAR, ERNST, ed. *Arnold Schönberg, Gedenkausstellung 1974.* Vienna: Universal Edition, 1974.

KELLER, HANS. "Portrait of Schoenberg." London: BBC. Interviews. 4 November 1965.

KLEIN, FRITZ HEINRICH. "Die Grenze der Halbtonwelt." *Musik* 17 (January 1925): 281–286.

LARESE, DINO. *Alfred Keller: Eine Lebensskizze.* N.p.: Amriswiler Bücherei, 1969.

MAHLER WERFEL, ALMA. *And the Bridge is Love.* New York: Harcourt Brace, 1958.

————. *Gustav Mahler: Memories and Letters.* 2nd ed. Edited by Donald Mitchell. Translated by Basil Creighton. London: John Murray, 1968.

———. *Mein Leben.* Frankfurt am Main: Fischer Taschenbuch Verlag, 1963.

MILHAUD, DARIUS. *Notes without Music.* Edited by Rollo H. Myers. Translated by Donald Evans. London: Dennis Dobson, 1952.

———. "To Arnold Schoenberg on His Seventieth Birthday: Personal Recollections." *Musical Quarterly* 30 (October 1944): 379–384.

MOLDENHAUER, HANS. *The Death of Anton Webern: A Drama in Documents.* New York: Philosophical Library, 1961.

MOLDENHAUER, HANS, and ROSALEEN MOLDENHAUER. *Anton von Webern: A Chronicle of His Life and Work.* New York: Alfred A. Knopf, 1979.

MUSEUM DES 20. JAHRHUNDERTS, VIENNA. *Schönberg-Webern-Berg: Bilder-Partituren-Dokumente.* Exhibition catalog 36, May–July 1969.

PEYSER, JOAN. *The New Music: The Sense behind the Sound.* New York: Dell, 1971.

PFITZNER, HANS. *Die neue Aesthetik der musikalischen Impotenz: ein Verwesungssymptom?* Munich: Süddeutsche Monatshefte, 1920. Reprinted in *Gesammelte Schriften*, vol. 2, pp. 99–281. Augsburg: Dr. Benno Filser-Verlag, 1926.

PISK, PAUL A. "Memories of Arnold Schoenberg." *Journal of the Arnold Schoenberg Institute* 1 (October 1976): 39–44.

RATZ, ERWIN. "Die Zehn öffentlichen Proben zur Kammersymphonie im Juni 1918 und der 'Verein für musikalische Privataufführungen.'" In *Arnold Schönberg, Gedenkausstellung 1974*, pp. 68–70. Edited by Ernst Hilmar. Vienna: Universal Edition, 1974.

REICH, WILLI. *Alban Berg.* Translated by Cornelius Cardew. New York: Harcourt, Brace and World, 1965.

———. *Schoenberg: A Critical Biography.* Translated by Leo Black. London: Longman Group, 1971.

RUFER, JOSEF. *The Works of Arnold Schoenberg: A Catalogue of His Compositions, Writings and Paintings.* Translated by Dika Newlin. London: Faber and Faber, 1962.

RUSSELL, JOHN. *Erich Kleiber: A Memoir.* London: Andre Deutsch, 1957.

SCHERLIESS, VOLKER. *Alban Berg, in Selbstzeugnissen und Bilddokumenten.* Reinbek bei Hamburg: Rowohlt Taschenbuch Verlag, 1975.

SCHNABEL, ARTUR. *My Life and Music.* New York: St. Martin's Press, 1961.

SCHÖNBERG, ARNOLD. *Berliner Tagebuch.* Edited by Josef Rufer. Frankfurt am Main: Propyläen Verlag, 1974.

———. *Gesammelte Schriften.* Vol. 1: *Stil und Gedanke, Aufsätze zur Musik.* Edited by Ivan Vojtech. Reutlingen: S. Fischer Verlag, 1976.

———. *Letters.* Edited by Erwin Stein. Translated by Eithne Wilkins and Ernst Kaiser. New York: St. Martin's Press, 1965.

———. *Schöpferische Konfessionen.* Edited by Willi Reich. Zurich: Verlag der Arche, 1964.

———. *Style and Idea.* Edited by Leonard Stein. Translated by Leo Black. London: Faber and Faber, 1975.

———. *Theory of Harmony.* Translated by Roy E. Carter. Berkeley: University of California Press, 1978.

SCHULLER, GUNTHER. "A Conversation with Steuermann." *Perspectives of New Music* 3 (Fall–Winter 1964): 22–35.

SIMMS, BRYAN R. "The Society for Private Musical Performances: Resources and Documents in Schoenberg's Legacy." *Journal of the Arnold Schoenberg Institute* 3 (October 1979): 127–149.

SLONIMSKY, NICOLAS. *Music Since 1900.* 3rd ed. New York: Coleman-Ross, 1949.

SMITH, JOAN ALLEN. "The Berg-Hohenberg Correspondence." In Franz Grasberger and Rudolf Stephan, gen. eds., *Alban Berg Studien.* Vol. 2: *Alban Berg Symposion Wien 1980: Tagungsbericht,* pp. 189–197. Edited by Rudolf Klein. Vienna: Universal Edition, 1981.

STEIN, ERWIN. *Orpheus in New Guises.* London: Rockliff, 1953.

STEIN, LEONARD. "The Privataufführungen Revisited." In *Paul A. Pisk: Essays in His Honor,* pp. 203–207. Edited by John Glowacki. Austin: College of Fine Arts, University of Texas, 1966.

STROBEL, HEINRICH. "So sehe ich Webern." *Melos* 32 (September 1965): 285–290.

STUCKENSCHMIDT, H. H. *Schoenberg: His Life, World and Work.* Translated by Humphrey Searle. New York: Schirmer Books, 1978.

SZMOLYAN, WALTER. "Die Konzerte des Wiener Schönberg-Vereins." *Oesterreichische Musikzeitschrift* 36 (February 1981): 82–104.

WALLER, AMALIE. "Mein Vater Anton von Webern." *Oesterreichische Musikzeitschrift* 23 (1968): 331–333.

WALTER, BRUNO. *Theme and Variations: An Autobiography.* Translated by James A. Galston. New York: Alfred A. Knopf, 1959.

WEBERN, ANTON. *Letters to Hildegard Jone and Josef Humplik.* Edited by Josef Polnauer. Translated by Cornelius Cardew. Bryn Mawr, Pa.: Theodore Presser; London: Universal Edition, 1967.

———. *The Path to the New Music.* Edited by Willi Reich. Translated by Leo Black. Bryn Mawr, Pa.: Theodore Presser; London: Universal Edition, 1963.

WELLESZ, EGON. London: BBC. Interview with Deryck Cooke. 26 April 1962.

———. *Arnold Schönberg.* Translated by W. H. Kerridge. London: J. M. Dent and Sons, 1925; reprint, New York: Da Capo Press, 1969.

———. "Schoenberg and Beyond." *Musical Quarterly* 2 (January 1916): 76–95.

WILDGANS, FRIEDRICH. *Anton Webern.* Translated by Edith Temple Roberts and Humphrey Searle. New York: October House, 1967.

Music Theory

BABBITT, MILTON. "Set Structure as a Compositional Determinant." *Journal of Music Theory* 5 (April 1961): 72–94. Reprinted in *Perspectives on Contemporary Music Theory,* pp. 129–147. Edited by Benjamin Boretz and Edward T. Cone. New York: W. W. Norton, 1972.

———. "Some Aspects of Twelve-tone Composition." *Score* 12 (June 1955): 53–61.

———. "Three Essays on Schoenberg." In *Perspectives on Schoenberg and Stravinsky,* pp. 47–60. Edited by Benjamin Boretz and Edward T. Cone. New York: W. W. Norton, 1968.

———. "Twelve-Tone Invariants as Compositional Determinants." *Musical Quarterly* 46 (April 1960): 246–259. Reprinted in *Problems of Modern Music,* pp. 108–121. Edited by Paul Henry Lang. New York: W. W. Norton, 1962.

———. Review of *Schoenberg et son école* and "Qu'est ce que la musique de douze sons," by René Leibowitz. *Journal of the American Musicological Society* 3 (Spring 1950): 57–60.

BARKIN, ELAINE. "A View of Schoenberg's Op. 23/1." *Perspectives of New Music* 12 (Fall–Winter 1973, Spring–Summer 1974): 99–127.

BORETZ, BENJAMIN, and EDWARD T. CONE, eds. *Perspectives on Contemporary Music Theory.* New York: W. W. Norton, 1972.
———, eds. *Perspectives on Schoenberg and Stravinsky.* New York: W. W. Norton, 1968.
BROWNE, RICHMOND. Review of *The Structure of Atonal Music,* by Allen Forte. *Journal of Music Theory* 18 (Fall 1974): 390–415.
CONE, EDWARD T. "Sound and Syntax: An Introduction to Schoenberg's Harmony." *Perspectives of New Music* 13 (Fall–Winter 1974): 21–40.
DEVOTO, MARK. "Some Notes on the Unknown *Altenberg Lieder.*" *Perspectives of New Music* 5 (Fall–Winter 1966): 37–74.
DEAN, JERRY. "Schoenberg's Vertical-Linear Relationships in 1908." *Perspectives of New Music* 12 (Fall–Winter 1973, Spring–Summer 1974): 173–179.
FENNELLY, BRIAN. "Structure and Process in Webern's Opus 22." *Journal of Music Theory* 10 (Winter 1966): 300–328.
FORTE, ALLEN. "Schoenberg's Creative Evolution: The Path to Atonality." *Musical Quarterly* 64 (April 1978): 133–176.
———. "Sets and Nonsets in Schoenberg's Atonal Music." *Perspectives of New Music* 11 (Fall–Winter 1972): 43–64.
———. *The Structure of Atonal Music.* New Haven: Yale University Press, 1973.
———. "A Theory of Set-Complexes for Music." *Journal of Music Theory* 8 (Winter 1964): 136–183.
HYDE, MARTHA M. *Schoenberg's Twelve-Tone Harmony: The Suite Op. 29 and the Compositional Sketches.* Ann Arbor, Mich.: UMI Research Press, 1982.
JARMAN, DOUGLAS. "Dr. Schön's Five-Strophe Aria: Some Notes on Tonality and Pitch Association in Berg's *Lulu.*" *Perspectives of New Music* 8 (Spring–Summer 1970): 23–48.
———. *The Music of Alban Berg.* Berkeley: University of California Press, 1979.
———. "Some Rhythmic and Metric Techniques in Alban Berg's *Lulu.*" *Musical Quarterly* 56 (July 1970): 349–366.
KASSLER, MICHAEL. "Toward a Theory That Is the Twelve-Note-Class System." *Perspectives of New Music* 5 (Spring–Summer 1967): 1–80.
KRAMER, JONATHAN. "The Row as Structural Background and Audible Foreground: The First Movement of Webern's First Cantata." *Journal of Music Theory* 15 (Double Issue 1971): 158–181.
LANG, PAUL HENRY, ed. *Problems of Modern Music.* New York: W. W. Norton, 1962.

LEIBOWITZ, RENÉ. *Schoenberg and His School.* Translated by Dika Newlin. New York: Philosophical Library, 1949; Da Capo Press, 1970.

——. *Introduction à la musique de douze sons.* Paris: L'Arche, 1949.

LESTER, JOEL. "Pitch Structure Articulation in the Variations of Schoenberg's Serenade." *Perspectives of New Music* 6 (Spring–Summer 1968): 22–34.

LEWIN, DAVID. "Inversional Balance as an Organizing Force in Schoenberg's Music and Thought." *Perspectives of New Music* 6 (Spring–Summer 1968): 1–21.

——. "*Moses und Aron:* Some General Remarks, and Analytic Notes for Act I, Scene 1." *Perspectives of New Music* 6 (Fall–Winter 1967): 1–17. Reprinted in *Perspectives on Schoenberg and Stravinsky,* pp. 61–71. Edited by Benjamin Boretz and Edward T. Cone. New York: W. W. Norton, 1968.

——. "Some Notes on Schoenberg's Opus 11." *In Theory Only* 3 (April 1977): 3–7.

——. "A Study of Hexachord Levels in Schoenberg's Violin Fantasy." *Perspectives of New Music* 6 (Fall–Winter 1967): 18–32. Reprinted in *Perspectives on Schoenberg and Stravinsky,* pp. 78–92. Edited by Benjamin Boretz and Edward T. Cone. New York: W. W. Norton, 1968.

——. "A Theory of Segmental Association in Twelve-Tone Music." *Perspectives of New Music* 1 (Fall 1962): 89–116. Reprinted in *Perspectives on Contemporary Music Theory,* pp. 180–207. Edited by Benjamin Boretz and Edward T. Cone. New York: W. W. Norton, 1972.

——. "Toward the Analysis of a Schoenberg Song (Op. 15, no. XI)." *Perspectives of New Music* 12 (Fall–Winter 1973, Spring–Summer 1974): 43–86.

MARTINO, DONALD. "The Source Set and its Aggregate Formations." *Journal of Music Theory* 5 (November 1961): 224–273. Addendum in *Journal of Music Theory* 6 (Winter 1962): 322–323.

PERLE, GEORGE. "An Approach to Simultaneity in Twelve-Tone Music." *Perspectives of New Music* 3 (Fall–Winter 1964): 91–101.

——. "Berg's Master Array of the Interval Cycles." *Musical Quarterly* 63 (January 1977): 1–30.

——. "*Lulu:* The Formal Design." *Journal of the American Musicological Society* 17 (Summer 1964): 179–192.

——. "*Lulu:* Thematic Material and Pitch Organization." *Music Review* 26 (November 1965): 269–302.

————. "The Music of *Lulu*: A New Analysis." *Journal of the American Musicological Society* 12 (Summer–Fall 1959): 185–200.

————. *The Operas of Alban Berg.* Vol. 1: *Wozzeck.* Vol. 2: *Lulu.* Berkeley: University of California Press, 1980, 1985.

————. Review of *Studien zur Entwicklung des dodekaphonen Satzes bei Arnold Schönberg. I. Chronologischer Teil. II. Analytischer Teil. III. Notenbeilage,* by Jan Maegaard. *Musical Quarterly* 63 (April 1977): 273–283.

————. *Serial Composition and Atonality: An Introduction to the Music of Schoenberg, Berg, and Webern.* 5th ed. Berkeley: University of California Press, 1981.

————. *Twelve Tone Tonality.* Berkeley: University of California Press, 1977.

————. "Webern's Twelve-Tone Sketches." *Musical Quarterly* 57 (January 1971): 1–25.

RAHN, JOHN. *Basic Atonal Theory.* New York: Longman, 1980.

ROTHGEB, JOHN. "Some Ordering Relationships in the Twelve-Tone System." *Journal of Music Theory* 11 (Winter 1967): 176–197.

RUFER, JOSEF. *Composition with Twelve Notes.* Rev. ed. Translated by Humphrey Searle. London: Barrie and Rockliff, 1961.

WESTERGAARD, PETER. "Some Problems in Rhythmic Theory and Analysis." *Perspectives of New Music* 1 (Spring–Summer 1962): 180–191.

Index

Page numbers in italic indicate oral history material.